Citation-based Plagiarism Detection

T0238473

Bela Gipp

Citation-based Plagiarism Detection

Detecting Disguised
and Cross-language Plagiarism
using Citation Pattern Analysis

 Springer Vieweg

Bela Gipp
Berkeley, USA

Dissertation Otto-von-Guericke University Magdeburg, Germany, 2013

ISBN 978-3-658-06393-1   ISBN 978-3-658-06394-8 (eBook)
DOI 10.1007/978-3-658-06394-8

The Deutsche Nationalbibliothek lists this publication in the Deutsche Nationalbibliografie; detailed bibliographic data are available in the Internet at http://dnb.d-nb.de.

Library of Congress Control Number: 2014944069

Springer Vieweg
© Springer Fachmedien Wiesbaden 2014

Printed on acid-free paper

Springer Vieweg is a brand of Springer DE.
Springer DE is part of Springer Science+Business Media.
www.springer-vieweg.de

Acknowledgements

This doctoral thesis would not have been possible without the collaboration and generous support of numerous individuals and institutions. I am especially grateful to my doctoral advisor, Professor Andreas Nürnberger, for his dedication to my success in writing this thesis and supporting me in all my research endeavors. I am thankful to Professor Claus Rautenstrauch for inspiring me to pursue a PhD in the first place. Furthermore, I am indebted to the professors Jim Pitman and Erik Wilde from the University of California, Berkeley for inviting me to complete my research at UC Berkeley from 2009–2013. Our open exchange of ideas and our collaboration on interesting projects such as Mr. DLib, led to several joint publications.

I especially acknowledge my research group at SciPlore: Joeran Beel, Corinna Breitinger, Mario Lipinski and Norman Meuschke, with whom it was a pleasure to work over the years. The close collaboration and joint publications with Norman while overseeing his master thesis, as well as during our subsequent research, have significantly contributed to the development of the CbPD approach. I also thank Joeran, Corinna and Mario for our joint projects indirectly related to my doctoral research, such as the development of the open source software, SciPlore Mindmapping, now known as Docear, the development of the machine-readable digital library, Mr. DLib, and the research on Co-citation Proximity Analysis. I wish to thank Christian Hentschel, Juliane Stiller and my research colleagues as mentioned above, for their valuable feedback and proofreading of the manuscript.

I wish to thank my past students at the OvGU Magdeburg, Wadi International University and the UC Berkeley, as well as my most recent students at the HTW Berlin, with whom I developed a web-based CbPD visualization prototype. Working with students in lecture, and supervising bachelor and master projects is a rewarding experience, which confirmed my desire to pursue a career in academia. I also thank the participants of the CbPD user study for their time.

I gratefully acknowledge the organizations that provided my colleagues and me with the funding to realize our research. I thank EXIST for a generous grant from

the German Federal Ministry of Economics and Technology. Moreover, I thankfully acknowledge a NSF grant that allowed us to work on a related project, Mr. DLib. I am indebted to the German Academic Exchange Service (DAAD) for their scholarship that allowed me to research at UC Berkeley, as well as my employer, the SAP-sponsored VLBA-lab at the OvGU. I also wish to thank the Google Scholar team and Bill Schilit for their collaboration, and for inviting me to present my citation-based approach to plagiarism detection at Google in Mountain View. I thank ACM, SIGIR, ECDL and JCDL for their conference-travel grants and I also gratefully acknowledge the State of Saxony-Anhalt for its financial support of the patent applications.
Finally, and most importantly, I thank my loving family and my wonderful girlfriend, for always supporting me in all my endeavors.

Contents

List of Tables

List of Figures

Glossary

AA – Authorship Attribution

Research field in computer science dealing with methods and systems to determine or verify the authors of a text.

API – Application Programming Interface

Software-to-software interface managing the seamless interaction between multiple applications.

BC – Bibliographic Coupling

Measure of global document similarity indicating the number of references two documents have in common in their bibliographies. BC considers references in the bibliography, but does not take into account the placement or order of citations in the full text, refer to page 48 for details.

c&p – Copy & Paste

Plagiarism form characterized by verbatim copying of text.

CbPD – Citation-based Plagiarism Detection

Approach used to identify plagiarism by analyzing citation sequence similarity – term coined by the author, details explained in the thesis.

CF-Score – Citing Frequency-Score

Scoring function taking into account citation frequencies of documents to aid in assessing a citation pattern's degree of suspicion for identifying potential plagiarism – term coined by the author, refer to page 84 and Equation 4.2 for details.

Cit-Chunk – Citation Chunking

Set of CbPD algorithms designed to identify citation patterns regardless of potential transpositions and/or scaling – term coined by the author, refer to page 73 for details.

CitePlag – Prototype of a Citation-based Plagiarism Detection System

Plagiarism Detection System prototype implementing the CbPD algorithms introduced in this thesis, programmed in Java and available under an open source license – refer to page 89 for details.

CLIR – Cross-Language Information Retrieval

Subfield of Information Retrieval dealing with data in multiple languages.

Cont.-Score – Continuity-Score

Scoring function taking into account the continuity of a citation pattern to aid in assessing a citation pattern's degree of suspicion for identifying potential plagiarism – term coined by the author, refer to page 85.

CPA – Co-citation Proximity Analysis

Approach using in-text citation proximities to identify related documents – term coined by the author, refer to page 52 for details.

DOI – Digital Object Identifiers

System for assigning unique character strings to published documents to enable their identification, maintained by the DOI Consortium.

ERM – Entity-Relationship Model

Modeling notation used for conceptual models, or more commonly data models.

GCT – Greedy Citation Tiling

CbPD algorithm adapted from the text string similarity function Greedy String Tiling (GST), explicitly for use with citations. GCT permanently links individually longest citation matches in citation sequences and stores them as a tile – term coined by the author, refer to page 70 for details.

IR – Information Retrieval

Research field in computer science dealing with methods for finding material of unstructured nature in large collections of data.

LCCS – Longest Common Citation Sequence

CbPD algorithm identifying the longest contiguous series of citations common to a set of documents – term coined by the author, refer to page 70 for details.

LSI – Latent Semantic Indexing

Technique in natural language processing to identify patterns in the relationships between the terms and concepts contained in text.

MDR – Match Detect Reveal

Plagiarism Detection System using substring comparisons developed by Monostori et al. [233].

MeSH – Medical Subject Headings

The U.S. National Library of Medicine's controlled vocabulary thesaurus.

NLM – U.S. National Library of Medicine

Organizational unit within the U.S. National Institute of Health.

NLP – Natural Language Processing

Research field in computer science addressing interactions of humans and machines that are related to human language.

NXML – National Library of Medicine XML

Texts in XML markup conformant to the Journal Archiving and Interchange Tag Suite.

PAN-PC – PAN International Competition on Plagiarism Detection

Annual scientific competition evaluating Plagiarism Detection Systems.

PD – Plagiarism Detection

Hypernym for computer based procedures supporting the identification of plagiarism.

PDS – Plagiarism Detection Systems

Hypernym for computer-based systems supporting the semi-automatic identification of plagiarism – also seen abbreviated as PDSs.

PMC® – PubMed Central

Digital archive of health and life science publications maintained by the U.S. National Library of Medicine.

PMCID – PubMed Central® Identifier

Unique numeric identifier assigned to records in the digital archive PubMed Central®.

PMC OAS – PubMed Central Open Access Subset

Collection of Open Access publications included in PubMed Central.

PMID – PubMed® Identifier

Unique numeric identifier assigned to records in the bibliographic database PubMed®.

POS – Part of Speech

The linguistic category of words and other terms that are part of natural language.

RefAuthKey – Reference Author Key

Fixed-length descriptor computed from author names given for references that are examined in the thesis.

RefTitKey – Reference Title Key

Fixed-length descriptor computed from the title given for references that are examined in the thesis.

SAX – Simple API for XML

Java Application Programming Interface for event-based, strictly sequential processing of XML documents.

s&p – Shake & Paste

Plagiarism form characterized by combining shorter sections of literally copied content from different sources.

SW-Tagger – Sentence-Word-Tagger

A subcomponent of CitePlag's parser, which identifies sentences and words in NXML texts and marks them with delimiters that do not impair the validity of the original XML markup – introduced by the author, refer to Appendix B.1 for details.

TF-IDF – Term Frequency–Inverse Document Frequency

Measure reflecting the importance of a word in a document.

UML – Unified Modeling Language

Modeling notation primarily designed for Object Oriented Software Development developed by the Object Management Group.

VSM – Vector Space Model

Document model representing textual content using weighted terms.

XML – Extensible Markup Language

Standard published by the World Wide Web Consortium defining a markup of information.

Abstract

This doctoral thesis addresses a problem in information retrieval, which has recently captured the attention of media – the software-based detection of disguised plagiarism forms. State-of-the-art plagiarism detection approaches are capable of identifying copy & paste, and to some extent, lightly disguised plagiarism. However, even today's best performing systems cannot reliably identify more heavily disguised forms of plagiarism, including paraphrases, translated plagiarism, or idea plagiarism. This weakness of current systems results in a large percentage of disguised scientific plagiarism going undetected. While the easily recognizable copy & paste-type plagiarism typically occurs among students and has no serious consequences for society, disguised plagiarism in the sciences, such as plagiarized medical studies in which results are copied without the corresponding experiments having been performed, can jeopardize patient safety.

To address the weakness of plagiarism detection systems, this thesis introduces Citation-based Plagiarism Detection (CbPD). Unlike existing character-based approaches, which perform text comparisons, CbPD does not consider text similarity alone, but uses citation patterns within documents as a unique, language-independent "semantic fingerprint" to identify potentially suspicious similarity among texts. The idea for CbPD originated from the observation that plagiarists commonly disguise academic misconduct by paraphrasing copied text, but typically do not substitute or significantly rearrange the citations. Motivated by these findings, the author developed various CbPD algorithms tailored to the different forms of plagiarism, and implemented them in the first citation-based plagiarism detection prototype capable of detecting heavily disguised plagiarism.

The advantages of the CbPD approach were demonstrated in evaluations using three document collections. CbPD's applicability for detecting strongly disguised plagiarism was first demonstrated using the plagiarized thesis of former German Minister of Defense, K.-T. zu Guttenberg. While conventional approaches failed to detect a single instance of translated plagiarism in this thesis, CbPD identified 13 of the 16 translations. The effectiveness of the approach was further demonstrated when applied to other authors and plagiarism forms in the VroniPlag Wiki.

The practicality of the CbPD approach was demonstrated by the successful identification of several plagiarism cases in the biomedical publication collection PubMed Central Open Access Subset. As a result of a user study utilizing the CbPD prototype, several plagiarism investigations have thus far been initiated. One medical study and a plagiarized medical case report have since been retracted. The evaluation also showed CbPD's visualization of citation pattern similarities to facilitate the verification of plagiarism. Additionally, it could be shown that CbPD has a superior computational efficiency compared to existing approaches, and produced significantly fewer false positives. CbPD is not a substitute for, but rather a complement to existing approaches. A combination of CbPD with current approaches into a hybrid system promises to ensure optimal detection of both short literal plagiarism, as well as heavily disguised or translated plagiarism.

Kurzfassung

Die vorliegende Dissertation adressiert ein Problem des Information Retrieval, welches aktuell viel Beachtung erfährt: Die softwarebasierte Erkennung verschleierter Plagiate. Bislang genutzte Erkennungsverfahren können lediglich exakte Kopien oder nur geringfügig veränderte Plagiate identifizieren. Selbst die leistungsfähigsten Systeme können verschleierte Plagiatsformen, wie z. B. Paraphrasen, Übersetzungs- oder Ideenplagiate, nicht zuverlässig erkennen, wodurch derartige Plagiate oft unentdeckt bleiben. Unverschleierte Plagiate werden zumeist von Schülern begangen und haben keine ernsten Folgen für die Gesellschaft. Stark verschleierte, nicht maschinell erkennbare Plagiate hingegen sind vor allem in wissenschaftlichen Arbeiten zu finden und können z. B. die optimale Behandlung von Patienten gefährden, wenn eine plagiierte medizinische Studie in Wirklichkeit nie durchgeführt wurde.

Durch Vorstellung eines neuartigen Erkennungsansatzes namens Citation-based Plagiarism Detection (CbPD) leistet die vorliegende Arbeit einen Beitrag zur Lösung dieses Problems. Im Gegensatz zu existierenden Erkennungsverfahren berücksichtigt CbPD nicht die zeichenbasierte Ähnlichkeit von Dokumenten, sondern die Position und Reihenfolge der zitierten Quellen (Zitationen) im Text. Auf Basis der Zitationen generiert CbPD einen sprachunabhängigen „semantischen Fingerabdruck" und nutzt diesen für einen Vergleich der zu untersuchenden Dokumente. Die Idee zur Entwicklung der zitationsbasierten Plagiatserkennung basiert auf der Beobachtung, dass Plagiatoren zwar Texte paraphrasieren um Plagiate zu verschleiern, jedoch die Zitationen üblicherweise weder ersetzen noch deren Reihenfolge signifikant verändern. Auf Basis dieser Erkenntnis wurden auf die unterschiedlichen verschleierten Plagiatsformen zugeschnittene CbPD-Algorithmen entwickelt. Die Algorithmen erkennen Transpositionen und Mehrfachverwendung (Scaling) von Zitationen und nutzen Heuristiken zur Berücksichtigung der Wahrscheinlichkeit eines gemeinsamen Auftretens von Zitationen sowie der Kontinuität von Zitationsmustern. Das CbPD-Konzept wurde in Form eines voll funktionsfähigen Prototyps unter Verwendung von Java und HTML5 realisiert.

Das CbPD-Verfahren wurde mittels dreier Testkollektionen evaluiert und mit existierenden Verfahren verglichen. Die prinzipielle Eignung wurde zuerst anhand der bekannten Doktorarbeit von K.-T. zu Guttenberg belegt. CbPD erlaubte die Erkennung von 13 der 16 enthaltenen Übersetzungsplagiate, während existierende Verfahren keines der Übersetzungsplagiate identifizieren konnten. Die Wirksamkeit des CbPD-Verfahrens für Arbeiten weiterer Autoren und andere Plagiatsformen konnte mittels der VroniPlag Wiki Kollektion belegt werden. Die Praxistauglichkeit der CbPD konnte bewiesen werden, indem mit Hilfe einer Nutzerstudie und des entwickelten Prototyps mehrere Plagiate in der biomedizinischen Volltextkollektion PMC OAS aufgespürt wurden. Sechs Untersuchungen der entdeckten Fälle wurden bislang eingeleitet und eine weitere medizinische Studie wurde inzwischen zurückgezogen. Die Evaluation zeigte, dass CbPD die Verifikation von Plagiaten durch die Visualisierung der Zitationsähnlichkeiten erleichtert. Ausserdem konnte gezeigt werden, dass CbPD gegenüber existierenden Verfahren eine signifikant bessere Laufzeiteffizienz sowie eine deutlich geringere Rate falsch-positiver Ergebnisse aufweist. Die Evaluation machte deutlich, dass CbPD kein Ersatz für existierende Verfahren ist, sondern diese komplementiert. Die Kombination von CbPD mit existierenden Verfahren zu einem Hybridsystem gewährleistet eine optimale Erkennung von sowohl kurzen wörtlichen, als auch stark verschleierten semantischen oder übersetzten Plagiaten.

1 Introduction

This doctoral thesis addresses an unsolved information retrieval problem: the automatic detection of disguised plagiarism forms, including paraphrases, translated plagiarism and structural and idea plagiarism.

Section 1.1 of this chapter introduces the problem setting of currently non-machine-detectable academic plagiarism. Section 1.2 describes my motivation for research, and Section 1.3 presents the resulting research objective pursued in this thesis. Section 1.4 provides an outline of the thesis.

1.1 Problem Setting

The problem of academic plagiarism[1] has been present for centuries. Yet the widespread dissemination of information and communication technology, including the Internet, has greatly contributed to the ease of plagiarizing. Many online services exist to facilitate student plagiarism, including essay databases, and text "synonymizer" tools, such as *synomizer.com*[2], which outputs input text with a list of synonyms for each word.

The most extensive study on plagiarism surveyed ~82,000 students at North American colleges. Approximately 40 % of the students admitted having plagiarized within the last year [220]. However, students are not the only group to plagiarize. In Germany, more than 30 prominent cases of academic dishonesty among politicians recently made headlines. The German politicians who plagiarized in their doctoral theses include former Minister of Defense, Karl-Theodor zu Guttenberg, and even the Federal Minister of Education and Research, Annette Schavan. The question arises why cases of plagiarism, which are apparent in hindsight, often remain undiscovered for so long. Why can academic misconduct not be caught much earlier using plagiarism detection software?

---

[1] Refer to Section 2.1.1, page 10, for a definition of plagiarism.
[2] http://www.synomizer.com

D. Weber-Wulff, who conducts regular performance evaluations for Plagiarism Detection Systems (PDS), gives a disillusioning summary regarding available systems:

"[...] Plagiarism Detection Systems find copies, not plagiarism."

([357], p. 6)

Substantial research on the approaches and systems aiding in the detection of plagiarism has been performed for almost two decades. Currently available PDS use sophisticated and highly efficient character-based text comparisons. These approaches are capable of detecting verbatim and moderately disguised copies of text reliably. However, the cleverly veiled and re-structured real-world plagiarism more commonly found in research contains insufficient character-based similarities, making it undetectable by current PDS.

Today, manual inspection of suspicious documents by experts or through crowd-sourced projects, such as the VroniPlag Wiki [350], an online platform used to expose plagiarism cases, represents the only reliable method to detect more heavily disguised plagiarism. However, the time commitment required to examine plagiarism manually is significant. The 48 cases[3] in the VroniPlag Wiki alone amounted to hundreds of hours, making manual inspection and crowd-sourced examination unfeasible for examining lower-profile plagiarism or for checking entire databases.

---

[3] As of 2013-07-04. The VroniPlag Wiki is an ongoing project.

1.2 Motivation

My motivation to research new approaches to plagiarism detection grew out of my disillusionment with the state-of-the-art systems. Current software solutions label themselves "plagiarism detectors". This is a misnomer because it leads users to believe the software is indeed capable of detecting real-world plagiarism, including the disguised plagiarism more common to research. In reality, however, this is not the case.

While I believe that plagiarism should not be tolerated in student assignments, I find that plagiarism in research – and particularly in the medical field – has far more serious consequences to society. An example of a plagiarized medical study[4] [165] in Table 1, illustrates this point. The plagiarism discusses the correct care for patients suffering from acute respiratory distress syndrome. The key difference between the plagiarism and the original study are the numbers stated in the results section. The excerpt from the medical study's results in Table 1 highlights the differences in reported values between the earlier and later publication in red. Both the original and the plagiarism were retrieved from an openly available subset of PubMed's medical publication database.

---

[4] This study was identified because it was retrieved among the top results by the approach presented in this thesis. As I later discovered, the study had already been retracted by the journal, although at the time of evaluation it was still available in the database. Visit http://citeplag.org/compare/5583/117324 for a visual comparison of the plagiarism and the original.

Table 1: Excerpt from a Plagiarized Section Describing Experimental Results

Original [48] PMCID: 1065018	Plagiarism [281] PMCID: 2772258
PEEP had no effect on CO_2 gap (median [range], baseline: 19 [2–30] mmHg; PEEP 10: 19 [0–40] mmHg; PEEP 15: 18 [0–39] mmHg; PEEP 20: 17 [4–39] mmHg; ideal PEEP: 19 [9–39] mmHg; $P = 0.18$). Cardiac index also remained unchanged (baseline: 4.6 [2.5–6.3] l min-1 m-2; PEEP 10: 4.5 [2.5–6.9] l min-1 m-2; PEEP 15: 4.3 [2–6.8] l min-1 m-2; PEEP 20: 4.7 [2.4–6.2] l min-1 m-2; ideal PEEP: 5.1 [2.1–6.3] l min-1 m-2; $P = 0.08$).	PEEP had no effect on CO_2 gap (median [range], baseline: 18 [2–30] mmHg; PEEP 10: 18 [0–40] mmHg; PEEP 15: 17 [0–39] mmHg; PEEP 20: 16 [4–39] mmHg; ideal PEEP: 19 [9–39] mmHg; $P = 0.19$). Cardiac index also remained unchanged (baseline: 4.7 [2.6–6.2] l min−1 m−2; PEEP 10: 4.4 [2.5–7] l min−1 m−2; PEEP 15: 4.4 [2.2–6.8] l min−1 m−2; PEEP 20: 4.8 [2.4–6.3] l min−1 m−2; ideal PEEP: 4.9 [2.4–6.3] l min−1 m−2; $P = 0.09$).

Plagiarized studies typically do not only copy text, but are also more likely to contain fictitious evaluations and results. Such fake medical studies jeopardize the quality of medical research and can prevent patients from receiving optimal treatment[5]. Furthermore, for the progression of scientific disciplines it is crucial that researchers can trust the outcomes of past research. This motivated me to develop a plagiarism detection approach better capable of detecting disguised plagiarism as it occurs in higher education and in scientific research.

1.3 Research Objective

Motivated by the limitations of existing plagiarism detection systems, the following research objective was defined:

---

[5] For examples of harmful studies, refer to Section 7.3.4.

Propose, implement, and evaluate a plagiarism detection approach capable of detecting non-machine-identifiable plagiarism forms, such as paraphrases, translated plagiarism, and idea plagiarism.

To achieve this objective the following research tasks were derived:

Task 1:   *Perform a comprehensive analysis of the individual strengths and weaknesses of state-of-the-art plagiarism detection approaches and systems.*

Task 2:   *Develop a plagiarism detection concept that addresses the identified weaknesses of current plagiarism detection approaches.*

Task 3:   *Design detection algorithms that employ the theoretical concept introduced and are fitted to detect the plagiarism forms currently not machine-detectable.*

Task 4:   *Implement a prototype of a plagiarism detection system that employs the developed algorithms to demonstrate the applicability of the approach in real-world scientific document collections.*

Task 5:   *Evaluate the proposed concept in identifying strongly disguised plagiarism forms by comparing detection performance, user utility, and computational efficiency to state-of-the-art systems. As proof of concept, identify unknown and currently non-machine-detectable plagiarism instances.*

1.4   Thesis Outline

Chapter 1 describes the problem setting, the research motivation, and the corresponding research objective. The research objective is divided into five research tasks pursued in this thesis.

Chapter 2 introduces the reader to the problem of academic plagiarism and the existing research on plagiarism detection. Following a definition of what constitutes plagiarism and the prevalent forms of plagiarism, the scope of plagiarism in the academic and scientific environments is discussed. A detailed examination of current plagiarism detection approaches is given, and the challenges of detecting disguised and translated plagiarism are explained. This chapter addresses Research Task 1 by reviewing and exposing strengths and weaknesses of available plagiarism detection approaches.

Chapter 3 provides background information on citation-based document similarity measures. After introducing relevant terminology, a review of the literature introduces important measures, including Bibliographic Coupling and Co-citation Analysis.

Chapter 4 presents the novel detection approach proposed in this thesis. I coined this approach Citation-based Plagiarism Detection (CbPD). CbPD addresses weaknesses of current plagiarism detection approaches. By analyzing citation similarities within documents, CbPD can machine-detect currently non-automatically detectable disguised forms of plagiarism. Chapter 4 addresses Research Task 2 and Task 3 by proposing CbPD as a plagiarism detection approach and designing detection algorithms using the introduced concept.

Chapter 5 describes the implementation of the Citation-based Plagiarism Detection approach in a prototype, thus addressing Research Task 4.

Chapter 6 describes the CbPD evaluation framework and presents the evaluation results. In the methodology section potential test collections, ground truths and limitations of the evaluation are discussed. Chapter 6 addresses Research Task 5 by evaluating the effectiveness of the proposed approach for both known and yet unknown plagiarism cases.

Chapter 7 provides a summary, discusses research contributions, and gives an outlook on future work. The appendix includes a list of related publications, the preliminary corpus analysis, the CPA/CbPD patent application, material related to the prototype, and other resources as listed below.

I will use "we" rather than "I" in the subsequent chapters of this thesis, since I published and discussed my ideas with others including my advisor and fellow researchers. For more information on joint projects and publications, please refer to the acknowledgements in Appendix D.

2 Plagiarism Detection

This chapter[6] provides a background on academic plagiarism. The rapid advancement of information technology and especially the dissemination of the Internet have drastically increased the availability of information – not only for legitimate purposes. Academic plagiarism is one form of undue information use simplified by the abundance of information and ease of information access [161].

In academia, plagiarism, i.e. using the words or ideas of another person and passing them off as one's own, has been described by some as a "cardinal sin" ([249], p. 1), maybe even the "ultimate sin" ([21], p. 57). Plagiarism deprives the original authors of the benefits of their work, including gaining academic reputation or acquiring research funding. Plagiarism may even shift these benefits to the plagiarist. Furthermore, plagiarism distorts the traceability of ideas, arguments and results within academic literature, and withholds valuable resources for discovering related material from the reader [306].

Given the volume of available information, detecting plagiarism through manual inspection is time-consuming and hardly feasible ([71], p. 9). Therefore, software capable of partially automating plagiarism detection has become increasingly popular. This section reviews the extensive and rapidly growing literature on research in academic plagiarism detection. Section 2.1 provides a definition, explains the forms of plagiarism, and discusses the prevalence of academic plagiarism. Section 2.2 gives a detailed description of plagiarism detection (PD) approaches currently in use, and an overview of the most effective PDS including performance evaluations follows in Section 2.3.

2.1 Academic Plagiarism

This section introduces the problem of academic plagiarism. Section 2.1.1 provides a definition, Section 2.1.2 characterizes the forms of academic

---

[6] An abridged version of the literature review in this chapter has been published with Norman Meuschke [228].

plagiarism, and Section 2.1.3 concludes with a summary of the severity of the problem.

2.1.1 Definition

Inspired by the five key characteristics of plagiarism according to Fishman[7] ([113], p. 5), we define plagiarism to encompass:

The use of ideas, concepts, words, or structures without
appropriately acknowledging the source to benefit in a setting
where originality is expected.

Other researchers commonly define academic plagiarism as literary theft, i.e. stealing words or ideas from other authors [102, 250]. Theft describes the deliberate appropriation of foreign property without the consent of the rightful owner ([120], p. 125). The definition used in this thesis does not necessarily characterize academic plagiarism as theft for the following reasons.

First, academic plagiarism need not be deliberate. Authors may inadvertently fail to properly acknowledge a source, e.g., by forgetting to insert a citation, or citing a wrong source; thereby committing plagiarism unintentionally [36, 219]. Additionally, a psychological memory bias called cryptomnesia can cause humans to unconsciously attribute foreign ideas to themselves [268].

Second, academic plagiarists may act in consent with another author, but still commit plagiarism by not properly acknowledging the original source. The term collusion describes the behavior of authors, who write collaboratively, or copy from one another, although they are required to work independently [71]. We include collusion in the definition of academic plagiarism.

---

[7]   Note, the five characteristics of plagiarism as defined by Fishman are: (1) the use of words, ideas, or work products (2) attributable to another identifiable person or source, (3) without attributing the work to the source (4) in a situation where there is a legitimate expectation of original authorship (5) in order to obtain some benefit, credit, or gain which need not be monetary ([113], p. 5).

2.1.2 Forms of Academic Plagiarism

Real-world observations of academic plagiarism reveal a variety of commonly found forms.

Literal plagiarism describes the undue copying of text with very little or no disguise.

- *Copy & paste (c&p)* is the most common form of literal plagiarism and is characterized by adopting text verbatim from another source [219, 358].

- *Shake & paste (s&p)* refers to the copying and merging of text segments with slight adjustments to form a coherent text, e.g., by changing word order, by substituting words with synonyms, or by adding or deleting "filler" words [357].

Disguised plagiarism subsumes practices to conceal unduly copied text [185]. We identified five forms of disguised plagiarism in the literature on plagiarism.

- *Paraphrasing* is the intentional rewriting of foreign thoughts in the vocabulary and style of the plagiarist without acknowledging the source [71, 185].

- *Technical disguise* refers to techniques that exploit weaknesses of current detection approaches to make plagiarized content non-machine-detectable. Examples include using homoglyphs, symbols that visually appear similar or identical, or inserting random letters in white font [151, 170].

- *Translated plagiarism* is the manual or automated conversion of text from one language to another with the intention of hiding its origin [357].

- *Structural and idea plagiarism*[8] encompasses the use of compositional elements or a broader concept without due acknowledgement of the source. Even if the text is in the author's own words, structural elements, such as outlines or the presentation of ideas or content, such as the chosen research approach, the experimental setup, the lines of argument or the background sources used, may be similar on a level that would have warranted acknowledgement [116, 219]. Inherent in its definition, structural and idea plagiarism is not "obvious" and thus it is not necessarily an indicator that a work is unoriginal or must be retracted. Thus, the term "plagiarism" for structural and idea similarity is justified often only for extreme cases. The presence of structural or idea similarity can rather be a potential quality indicator, e.g., to determine if a work qualifies to be published in a top-journal or a mediocre journal, or if a dissertation meets the highest demands or only satisfies the necessary requirement. We combine structural and idea plagiarism into a single plagiarism form, since it is extremely difficult for human examiners to judge if potential structural plagiarism also copied ideas. Structural and idea plagiarism represent one of the most controversial forms of plagiarism to verify [362], because the decision on whether structural or topical similarities exceed a legitimate level is highly subjective.

---

[8] There is no consensus on whether structural and idea plagiarism should be categorized as a form of disguised plagiarism. However, for the definition of disguised plagiarism in this thesis, i.e. forms of plagiarism containing little or no verbatim text overlap and thus not being reliably detectable by PDS, structural and idea plagiarism can reasonably be included in this category. Note that exceptional cases in which structural plagiarism or idea plagiarism also contains paragraphs or sentences copied in their entirety exist; however, this holds true for all plagiarism forms, they do not have to be exclusive.

Self-plagiarism is the partial or complete reuse of one's own writings without such reuse being justified. Presenting updates or providing access to a larger community may justify re-publishing one's own work, but still requires appropriate acknowledgement of the previously published work [40]. Unjustified reasons include trying to artificially increase one's citation count [77].

2.1.3 Prevalence of Plagiarism in the Academic Environment

Academic plagiarism is not a new phenomenon. Since the 1920s, researchers have analyzed the problem, focusing mainly on North American colleges. The following studies give empirical evidence of the problem by providing reviews on academic dishonesty in general [44, 74], collegiate cheating behavior [82, 364] and plagiarism in particular [102, 250].

The majority of studies use self-report surveys to evaluate plagiarism behavior. The most extensive study on U.S. and Canadian campuses questioned around 80,000 students over three years from 2002 to 2005 [220]. McCabe reports 38 % of undergraduates and 25 % of graduate students self-reporting to have paraphrased or copied at least a few sentences without indicating the written source in the 12-month period prior to being questioned [220]. McCabe assumes the true numbers to be higher, because students were more concerned about their anonymity in this web-based assessment compared to earlier paper-based surveys [221, 222]. We agree with this assumption, since self-reports show a tendency to understate misbehavior [284].

The self-report studies often did not distinguish between the different forms of concealed plagiarism or the degree of plagiarism obfuscation. However, for studies indicating the prevalence of specific plagiarism forms, copy & paste and shake & paste plagiarism, a few sentences in length, dominates [176, 220, 222, 223, 273]. Around 20 % of participants admitted to having plagiarized large parts of a document or having obtained texts from fellow students or Internet essay banks [176, 220, 273].

Other studies completed outside of North America that employed plagiarism detection systems consistently found 20 % or more of the inspected documents to contain suspicious content [23, 83, 329]. However, the fraction out of total plagiarism represented by the detected plagiarism remains unknown. The presented studies only serve as "spotlights" on student plagiarism in different countries. Yet, by reviewing these studies, as well as other extensive research and particular cases observed in the literature [74, 82, 102, 250], we conclude that plagiarism among students is a serious problem.

Assessments of academic dishonesty among post-graduate researchers are rare. One large-scale survey of 2,000 doctoral students and their 4,000 associated faculty members reported that 28 % of faculty members witnessed doctoral students committing plagiarism. Seven percent of doctoral students and 8 % of faculty members reported they had experienced plagiarism by faculty members [324]. Another survey of approximately 3,250 scientists asking about personal misbehavior yielded lower admitted incident rates. Only about 1 % of the respondents self-reported having committed plagiarism. Martinson and Anderson assess these results as "[...] *conservative estimates* [...]" of the true frequency ([215], p. 738). They assume understatements and a response bias from plagiarists who refused to participate.

Fröhlich, Martin and Williams, experts in the field of academic plagiarism, agreed that persons and institutions that discover academic misbehavior often treat such incidences in a clandestine manor. Therefore, only a small fraction of incidences becomes public [116, 214, 366]. The aforementioned experts deduct reasons that substantiate this assumption from known cases of misconduct. *Personal dependence and the fear of retaliation* by the accused, or peers related to the accused, may keep researchers from reporting or publicizing academic misbehavior. *Aversion of engagement* in the laborious and time-consuming inquiry needed for verifying misconduct is another obstacle to reporting. *Fear of losing credibility and scientific reputation* often keeps institutions, including universities, research centers or conferences, from publicizing cases of misconduct or handling them as rigorously as they should.

Despite these obstacles, numerous cases of plagiarism in academia have become public. Price reviews 19 cases of plagiarism, which the U.S. Office of Research Integrity publicized as a result of evaluating medical research projects between 1992 and 2005 [269]. Gutbrodt reports that the IEEE INFOCOM 2006 conference, rejected 12 out of about 1,000 submitted papers after a scan using a PDS revealed suspicious similarities [145].

Sorokina et al. used a self-developed PDS to scan approximately 285,000 texts in the scientific document database arXiv.org [307]. They found more than 500 documents to contain likely cases of plagiarism and approximately 30,000 documents (20 % of the collection) to likely be duplicates or to contain "[...] *excessive self-plagiarism* [...]" ([307], p. 12). Sorokina et al. categorized documents in the excessive self-plagiarism class if their largest contiguous amount of copy-free text was less than 20 % of total document length. As the consequence of a different investigation, arXiv.org deleted 65 articles from 14 different authors for containing substantial plagiarism [15].

The project Déjà Vu [92, 104, 105, 114, 202, 321] used a text similarity scanner [191, 254] to analyze abstracts of bioscience articles in MEDLINE® and their full-texts in PubMed Central® (PMC) if available. MEDLINE is a bibliographic index and PMC a digital full-text archive [335, 338]. The Déjà Vu project identified 79,383 articles with highly similar abstracts. Manual checks of 4,515 full-texts identified 252 cases of likely plagiarism and 89 likely cases of self-plagiarism [92]. Many reviews presented further plagiarism cases committed in part by renowned senior scholars [69, 116, 214, 313, 361, 366].

Recently, the investigations of two crowd-sourcing projects, the GuttenPlag Wiki and the VroniPlag Wiki exposed plagiarism in the doctoral thesis of former German Federal Minister of Defense and documented 48 cases of plagiarism, respectively[9] [147, 350]. Some cases in the VroniPlag Wiki involve high-ranking politicians, including the dissertations of members of the German Federal Parliament [348], the European Parliament [64], and the former Vice President of the European Parliament [226]. To date, the responsible universities have verified and retracted the doctorates of nine offenders[10] [350].

---

[9] As of 2013-07-04. The VroniPlag Wiki investigations began in March 2011 and are ongoing.

[10] As of 2013-07-04. For a complete and up-to-date listing of retractions visit: http://de.vroniplag.wikia.com/wiki/Übersicht

In a similar case, a Hungarian magazine accused Hungary's president, Pál Schmitt, of having committed substantial plagiarism in his doctoral thesis. The responsible university investigated the allegations, confirmed plagiarism on 197 of the 215 pages in the dissertation, and rescinded Schmitt's doctorate [292].

Ironically, even two European ministers of education, were recently found to have plagiarized. The Romanian Minister of Education, Ecaterina Andronescu, was accused of plagiarism and falsification of data in 2012 [163]. The same year in Germany, Annette Schavan, the German Federal Minister of Education and Research was accused of plagiarism in her doctoral thesis. The accusations of Schavan's dissertation sparked a lengthy and heated political debate. The final decision on the presence of plagiarism was made almost a year later, in February 2013, when the Heinrich-Heine University of Düsseldorf rescinded the doctorate by a nearly unanimous vote on the grounds of "willful deceit" [153]. A. Schavan stepped down from her political position but vowed to take the decision to court [309].

We conclude that academic plagiarism is a pressing unsolved problem, also among graduate and post-graduate researchers, although plagiarism research has focused mainly on undergraduate students. Applying automatic detection systems to student assignments is already common practice at many institutions [18]. Scholarly publications, however, are checked far less routinely. By applying string matching to the MEDLINE® database, the Déjà Vu project identified numerous likely cases of plagiarism [104, 114]. Investigations like these can only lead to speculations on the quantity of well-disguised plagiarism in research that goes undetected. Empirical studies on plagiarism frequencies are listed in Appendix H.

The following section describes current plagiarism detection approaches. By pointing out the strengths and weaknesses of existing systems, we find that a substantial number of plagiarism incidences are likely to remain undetected.

2.2 Plagiarism Detection Approaches

This section first gives an overview of the generic mode of operation for all plagiarism detection systems (PDS) and second presents technical descriptions of the detection approaches employed by PDS.

2.2.1 Generic Detection Approach

Plagiarism detection is a hypernym for computer-based approaches, which support the identification of plagiarism [318]. PD is an information retrieval (IR) task supported by specialized IR systems, called plagiarism detection systems (PDS). PDS implement one of two generic detection approaches: *external* or *intrinsic*.

External PDS compare a suspicious document with a reference collection, which is a set of genuine documents [318]. The comparison requires a document model with defined similarity criteria. The task is to retrieve all documents that contain passages that are similar, beyond a chosen threshold, to segments in the suspicious document [319].

Intrinsic PDS statistically examine linguistic features of a text, a process known as *stylometry*, without performing comparisons to other documents. Intrinsic PDS report changes in writing styles as indicators for potential plagiarism [97].

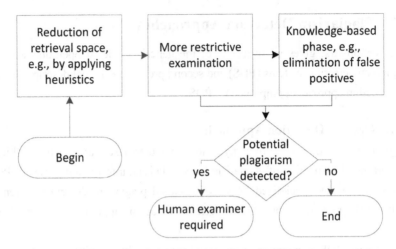

Figure 1: Generic Plagiarism Detection Process

Most external PDS follow a three-stage retrieval process as illustrated in Figure 1. In the first stage, PDS commonly apply computationally inexpensive heuristic document models to reduce the retrieval space. The goal of this stage is to identify a small fraction of the reference collection as candidate documents from which the suspicious text could originate. Coarser fingerprinting (see Section 2.2.3), string matching (see *String Matching*, page 26) or vector space models (see *Vector Space Models*, page 28) are common detection approaches used by PDS for this purpose.

In the second stage, candidate documents retrieved in the first stage undergo a computationally more expensive detailed comparison. PDS usually apply finer-grained variants of the detection approaches we will explain in Sections 2.2.3–2.2.4. PDS can either rely on a single detection approach, or implement a combination of approaches. For example, a PDS may use a coarser fingerprinting method or a vector space model for the initial retrieval stage and a more fine-grained implementation of the same detection approach for the detailed comparison stage. Likewise, a PDS may employ fingerprinting or vector space model-based retrieval for the initial retrieval stage and an elaborate string-matching procedure for the detailed comparison stage.

In the third stage, PDS apply domain-specific, knowledge-based, post-processing procedures to text segments retrieved in the second stage. The goal of this stage is to eliminate false positives, which the specific detection procedures in the previous stages are prone to produce. Typical cases of false positives are correctly cited passages with high character based similarity [317]. The design of the procedures applied in the third stage depends highly on the characteristics of the detection approach in the previous retrieval stages.

Many plagiarism detection approaches involve the comparison of billions of lines of text in large reference collections, which inevitably leads systems to face a trade-off between computational effort and accepting some degree of information loss. The computational efficiency of systems, both in terms of time and use of storage space, is thus an important consideration.

The literature on plagiarism detection emphasizes that no PDS are capable of reliably identifying plagiarism without human review. An examiner is always required to check the results of the automated retrieval and to verify if plagiarism is present [185, 218]. Additionally, the perceptions of human assessors regarding what constitutes plagiarism differ widely [275, 323]. Therefore, PDS cannot fully automate the identification of plagiarism. These systems are only the first step in a semi-automated plagiarism detection and verification process, which requires careful consideration on a case-by-case basis [185].

2.2.2 Overview of Plagiarism Detection Approaches

This section gives an overview of PD approaches. We classify available approaches by the type of similarity assessment they most prominently apply, as either performing a *local* or a *global* similarity assessment, as shown in Figure 2.

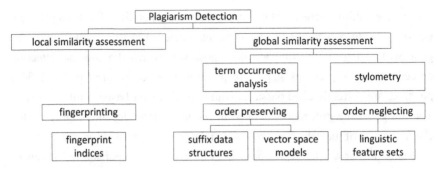

Figure 2: Classification of Plagiarism Detection Approaches

The leaves of the tree diagram in Figure 2 show the detection approaches typically used in local and global document similarity assessment. All detection methods require a reference collection to run comparisons, except for stylometry. The stylometry approach analyzes document suspiciousness intrinsically without performing comparisons to other documents.

Local similarity assessment approaches analyze matches of confined text segments in suspicious texts [316]. Section 2.2.3 describes fingerprinting, the most common approach in this class of detection approaches.

Global similarity assessment approaches examine characteristics of longer text sections, or the complete document, and express the degree to which two documents are similar to each other in their entirety [316]. PD approaches that employ term occurrence analysis typically make use of the entire text, i.e. operate at the global level. Vector space models (VSM) or suffix data structures are commonly used global document similarity assessment methods, as explained in Section 2.2.4.

Figure 3 visualizes the concept underlying the global versus local similarity assessment approach. In the left example, the text is processed according to local similarity analysis, where all contiguous matching sequences, which share a minimum number of words or characters with another document – not shown in the figure – are highlighted. In the right example, the same text is marked up according to a global similarity analysis approach, where only the word stems held in common with another similar document are used to form global term vectors.

Local similarity analysis	**Global similarity analysis**
At the first sight ``knowledge over search'' is obvious on the one hand, but too simple on the other: Among others, the question remains whether or not he could believe the alleged claim. However, most of us think that it develops from the search-plus-simulation paradigm. This way one could gain the maximum impact for automated diagnosis problem solving, simply by untwining the roles of search and simulation.	At the first sight ``knowledge over search'' is obvious on the one hand, but too simple on the other: Among others, the question remains whether or not he could believe the alleged claim. However, most of us think that it develops from the search-plus-simulation paradigm. This way one could gain the maximum impact for automated diagnosis problem solving, simply by untwining the roles of search and simulation.
Concept:	**Concept:**
contiguous matching word sequences analyzed	shared word stems analyzed, stop words excluded

Figure 3: Local vs. Global Document Similarity Analysis

Source: Stein and Meyer zu Eissen [316]

The classification in Figure 2 reflects the most common application of the presented detection approaches as part of a plagiarism detection system. For example, PDS commonly apply vector space models or string-matching procedures to the entire document. The procedures flag documents as suspicious if the detected text matches exceed a certain fraction of the entire document length. However, PDS can also employ vector space models or string-matching procedures to analyze fragments of a text to detect more local similarities. Figure 2 applies to the monolingual PD setting and omits cross-language PD (CLPD) for simplicity. CLPD approaches partially adapt building blocks from the monolingual setup and partially use specifically designed cross-language similarity assessments.

We present all detection approaches, including CLPD, in the following sections. For each approach, we present typical characteristics that influence its detection capabilities. However, the detection performance achieved by individual approaches depends heavily on their individual implementation and the test collection chosen for evaluation. We highlight characteristic strengths and weaknesses of detection approaches by presenting results of impartial PDS performance comparisons in Section 2.3.1.

2.2.3 Fingerprinting

Fingerprinting is currently the most widely applied external plagiarism detection approach [97]. Fingerprinting approaches represent a document by segmenting it into substrings and selecting a subset of all the substrings formed. The substring set is the fingerprint; its elements are called minutiae [158]. PDS often apply hash functions to transform minutiae into space-efficient byte strings. PDS compare a document by computing the document's fingerprint and querying each of the minutiae with a pre-computed index of fingerprints for all documents in a reference collection, as Figure 4 shows.

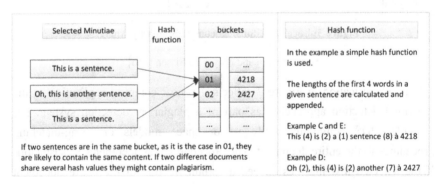

Figure 4: Concept of Fingerprinting

Minutiae that match with other documents indicate shared text segments and suggest potential plagiarism when exceeding the chosen similarity threshold [41]. The fingerprinting methods proposed for PD differ in the parameters:

chunking unit, chunk size, fingerprint resolution, chunk selection strategy and the similarity function.

The *chunking unit* defines the segments into which a fingerprinting method divides a text, and whether these segments are combined into larger composites, called chunks. For example, the chunking units used in Figure 4 are sentences. Table 2 summarizes chunking units proposed for fingerprinting methods.

Table 2: Overview of Chunking Units Proposed for Fingerprinting Methods

Chunking Unit		Used in
Character n-grams (n consecutive characters)		[51, 57, 142, 154, 245, 285, 371]
Words	All words	[33, 42, 111, 172, 203]
	Stop words removed	[68, 158, 173, 297]
	Stop words alone	[312]
Sentences		[41, 253]
Hybrid terms	Word-bound n-grams	[293]
	Sentence-bound character n-grams	[56, 57]
	Sentence-bound word n-grams	[307]

The *chunk size* determines the granularity of a fingerprint. Larger chunk sizes are more restrictive selectors and thus benefit detection accuracy, because the probability that documents share substrings decreases with increasing substring length. Larger chunks are also computationally more efficient, because fewer chunks must be stored for each document. Yet, large chunks are susceptible to failure in detecting disguised plagiarism, because changing one character alters the fingerprint of a rather long text segment. Small chunks better deal with modifications, but require higher computational effort and tend to yield false positives when matching common substrings that documents share by chance

[154, 158]. Due to these trade-offs, chunk sizes differ. Table 3 lists the chunk sizes of common fingerprinting methods found in the literature.

Table 3: Overview of Chunk Sizes Proposed for Fingerprinting Methods

Chunk Size	Used in
3-4 characters	[57]
single content words	[297]
3-5 content words	[158, 172, 203, 298]
7-10 content words	[42, 307]
8-11 stop words	[312]

The *resolution* is the number of minutiae, i.e., the number of hashed substrings a fingerprint contains and can be either fixed or variable. More minutiae are equivalent to encoding longer sections of the text. Thus, a higher fingerprint resolution is positively correlated with detection accuracy, yet is computationally more expensive [42, 158, 286].

Fixed-resolution fingerprints are computationally efficient, but yield lower detection accuracy, especially for long documents [154]. When using fixed-resolution fingerprints, a book may not share enough minutiae with a paragraph copied from it to be detectable [286].

Variable-resolution fingerprinting methods compute more minutiae the longer the document and thus encode a higher percentage of the text. This increases detection accuracy, but requires higher computational effort. Full fingerprinting considers all minutiae. However, the fingerprint index for a full-resolution fingerprinting PDS requires eight or more times the disk space of the original document collection and significant processing time [33, 286]. Therefore, full-resolution fingerprinting PDS are not practical for collections

containing millions of documents. Table 4 lists fixed or variable resolution
fingerprinting methods.

Table 4: Overview of Fixed and Variable-Resolution Fingerprinting Methods

Resolution	Used in
fixed	[154]
variable	[33, 41, 42, 57, 143, 173, 203, 208, 285, 297, 307]

The *chunk selection strategy* determines which text sections the fingerprint
encodes and thereby makes them comparable to other documents. A selection of
chunks is necessary, because the computational requirements of full-resolution
fingerprinting are too high for most practical use cases. Table 5 lists three
common chunk selection strategies described in the literature.

Table 5: Overview of Chunk Selection Strategies for Fingerprinting Methods

Chunk Selection	Used in
Common substrings	[208]
Probabilistic selection	[41, 42]
Frequency-based selection	[154, 235, 286]

The *similarity function* considers the minutiae that a suspicious text shares
with a document in the reference collection to calculate a similarity score.
Documents of the reference collection that exceed a certain threshold score
represent potential plagiarism sources [158]. One basic similarity function, as
used by Kasprzak and Brandejs, defines a fixed number of matching minutiae as
the threshold [172].

Another intuitive similarity function considers the fraction of all minutiae
$M(d)$ of a suspicious document d_s that overlap with minutiae of a genuine
document d_g. Broder et al. coined this measure containment $c(d_s, d_g)$, see

Equation 2.1, because it represents the share of a suspicious document contained within a source [42]. Broder et al. proposed using containment in conjunction with a measure they termed *resemblance, $r(d_s, d_g)$*, see Equation 2.2.

$$c(d_s, d_g) = \frac{|M(d_s) \cap M(d_g)|}{|M(d_s)|} \tag{2.1}$$

$$r(d_s, d_g) = \frac{|M(d_s) \cap M(d_g)|}{|M(d_s) \cup M(d_g)|} \tag{2.2}$$

Resemblance is the Jaccard coefficient for the sets of minutiae and hence expresses the global similarity of the two sets. Resemblance and containment have found frequent use in PD research along with other similarity measures [33, 41, 42, 67, 111, 203, 253]. More sophisticated similarity functions use the length of documents [33], relative frequencies of minutiae [285], or maximal differences in minutiae vectors [371].

The inherent challenge of all fingerprinting methods is to find a document representation that reduces computational effort and limits the information loss incurred, in order to achieve acceptable detection accuracy [97]. The parameter choice of fingerprinting methods reflects this challenge. The combinations of parameters that perform best depend on the nature and size of the collection, and on the expected amount and form of plagiarism present.

2.2.4 Term Occurrence Analysis

Checking documents for verbatim text overlaps is an intuitive approach to external plagiarism detection. Researchers frequently adopt the classical computer science concepts of string matching and vector space models to check for verbatim text overlaps. This section explains the principles of both approaches and outlines their capabilities and limitations when used in PDS.

2.2.4.1 *String Matching*

String matching refers to searching for a given character sequence, or "pattern", in a text. PDS employing string-matching approaches commonly use suffix document models. Suffix data structures store each substring of a text and allow for efficient comparisons. Using string matching for PD requires the computation of suffix document models for the suspicious document and for all documents in the reference collection. Because the pattern to search for is initially unknown in a PD setting, the detection procedure must select portions of the suspicious text and check them against all other suffix models [20].

Baker was among the first to employ suffix trees for PD [19]. She augmented the trees' vertices with positional information that allowed detecting all matching strings of maximum length. Baker defined a heuristic similarity threshold and tailored her procedure to check source code for plagiarism. She suggested an adaption of the algorithms to text plagiarism detection, but did not pursue this application [20]. The Match Detect Reveal (MDR) system also employed string matching for PD [232]. MDR adopted Ukkonen's algorithm [336], which only considers suffixes of full words for constructing the tree [234]. MDR used the matching statistics algorithm of Chang and Lawler for overlap computation [63]. Khmelev et al. constructed a PDS using suffix arrays for document representation and the "R-measure", i.e. the normalized sum of repeated substrings, for similarity calculation [175]. Goan et al. used String B-Trees and similarity assessments leveraging "[…] *knowledge of common text patterns* [...]" ([137], p. 693) for PD. The authors presented no additional implementation details.

The strength of substring-matching PD approaches is their accuracy in detecting verbatim text overlaps. Suffix document models encode the complete character information of a text, which distinguishes them from the document models that most fingerprinting methods employ. If two documents share substrings, suffix document models enable the detection of this overlap through string matching.

The major drawbacks of string matching in a PD context are the difficulty of detecting disguised plagiarism, which is attributable to the exact matching approach, and the high computational effort required. At the time of writing, the most space-efficient suffix tree [183], suffix array [177] and suffix vector [236] implementations allow searching in linear time and require on average approximately $8n$ of storage space, with n being the number of characters in the original document. String B-Trees allow searching in $O(\log n)$, but also require multiple times the storage space of the original documents [183]. Additionally, pre-computing suffix models is computationally expensive.

For very large document collections, the computational requirements prohibit the practical application of elaborate string matching. Therefore, PDS commonly apply computationally less expensive approaches, such as fingerprinting methods to limit the document collection in the heuristic retrieval phase and subsequently employ string matching in the detailed analysis phase (see Figure 1 in Section 2.2.1).

2.2.4.2   Vector Space Models

Vector Space Models (VSM) are a standard IR concept. VSMs consider the terms of a text as unordered sets, represent the sets as vectors and compare the vector representations using vector-based measures ([209], p. 120). We briefly outline the basic building blocks of VSMs, their application for PD and the strengths and weaknesses of the approach.

Most commonly, PDS use only one vector space model to encode the entire document. However, some PDS employ multiple models that encode paragraphs or sentences to perform a more local similarity assessment. This approach increases detection accuracy, but is computationally more expensive. Table 6 lists publications describing either global or local VSM as part of a PDS.

Table 6: Overview of Local and Global VSM Proposed for Plagiarism Detection

Scope	Used in
global (document)	[88, 94, 158, 230, 299]
local (sentences)	[150, 171, 238]

Most VSM consider words as terms, yet any unit of text can quantify as a *term unit*. Terms most often undergo *preprocessing*, i.e. a normalization and selection process, prior to constructing the model. Preprocessing may include stemming of words, de-capitalization, stop word and punctuation removal, number replacement or part-of-speech tagging [67, 150, 238, 252, 299]. Table 7 lists publications describing VSM for PD purposes using different term units.

Table 7: Overview of the Term Units of VSM Proposed for Plagiarism Detection

Term Unit	Used in
words	[94, 230, 299]
word n-grams	[24, 88]
Sentences	[150, 171, 238]

A *term weighting scheme* is a crucial part of all vector space document models, because it determines the most relevant terms to check. PDS commonly apply the classic *tf-idf* scheme, which considers a term's frequency (*tf*) in a document and normalizes it by the term's inverse frequency in all documents of the collection (*idf*) [94, 150, 171, 299]. The *tf-idf* scheme assigns high weights to terms that occur frequently within the analyzed document, but infrequently in the entire collection. The idea is that such terms are likely specific content words that characterize a topic, which few other documents in the collection address.

The *similarity function* defines how matching terms of documents contribute to the calculation of a similarity score. Numerous works use the standard cosine similarity measure [94, 150, 238, 299]. More complex similarity functions incorporate semantic information to increase the probability of identifying disguised plagiarism, for example, by considering word synonyms. Kang et al. propose a similarity function that assesses word matches, including synonyms and vector overlap on the sentence level [171]. The similarity functions of Tsatsaronis et al. [333] and Pera and Ng [252] give additional weight to co-occurring, semantically related terms. Both works use the WordNet ontology [109] to pre-compute the semantic relatedness of terms and the Wikipedia encyclopedia [365] to calculate co-occurrence frequencies.

VSM are well-researched and well-performing approaches for identifying verbatim text overlaps. The global similarity assessment on the document level that most VSM perform tends to be detrimental to detection accuracy in PD settings. This is because verbatim plagiarism more often encompasses smaller, confined segments of a text, which favors local similarity analysis.

2.2.5 Stylometry

Stylometry subsumes statistical methods to quantify and analyze an author's writing style [160, 169]. Authorship attribution (AA) is the dominant field of application for stylometry and a prolific area of research beyond the scope of this thesis. Juola and Stamatatos perform extensive surveys on the state of the art in AA [169, 310].

Authorship verification is a problem class within AA and related to intrinsic and external PD [169, 178, 319]. Authorship verification addresses the binary decision problem of whether an alleged author wrote a given text or not. Conducting stylometric comparisons in one of three possible categories can solve this problem. According to Koppel and Stein [178, 319], these categories include:

1. Comparing existing documents from the author in question with a text doubtfully originating from the same author. This represents the classical authorship verification problem.

2. Comparing a text of the author in question to other texts written by different authors in order to identify similar sections. This corresponds to the problem of external PD.

3. Comparing different text segments allegedly written by the author in question to other text segments within the same documents in order to identify suspicious differences. This represents the intrinsic approach to PD, because it requires no external sources.

The following section outlines the characteristic strengths and weaknesses of stylometry and its contribution to intrinsic PD. We identified no applications of stylometry for external PD, arguably because other PD approaches achieve a better detection performance, refer to Section 2.3.1. We do not cover the classical authorship verification problems, because we cannot assume writing samples from the author in question to be widely available in a PD setting.

2.2.5.1 Stylometry for Intrinsic Plagiarism Detection

Intrinsic PD approaches construct and compare models that quantify an author's characteristic writing style for individual segments of a text. The goal is to identify sections that are stylistically different from other sections, and thus potential indicators of plagiarism [97]. Technically, intrinsic PD approaches solve a one-class classification problem. Genuine text segments that share characteristic attributes represent the target class, while plagiarized segments form outliers with divergent attributes. An automatic classification method must learn the characteristics of the target class and use them for rejecting outliers [260, 274, 319]. According to Stein et al., intrinsic plagiarism detection procedures generally contain the following components [319]:

A *decomposition strategy* defines the segments compared by the detection procedure. Using fixed-length segments based, for example, on character [311] or word counts [97, 144, 319], is a basic strategy [310]. Another common practice is structural segmentation, on the sentence [238], paragraph [322] or chapter [339] level.

A *style model* defines the set of linguistic features analyzed by the detection procedure. Style models generally use a unique combination of features selected from over 1,000 features proposed for stylometry [144, 279, 319]. The majority of features fall into one of the following categories [310, 319]:

- *Lexical features* appear on the character level, e.g., *n*-gram frequency, or on the word level, e.g., average word lengths or syllables per word.

- *Syntactic features* include word or part-of-speech frequencies.

- *Structural features* include average paragraph length or punctuation frequency.

An *outlier detection procedure* operates on the feature vectors of the segment and the overall document to identify significantly different elements. Many classifiers for one-class classification problems are available [319]. Intrinsic PD approaches commonly use traditional measures of dispersion, for example, standard deviation or median absolute deviation [322], and vector comparisons using cosine similarity [239]. Meyer zu Eisen et al. demonstrated machine-learning approaches capable of learning the relative differences in feature vectors [98]. Stein et al. applied methods using estimated feature distributions in the target and outlier class [319].

An *outlier post-processing procedure* determines whether multiple outliers form a larger section and are suspicious enough to be reported. Heuristic voting [322] or meta-learning [319] are two approaches used to solve this task.

The advantage of intrinsic PD is its independence from a reference collection. Thus, in theory, intrinsic PDS can give a quick overview of document segments that need further assessment in a plagiarism investigation. The accuracy and reliability of automated stylometric analyses depends on multiple factors, including the observed linguistic features, genre, volume, and purity of the analyzed text. For instance, quoted text, headings, tables or figures can significantly skew style statistics [169, 310]. Joint publications are another obstacle to text purity. Detecting writing style differences that signal potential plagiarism, and not simply multiple authorship, is a challenge for these kinds of documents [219]. Section 2.3.1 gives an overview of performance for state-of-the-art intrinsic PDS.

2.2.6 Cross-Language Plagiarism Detection

Cross-language plagiarism detection (CLPD) aims to identify documents plagiarized by translation from source documents in another language [259]. To scale to large document collections, CLPD approaches should follow the three-stage PD process composed of a heuristic retrieval, a detailed analysis and a knowledge-based post-processing phase (see Section 2.2.1) [259].

For the *heuristic retrieval* phase, a CLPD approach may construct a monolingual keyword index for the reference collection, extract, and machine-translate keywords from a suspicious document in another language, and query the index with the translated keywords. Alternatively, a CLPD approach could machine-translate the entire suspicious document prior to extracting keywords and querying the index. In the second case, the detection approach could also use a fingerprint index instead of a keyword index [259, 263].

For the *detailed analysis* phase, detection procedures can apply a number of retrieval models from Cross-Language Information Retrieval (CLIR). Such models can either use pre-computed dictionaries [59, 266, 320], or character similarities if the languages of the reference collection and the suspicious document share sufficient syntactical similarities [224]. Dictionaries can be trained by analyzing parallel [58, 257] or comparable corpora [259].

A detailed review of CLIR models is beyond the scope of this thesis. Potthast et al. present such a survey and compare three models they regard as promising for CLPD [263]. Both McNamee & Mayfield and Potthast et al., propose approaches to cross-language text similarity comparison that are promising for the detailed analysis phase of the CLPD process [224, 259].

As Section 2.3 shows, some prototypical PDS [172, 239, 371] machine translate all documents in the reference collection prior to applying monolingual PD approaches. However, this approach is only feasible for smaller local collections [261].

Currently, CLPD attracts less attention than monolingual PD and most research focuses on the similarity assessment in the detailed analysis stage [263]. We found no PDS that implements the complete CLPD process. Potthast et al. view CLPD research as being *"[...] still in its infancy"* ([263], p. 15).

2.3 Plagiarism Detection Systems

The plagiarism detection software business is large, fast-paced and growing. Companies offer an increasing variety of plagiarism detection systems, but many cease to exist after a short life cycle [18, 356]. Available systems perform external PD. We found no PDS in practical use that performed intrinsic PD. PDS either compare documents within a user-defined corpus or check texts against an external collection, which usually includes some subset of the Internet. Appendix J contains an overview of widely used systems.

2.3.1 Evaluations of PDS

Comparing the detection performance of PDS is challenging. Authors proposing PDS prototypes often use non-standardized evaluation methods. In a review of 139 publications on PD, Potthast et al. found that 80 % of the papers used individual corpora for evaluation and less than 50 % offered comparisons to prior research [262].

We found two projects that address this lack of comparability. Both benchmark PDS using standardized collections. The first project is the annual PAN International Competition on Plagiarism Detection (PAN-PC), initiated in 2009 [260]. PAN is an acronym for "Plagiarism Analysis, Authorship Identification, and Near-Duplicate Detection". Competitors in the PAN-PC primarily present research prototypes. The second project is a comparison of commercial and otherwise publicly available PDS, which a research group at the HTW University of Applied Sciences in Berlin performs periodically [356]. We will refer to this test series as the HTW PDS Tests. We will present results from the PAN-PC in 2011 to point out the capabilities of state-of-the-art PDS prototypes and subsequently discuss the findings from the latest HTW Test for external PDS to highlight the strengths and weaknesses of PDS available to the public.

2.3.1.1 Research Prototypes

The PAN-PC offers tasks for external and intrinsic plagiarism detection. The evaluation corpus of PAN-PC'11 contained 26,939 documents, of which 50 % were suspicious texts, and the remainder formed the reference collection. Suspicious documents contained 61,064 artificially plagiarized sections, of which 82 % were obfuscated by applying the following techniques:

- Using automated or manual English translations of German and Spanish text sections;

- Performing random shuffles, insertions, deletions or semantic substitutions of terms;

- Asking humans to paraphrase sections [264].

Figure 5 illustrates the results of the PAN-PC'11. The figure shows the plagiarism detection (*plagdet*) scores of the five best performing external PDS grouped by the obfuscation technique applied to the plagiarized text segments.

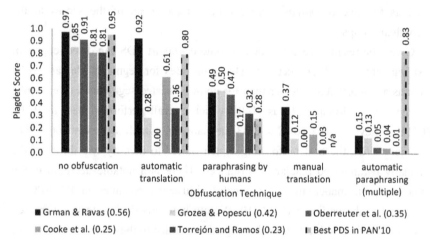

Figure 5: Plagdet Scores for External PDS in PAN-PC'11

Source: [264]

The *plagdet* score considers the F-measure, which is the equally weighted harmonic mean of precision (P) and recall (R), and combines this mean with the granularity (*gran*) of the detection algorithm. Precision denominates what percentage of all instances reported as suspicious by an algorithm are actually plagiarism. Recall denotes what percentage of all plagiarized instances in the collection a detection algorithm reports. The granularity reflects whether the detection algorithms identified the plagiarized instance as a whole or in multiple parts. The interval of the score is [0,1]. For the computation of the score, refer to [261].

For each of the five obfuscation techniques in Figure 5, the rightmost bars with a dashed fill show the *plagdet* score of the best performing system in the competition of the previous year: PAN-PC'10. However, these rightmost bars meant for comparison are only a rough indicator of the advancement of detection performance, because the evaluation corpus of PAN-PC'11 included more obfuscated segments than the corpus of PAN-PC'10. Moreover, the corpus of PAN-PC'11 included manual translations, whereas the corpora of all previous competitions included only automatic translations. Each legend entry states in brackets the overall *plagdet* score, which is the mean of the scores in the individual groups.

Given the results, we conclude that state-of-the-art PDS can detect copies of text segments with high accuracy. Detection rates for segments plagiarized by humans are substantially lower than for non-obfuscated segments. For example, the system of Grman & Ravas [140], which overall performed best in PAN-PC'11, achieved a recall of $R = 0.33$ for manually paraphrased segments [264]. In other words, the best performing system failed to identify two-thirds of the manually paraphrased plagiarism instances. There is a notable decrease in the detection performance for automatically obfuscated passages in PAN-PC'11 compared to the earlier PAN-PC'10. We attribute this decline to the increased amount of obfuscated test cases that organizers added to the evaluation corpus of PAN-PC'11.

The seemingly good detection performance for automatically translated text segments is misleading. The systems that performed well used automated services for translating foreign language documents in the reference collection into English. The employed services, such as Google Translate, are similar or identical to the ones used to construct the translated, plagiarized sections in the first place [263, 264]. The detection rate for manually translated plagiarism is substantially lower. For instance, the best performing system of Grman & Ravas achieved a recall $R = 0.26$ for manually translated segments [264]. We hypothesize that the translation undertaken by real authors when obfuscating their plagiarism is more complex and versatile, and hence harder to detect by the tested systems.

Figure 6 displays the *plagdet* scores of the four systems participating in the intrinsic detection track of PAN-PC'11. All systems performed significantly worse than those in the external track.

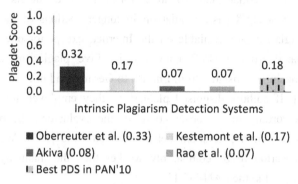

Figure 6: Plagdet Scores for Intrinsic PDS in PAN-PC'11

Source: [264]

The organizers attribute the good relative performance of the system presented by Oberreuter et al. to exploiting the artificial way of creating most plagiarized sections in the evaluation corpus. Artificial plagiarism in the evaluation corpus was created by copying text from source documents regardless of topical relatedness. This benefits the system of Oberreuter et al., which evaluates the uniqueness of words relative to the rest of the analyzed documents [246]. This approach is most likely not reproducible in realistic settings [264]. The performance of the remaining systems is in line with earlier PAN competitions. For comparison, a naïve baseline approach of classifying all segments as plagiarized achieved a recall $R = 0.46$, precision $P = 0.23$ and plagdet score of 0.24 in 2009 [260].

Intrinsic PD requires longer texts to work reliably. Stein et al. analyzed a subset of the PAN-PC'09 evaluation corpus. They excluded documents under 35,000 words from their evaluation for not being reliably analyzable. Stein et al. report precision values ranging from $0.72 - 0.98$ with corresponding recall values ranging from $0.30 - 0.60$ depending on the used sub-collection [319].

2.3.1.2   Systems Available to the Public

The latest HTW PDS Test for external detection systems in 2010 evaluated 26 publicly available systems using 40 manually fabricated essays – of which 30 were written in German and 10 in English. Most documents contained copy & paste or shake & paste plagiarism in longer sections of the text. The sources of plagiarism are available on the Internet, except for one document, which originated from a DVD encyclopedia. Five plagiarism cases were manually or machine translated from English to German and one from French to English [356]. If authors disguised plagiarism, they employed moderate text alterations. According to the observations of the evaluators, the obfuscation resembles the common plagiarism behavior of students [357]. We view the resulting obfuscation to be comparably weaker than the manually rewritten segments contained in the PAN-PC'11.

The organizers use a three-class scale to benchmark the reliability of tested PDS. The exact scoring criteria depended on the individual test documents. For instance, the organizers judged whether a PDS could identify all sources of a plagiarism (3 points), nearly all sources (2 points), some sources (1 point) or no sources (0 points) [357].

Figure 7 displays the number of test cases discovered by the top five systems in the HTW PDS Test 2010. Most undetected cases resulted from the six translations in the corpus. Due to the light obfuscation, the systems identified most other plagiarism cases more or less completely.

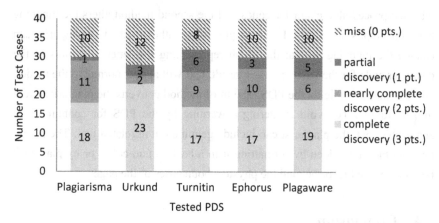

Figure 7: Performance of the Top Five Publicly Available PDS

Source: [356]

2.3.2 Technical Weaknesses of PDS

Technical weaknesses can significantly decrease the detection accuracy of PDS. The term technical disguise subsumes techniques to obfuscate plagiarism by exploiting technical weaknesses of PDS. Technical disguise solely affects the machine internal representation of text, which the PDS processes, while keeping the text unaltered to the human eye.

One example of technical disguise is inserting characters with font color identical to the background into plagiarized text. This renders the text as nonsense to the PDS. A similar disguise for plagiarized text is replacing letters from the original alphabet with letters from foreign alphabets that feature visually identical glyphs [248].

Heather demonstrated three methods of technical disguise that are especially suitable for altering documents in PDF format [151]. The first two methods both alter the mapping between visible glyphs to machine-processable characters. PDF files store text as a sequence of numerical character identifiers (CIDs). Special mappings in the PDF link CIDs to both the visible glyphs, i.e. the character shapes, as well as their machine-processable character codes. The first method Heather describes alters a PDF's mapping between CIDs and machine-processable character codes and the second method alters the mapping between glyphs and CIDs. For example, using either method, a plagiarist can change the mapping so that the glyph representing the letter 'e' points to the character code for the letter 'x'. As a result, text will appear normal to the reader, but is uninterpretable by the PDS. The third method converts the plagiarized text into a graphic. To avoid triggering a warning by the PDS for containing no analyzable text, the plagiarist can include genuine but unrelated text. The phony text can then be hidden by formatting it in a background color, or by placing it behind the graphic, or beyond the physical boundaries of the page.

2.4   Conclusion

In reviewing the research on plagiarism among students, we showed that the issue has been generating concern for decades. Compared to plagiarism among students, plagiarism among post-graduate scholars received less research attention. However, sporadic studies showed that post-graduate scholars do engage in plagiarism. Evidence from various cases of plagiarism also suggested that plagiarists in the sciences tend to disguise their misconduct more sophisticatedly and therefore are caught less often. In recent years, an increasing number of journals and conferences have begun to employ plagiarism detection systems to check submitted manuscripts routinely.

   Our review of detection approaches and their performance shows that PD approaches face an inevitable tradeoff between detection accuracy and computational effort. Table 8 summarizes the capabilities of current PD approaches in detecting the different forms of plagiarism.

Table 8: Capabilities of Current Plagiarism Detection Approaches

Detection Approach	Application				Form of plagiarism						References
	Extrinsic PD	Intrinsic PD	Mono-lingual PD	Cross-lingual PD	Copies	Near copies	Shake & Paste	Undue Paraphrase	Translated	Idea	
Character-based (Char.)	X		X								
Exact String Matching											[19, 137, 175, 232]
Approximate String Matching											[285, 370]
Fingerprinting											[57, 142, 245, 293, 307]
Vector Space Models											[24, 238, 252, 328, 333]
Semantic Enhancements											[22, 190, 252, 333]
Cross-language (CLPD)	X			X							[172, 239, 263, 371]
Stylometry (Style)		X	X								[97, 238, 319, 322]

Detection rate: | Good | Fair | Poor | Unfit |

We showed that all external monolingual PD approaches rely on character-based similarity between documents. Therefore, the detection accuracy of these methods decreases with increasing disguise of plagiarism. String-matching methods exhibit the strongest dependence on character-based similarity. By applying suitable term selection, fingerprinting or vector space model approaches are more stable against character alterations, but incur information loss and fail when character-based similarity falls below a certain level. The lack of textual overlap also makes translations and idea plagiarisms impossible to detect for character-based methods.

External, cross-language plagiarism detection is not mature or reliable at the time of writing [263]. Machine translating all documents in the reference collection not written in the target language, an approach applied by some prototypes in the PAN-PC is not scalable in practice [261].

The results of the PAN competitions, the HTW PDS Test and other studies [157, 170, 218, 282] prove that state-of-the-art PDS, which implement external detection methods, find incidences of verbatim and slightly modified copying with high accuracy, given the sources are accessible to the PDS. D. Weber-Wulff summarizes the current state of PDS as follows:

"[...] PDS find copies, not plagiarism." ([357], p. 6)
"[...] for translations or heavily edited material, the systems are powerless [...]" [360]

Aside from text alterations, technical disguise can fool existing PDS. The major systems seem to have implemented no countermeasures yet, but we expect that integrating additional checks to reveal technical disguise will present a minor challenge to future PDS.

Many researchers recognize the need to incorporate semantic information into similarity checks to allow detecting disguised plagiarism [22, 190, 252, 333]. In the experiments of Bao et al., considering synonyms increased detection performance by factor two to three. However, the processing time increased by factor 27 [22]. We regard current character-based PD approaches that include semantic analysis as computationally too expensive for most practical PD tasks.

Intrinsic plagiarism detection using stylometry is another approach that can overcome the boundaries of character-based similarity by comparing linguistic similarity. Given that the stylistic differences between plagiarized and original text are significant, and not due to legitimate multiple authorship, stylometry is a capable aid in identifying disguised plagiarism. When a plagiarist paraphrases text to the point where it resembles the expressions of the plagiarist, stylometry fails. The results of PAN-PC 2010, PAN-PC 2011, and the experiments by Stein et al. [319] indicate that stylometry only works reliably for document lengths of at least several thousand words. This restricts the applicability of this method for PD. We found no PDS in practical use that performed intrinsic PD.

In conclusion, the research on academic plagiarism detection has led to the development of PDS capable of detecting literal plagiarism, for example copy & paste or shake & paste type plagiarism. However, PDS remain unable to reliably detect strongly disguised plagiarism forms, such as paraphrases, translated plagiarism and idea plagiarism.

3 Citation-based Document Similarity

This chapter describes related work on citation-based similarity measures and relevant terminology. While Citation-based Plagiarism Detection (CbPD) makes use of citations for similarity computation, the related work section is relatively short for the following reasons:

- To date, citation analysis has been used mainly to identify semantically related documents and not for plagiarism detection purposes. Therefore, no directly related prior work is available.

- To date, almost all citation-based similarity measures analyze citation relationships on the document level. This global citation analysis is insufficient for the purpose of plagiarism detection, which requires analyzing intra-document citation relationships, including the order and proximity of citations to pinpoint *local* similarities.

- Co-citation Proximity Analysis (CPA), an approach proposed by the author of this thesis, presents the first citation-based similarity measure that considers the relative position of citations within a document's full-text to improve the accuracy of Co-citation analysis (see the patent application in E and [126]).

This chapter is structured as follows. Section 3.1 reviews terminology relevant to citation-based document similarity measures. Section 3.2 introduces citation-based document similarity measures relevant for the development of the CbPD approach. As a supplement to Section 3.2, Appendix I gives a summary of studies evaluating the performance of existing citation-based document similarity measures. This chapter concludes by placing the different similarity measures in context and explaining their role for the development of the CbPD concept.

3.1   Terminology

This section introduces relevant terminology for citation-based similarity computation and places the terms in context of the pursued research.

3.1.1 Citation vs. Reference

The terms *citation* and *reference* are often used inconsistently, although they have distinct meanings in library and information science as discussed in ([187], pp. 42-45). Technically speaking, a *reference* in a document A is a bibliographic note that describes a document B. If document A contains a reference to document B, then B receives a *citation* from A ([96], p. 204).

However, authors commonly use the term citation ambiguously to express "receiving a citation", e.g., [168, 187], to express "giving a citation", e.g., [199, 330], or to refer to an "in-text citation", i.e. to refer to the position at which a source is cited in the text, e.g., [99, 106]. An in-text-citation is a short text string in the body of academic texts that serves as a marker and points to an entry (reference) in the bibliography [155]. Overcoming the ambiguity of the term citation is difficult, because no widely accepted terminology exists to distinguish clearly between the different notions of "citation". As Larsen points out, a clear terminological distinction would require coining new terms ([187], p. 43).

We abstain from introducing new terms, to avoid confusion for domain experts. Instead, we use the term *reference* to refer to entries in the bibliography and the term *citation* either to refer to in-text markers, which point to references, or to denote the number of times a document is referenced by other documents. We clarify the desired notion by giving appropriate context. If a distinction between citation and reference is unnecessary, we use the more common expression, citation. For instance, we refer to similarity approaches that use citations, references, or a combination thereof as *citation analysis* or *citation-based* approaches. We use the verbs *citing* and *referencing* synonymously to indicate that a document refers to another work. Similarly, we use *being cited* and *being referenced* interchangeably to describe works that were credited by another work.

Figure 8 illustrates this terminology. There is a 1:1 relationship between a document and each of its references and a 1:n relationship between a single reference and corresponding in-text citations.

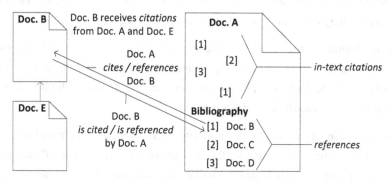

Figure 8: Citations and References in Scientific Documents

3.1.2 Similarity vs. Relatedness

The terms *similarity* and *relatedness* are used interchangeably in current literature. However, in certain situations, the connotation of these terms can be quite different. Similarity in lexical and structural characteristics can point to potential plagiarism. This is why text similarity can have a negative connotation in the academic community. Text relatedness has no such negative connotation, implying only a content-based, semantic similarity between documents. We find this connotation of the terms significant, although by no means universal. Each individual having his or her own definition of these generically used terms further challenges a clear definition. For these reasons, we will not dissect the nuanced meanings of similarity and relatedness, but rather regard the terms as equivalent and use only "similarity".

3.1.3 Dimensions of Similarity: Lexical, Semantic, Structural

Similarities between texts can take on several forms. The majority of current publications on information recommendation and retrieval systems simply use the term *document similarity* without giving much attention to the types of similarity. For example, many authors use the terms *lexical* and *structural,* or *subject* and *topical similarity* interchangeably. The distinctions between similarity forms, however, are of importance for this work.

For the purpose of this work, we distinguish between three distinct similarity dimensions for documents: *lexical, semantic,* and *structural.* These dimensions of similarity may occur individually, or in combination.

Lexical similarity measures the degree to which a set of words in two documents or document sections, e.g., sentences or paragraphs, is similar. For example, if the lexical similarity of two sentences is 1, they exhibit a 100 % overlap in their vocabularies and word order.

Semantic similarity measures the similarity of two or more texts based on their conceptual meaning. For example, the statements "the earth is round" and "the world is a globe" are not lexically similar, because they share no words aside from "the" and "is". Yet, the statements are semantically similar, because their meaning is synonymous.

Distinguishing lexical from semantic text similarities is a common problem in information retrieval. Tsatsaronis quantified lexical text similarities by using a VSM (see Section 2.2.4 on page 26) and similarity measures including Cosine, Jaccard, Dice and TF-IDF [334]. These approaches solely compare the textual representation of words and not their semantic content. Resnik [276], O'Shea [247], and Charles [231] discussed different dimensions of semantic similarity. We define two papers as semantically similar if they address the same or a similar research objective.

Structural similarity[11] in texts is a term we use to describe similarities in the composition of two or more documents. Structural similarities in text can take on various forms as discussed in the following chapters. An example of document structural similarity is the occurrence of shared citations in similar order in two documents.

---

[11] The term is unrelated to the structural similarity (SSIM) index; a concept for measuring similarity between two images, see http://en.wikipedia.org/wiki/Structural_similarity.

3.2 Citation-based Similarity Measures

This section presents link- and citation-based similarity measures. These measures are independent of the lexical, syntactical and style characteristics of a text. So far, citation-based measures have not been used for the purpose of plagiarism detection. Therefore, no related work using citations for plagiarism detection exists. This section presents citation-based measures that were introduced for general document similarity computation purposes.

Of the citation-based measures, Bibliographic Coupling, Co-citation, and Co-citation Proximity analysis are the measures with most direct relevance to the CbPD approach. Although these measures were not developed with the aim to detect plagiarism, reviewing them contributes to the understanding of the CbPD approach proposed in this thesis. A summary of studies examining the applicability of the citation-based similarity measures introduced in this section for different retrieval tasks is provided in Appendix I.

3.2.1 Direct Citation

Direct citation is the most intuitive approach to measure citation-based similarity. Direct citation, also known as intercitation, considers two documents similar if one cites the other. Each citation relationship is bidirectional as illustrated in Figure 9.

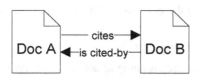

Figure 9: Doc A cites Doc B, while Doc B is cited-by Doc A.

Figure 10 visualizes the direct citations in a citation graph [17]. The node on the left is a paper from 1986. Nodes to the right represent more recent papers that either directly cited the 1986 paper, or that cited the 1986 paper indirectly by citing a paper which cited the 1986 paper further down the line. In this way, citation graphs can visualize valuable information about the popularity of publications.

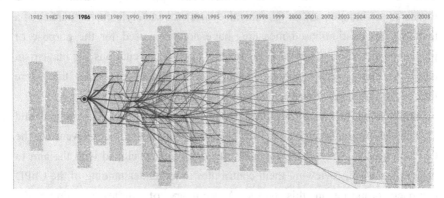

Figure 10: Visualization of a Citation Graph

Source: [17]

Search engines for scientific documents typically use the *cited-by* relationship to identify topically related documents or to rank search results. Topically related documents that are more recent can be identified by browsing cited-by relations, since cited documents are generally published earlier than the documents that cite it. High *cited-by* scores indicate higher popularity and relevance of a document [26]. Traversing *cite* relationships is useful for verifying information by checking the cited source or to identify further reading.

3.2.2 Bibliographic Coupling

In 1956, Fano suggested the grouping of academic papers using citation relations rather than on content [108]. Kessler coined this concept *Bibliographic Coupling* and argued for its usefulness as a measure for subject similarity. Documents are bibliographically coupled if they both cite at least one identical reference. The coupling strength represents the number of shared references. In Figure 11, the coupling strength of documents A and B equals 2, since both cite documents C and D.

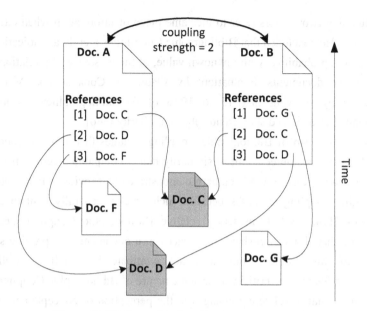

Figure 11: Bibliographic Coupling between Documents

Bibliographic Coupling strength (BCS) can be expressed as the Jaccard Index of the references in two documents, as shown by Equation 3.1:

$$BCS(d_1, d_2) = \frac{|R_{d_1} \cap R_{d_2}|}{|R_{d_1} \cup R_{d_2}|} \tag{3.1}$$

In this notation, d denotes a document and R_d the set of documents, which are cited by d, i.e., the references of d. The more references two documents d_1 and d_2 have in common, the more they are related. If the sets R_{d_1} and R_{d_2} are empty, the coupling strength is zero.

Bibliographic Coupling expresses a relationship between documents based on earlier documents as established by the authors when choosing their references. This relationship is static and intrinsic to the coupled documents, since it solely depends on the references in the respective works and does not change over time [304].

Several researchers questioned the usefulness of Bibliographic Coupling as a similarity measure. Martyn criticized that Bibliographic Coupling cannot guarantee that two authors refer to the same piece of information when citing a work [216]. He concluded that Bibliographic Coupling is merely an indication of there being a probability, with unknown value, of the existence of a relationship between two documents. Evaluations by Vladutz & Cook support Martyn's conclusion by showing that 15 to 19 % of the bibliographically coupled documents they analyzed showed no subject similarity [346].

Further criticism of Bibliographic Coupling includes that absolute coupling strength cannot guarantee a unit of similarity that is comparable across different document pairs. Kessler and Weinberg demonstrated that review articles tend to have higher coupling strengths because such articles generally contain more references [174, 363]. Considering relative Bibliographic Coupling, i.e. the fraction of shared and non-shared references in a document, can provide some remedy to this problem, but does not eliminate it. Small as well as Marshakova-Shaikevich criticized the static nature of Bibliographic Coupling for being suboptimal in reflecting changes in the perception of concepts and ideas expressed in the respective articles [213, 301]. This can be detrimental to mapping emerging trends and the evolution of a research field.

3.2.3 Co-citation

In an effort to address the static nature of *Bibliographic Coupling*, both Small and Marshakova-Shaikevich independently published the Co-citation concept in 1973 [213, 301].

Two documents are co-cited if they are jointly cited by at least one later work. The number of documents that jointly cite the two earlier documents determines the strength of the co-citation relationship and the cardinality of the co-citation score. Figure 12 demonstrates Co-citation for the document pair *A* and *B* Documents *A* and *B* are jointly cited by documents *C* and *D*, and hence have a co-citation strength of 2.

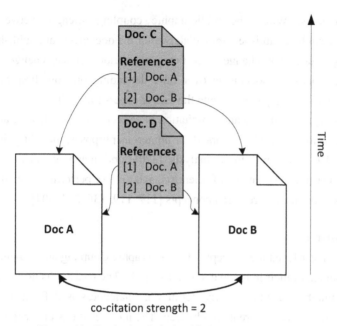

co-citation strength = 2

Figure 12: Co-citation Relationship between Documents

Alternatively, co-citation strength (CCS) can be expressed as a fraction, as shown in Equation 3.2:

$$CCS(d_1, d_2) = \frac{|C_{d_1} \cap C_{d_2}|}{|C_{d_1} \cup C_{d_2}|} \qquad (3.2)$$

In this notation, C_{d_i} stands for the set of "citing" documents, i.e. the pool of other documents that cite document d_i. The number of citing documents that two cited documents d_1 and d_2 have in common determines their subject similarity.

A co-citation relationship between two documents is extrinsic to the documents in question because the co-citation relationship is established using "incoming" links. Co-citation strength depends on the frequency with which other texts – that is subsequently published works – cite earlier publications. For this reason, co-citation has a tendency to fail for very recent publications. In contrast, Bibliographic Coupling measures the static "outgoing" links shared by two documents. While the bibliographic coupling strength between two documents can be established immediately after the documents are published and the strength does not change over time, co-citation reflects changes in the relationship between documents over time depending on how frequently the authors of subsequent papers co-cite the earlier papers [301, 304].

Bibliographic Coupling and Co-citation have received considerable attention in research and were rapidly adapted for numerous purposes, including literature retrieval [103], research front analysis [270], and mapping science, which includes measuring the impact of scientists, and diverse performance evaluations of articles, journals, and research concepts [117, 119, 136, 294, 304].

3.2.4 Amsler

In 1972, Amsler fused the concepts of Bibliographic Coupling and Co-citation to take advantage of their individual strengths[12] [13]. The measure is normalized by the total number of citations. By definition, relatedness is defined as zero if neither d_1 nor d_2 have parents or children. The more citations either the parents or children share, the more related they are. Equation 3.3 defines the Amsler measure:

$$Amsler\ (d_1, d_2) = \frac{|(C_{d_1} \cup R_{d_1}) \cap (C_{d_2} \cup R_{d_2})|}{|(C_{d_1} \cup R_{d_1}) \cup (C_{d_2} \cup R_{d_2})|} \tag{3.3}$$

A similar approach proposed in 2010 is *Inter-Connection* [368]. It also uses both incoming and outgoing citations (links) by transforming them into undirected links.

3.2.5 Co-citation Proximity-based Methods

Co-citation Proximity Analysis (CPA) was proposed in 2006 by the author of this thesis [122, 126]. This similarity measure builds on the co-citation analysis

---

[12] The definition is based on a paper of Couto [79], because the original technical report of Amsler is neither available in common literature databases, nor available from the department where it was published. We contacted other authors who cited the report, but found that they had not seen the original publication either and instead relied on descriptions from other papers.

approach, but differs in that it exploits the information implied in the placement of citations within the full-texts of documents. CPA rests on the assumption that documents cited in close proximity to each other within a document's full-text also tend to be more closely related than documents cited farther apart.

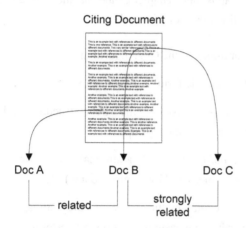

Figure 13: Co-citation Proximity Analysis

Figure 13 illustrates the concept. CPA rates documents B and C as more strongly related than documents B and A, because the citations to B and C are within the same sentence, while the citations to B and A are separated by several paragraphs.

The advantage of the CPA measure, compared to Co-Citation, is an improvement in precision [55, 106, 126, 198, 199, 351]. Other widely used citation analysis approaches – Bibliographic Coupling, Co-citation or the Amsler measure – do not take into account the location or proximity of citations within documents. The CPA measure allows a more granular automatic classification of documents and can be used to identify not only related documents, but also the specific sections within texts that are most related.

The CPA similarity measure calculates a *Citation Proximity Index (CPI)* for each set of documents cited by an examined document. Cited documents are assigned a weight of $\frac{1}{2^n}$, where n stands for the number of structural components separating the citations. Structural components can be measured in various increments, depending on the "resolution" of document similarity to be examined, for example, local versus global similarity. We define the smallest structural components for CPI calculation as citation groups, then sentences, followed by paragraphs and chapters, and at the highest level the entire document or even all volumes of a journal.

There are several variations of the CPA algorithm:

-   *Basic-CPA* – the basic form described above

-   *Extended-CPA* – considers the tree structure and citation arrangement within citation groups

-   *Multidimensional-CPA* – uses additional information, including the impact (e.g., measured by citation counts)

-   *Hybrid-CPA* – combines the CPI with other similarity measures, e.g., character-based measures. This boosts performance especially for documents with insufficient citation information.

3.3   Conclusion

Various citation-based measures for document similarity computation exist. Currently, these measures are used to identify related literature, for example, in recommender systems for academic literature. No citation-based similarity measure has so far been used for the purpose of plagiarism detection. Nonetheless, the citation-based approaches presented in this chapter are relevant for the following reasons:

Bibliographic Coupling – In addition to identifying topically similar papers, Bibliographic Coupling is suitable to be expanded to additionally reflect structural document similarity. We consider this similarity measure suitable as a baseline approach, see Section 4.2.1, to represent a very simple citation-based plagiarism detection approach, although Bibliographic Coupling was not developed, or previously used, for this purpose.

Co-citation – This similarity measure is only indirectly relevant for the purpose of plagiarism detection, since it measures relatedness between two documents on the global document level from the perspective of citing authors. It is suitable to identify documents that address, for example, the same research question, but is not suitable to identify documents that share structural similarity. This measure however is relevant, since it provides the basis for the CPA measure.

Co-citation Proximity Analysis (CPA) – The CPA measure is relevant for the understanding and development of the CbPD approach for two reasons:

1. CPA was the first citation-based similarity measure that considered the position of citations and their proximity to each other within the full-text of a document. Given the novelty of the approach, the author filled a patent application (see Appendix E). This citation position information allows identifying similar citation patterns between documents, which provide the basis for the CbPD approach proposed in this thesis (see Section 4.1).

2. CPA is used by the CbPD approach to identify citation substitutions as discussed in Section 7.3.2, page 214.

4 Citation-based Plagiarism Detection

When the author first considered the use of citation information as a method to detect plagiarism, he assumed this concept had already been explored or even integrated into today's plagiarism detection systems (PDS). After all, citations and references of scholarly publications have long been recognized as containing valuable semantic relatedness information for documents, as demonstrated in Section 3.2.

However, no publications or available systems considered the use of citation information for plagiarism detection purposes, despite plagiarism detection being a well-researched field with hundreds of publications. Given that this application of citation information had not yet been explored, the author proposed a citation pattern analysis approach for plagiarism detection and coined it Citation-based Plagiarism Detection (CbPD) [127].

Citation-based Plagiarism Detection (CbPD) subsumes methods that use citations and references to determine similarities between documents in order to identify plagiarism.

The underlying concept of CbPD is introduced in Section 4.1 and the citation characteristics analyzed by the CbPD algorithms are described in Section 4.2. Challenges to citation pattern identification and the potential transposing and scaling of copied citations by plagiarists is addressed in Section 4.3. Section 4.4 introduces an adaption of Bibliographic Coupling for plagiarism detection and describes the design of the CbPD algorithms. Section 4.5 summarizes the projected applicability of each of the introduced algorithms to detect the various forms of academic plagiarism and Section 4.6 introduces two additional scores for assessing the degree of suspicion for the citation patterns identified by the CbPD algorithms[13].

---

[13] Parts of these sections have been published with Norman Meuschke [129].

4.1 Concept

Ideally, plagiarism detection systems should detect both lexical and semantic similarity among documents. The detection capabilities of a PDS heavily depend on the similarity assessment performed by the PDS, which can be expressed in terms of a similarity function. The similarity function defines which *characteristics* of which textual *markers* are to be analyzed and how those characteristics are to be considered for computing a numeric similarity score. Each identifiable element of a text is a potential marker. We distinguish between two types of markers:

- *language-dependent markers* (e.g., character-*n*-grams, words, or other terms) and

- *language-independent markers* (e.g., citations, formulas, or dates).

Markers with defined characteristics represent a *pattern*. Commonly used characteristics to distinguish patterns and quantify the similarity of patterns include:

- marker *overlap*, i.e. the percentage of markers that documents share in common

- marker *distinctiveness*, i.e. how common are markers that documents share within the entire collection

- marker *order*, i.e. how similar is the order of occurrence for shared markers in the text

- marker *proximity*, i.e. how close to each other do shared markers occur in the text

As discussed in Section 2.3.1, current PD approaches can only reliably identify lexical similarity, i.e. character-based similarity as it is common in copy & paste plagiarism. The reason for this limitation is that current approaches consider only language-dependent markers and a limited set of characteristics for similarity computation. For instance, vector space models (VSMs) consider the overlap and distinctiveness of document terms. These approaches also consider the proximity of terms to some degree by constructing several VSMs for specific sections within a document. Fingerprinting methods are specialized index retrieval procedures, which consider the overlap, distinctiveness, and order of terms within patterns, yet they ignore the order of patterns.

Researchers initially explored attempts to detect semantic similarity (disguised plagiarism) by extending the set of considered language-dependent markers, for example, through Latent Semantic Indexing (LSI) or by including thesauri in the detection procedure to identify synonym replacements. However, such approaches are currently not practically feasible for plagiarism detection due to their computational complexity (refer to Section 2.3).

Because semantic similarity is very difficult to machine-detect, the idea motivating the research presented in this thesis is to measure structural similarity as an approximation for semantic similarity. The overarching concept of CbPD, which the author termed *Sequential Pattern Analysis*, is to consider a combination of language-independent and language-dependent markers, as well as the combination of all four similarity characteristics: overlap, distinctiveness, order and proximity for performing a similarity assessment.

Employing Sequential Pattern Analysis to detect strongly disguised academic plagiarism requires language-independent markers in academic texts. For this purpose, we regard using citations, and the citation patterns[14] that result, as a coherent approach for the following reasons:

- Citations are widely available in academic texts. Scientific publications without citations are rare, because presenting research without referring to any prior or related work is hardly possible.

- Citations are language-independent and less ambiguous than words. Paraphrasing or even translating allows expressing the

---

[14] Citation patterns are sub-sequences of the complete citation sequences, which contain shared citations between two documents and potentially intermediate non-shared citations.

same content in many different ways. However, the publications an author cites to back a given fact are often very specific. Even if citations are substitutable, identifying them will require knowledge of existing literature.

- Citations allow inferring semantic information. This inferable information becomes even more rich, if we take into account the exact placement of all citations within the full text of a document. However, even if the positions of citations within a document are unknown and only the bibliography is available, it is usually easy for an expert to recognize the research focus of a scientific paper.

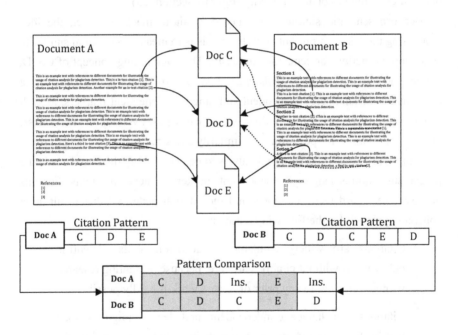

Figure 14: Depiction of CbPD Concept

Figure 14 depicts the general concept of citation pattern analysis for plagiarism detection. Document A and document B are shown as citing the documents C, D and E. Given their shared references, documents A and B likely discuss semantically similar content. More interestingly, however, they cite the three sources in a similar order within their full texts. Document B simply scales the citations to document C and D, see dashed lines in Figure 14. When comparing the citation patterns of documents A and B, i.e. their unique fingerprints, a citation pattern agreement of length three results, see gray highlights in Figure 14. The concept of CbPD thus allows for a document similarity computation even in the absence of text-based similarity among documents.

The concept behind CbPD is demonstrated by means of an example in the following thought experiment in which the reader may partake.

Experiment

Randomly open any set of 2-5 pages from the previous pages in this thesis.

- First, estimate the time it would take to paraphrase these pages to make the text unidentifiable by current PDS.
- Next, estimate the time it would take to research alternative works for each citation.

We estimate that paraphrasing a single page would take a plagiarist no more than an hour. However, finding alternative sources, which state *"x was the first to propose y"* or *"study a contradicts study b and c"* requires either expert knowledge, or time invested into research. Some sources are impossible to substitute, since only one source can be cited, for example, in the case of well-known theories, a certain painting, experiments or mathematical proofs, and initial papers introducing a new concept. Similarly, when plagiarizing content summarized in tables and figures, citations cannot be substituted without losing informational value.

In the case of this thesis, the author assumes that at least half of all citations are not substitutable without major rewriting, or without raising suspicion among knowledgeable readers. Certainly, it is possible to paraphrase scientific text and to delete all hard-to-substitute citations, but this significantly lowers the quality, and likely raises suspicion among the reviewers, making it difficult to publish an article at a reputable venue.

4.1.1 Citing Behavior

To understand the suitability of using citations to identify semantic similarity between documents, one must consider the reasons why authors cite. Garfield pioneered the field of author citing behavior, publishing the earliest paper detailing possible motivations for author citation [118], and found that authors cite for complex reasons. Garfield's list is extensive, but can be summarized into seven overarching motivations, defined by Brooks as [43]:

- *persuasiveness* – using references to convince peers of research validity

- *positive credit* – paying homage and giving credit to previous work

- *negative credit* – criticizing, correcting or disputing other works

- *currency* – the "prestige" factor that is associated with referring to the most current publications in a field

- *operational information* – references to the concepts, theories, and techniques borrowed from another author

- *reader alert* – providing readers with background information, or pointing to new findings

- *social consensus* – references chosen dependent on the author's belief of accepted norms or consensus in an academic field

We found the research on citation motivations to confirm the assumption that academic citations are carefully considered, independent markers, suitable for creating a digital fingerprint. This naturally makes citations difficult to substitute. While authors choose their citations for more than a single reason, for example, the scholars questioned by Brooks attributed 70.7 % of their references to multiple citation motives [43], Brooks nonetheless found that authors choose each citation with very specific goals in mind.

The following section explains which citation characteristics the CbPD algorithms analyze to identify suspiciously similar citation patterns for creating a document's citation-based fingerprint.

4.2   Citation Characteristics Considered

Identical citations in two documents do not automatically indicate plagiarism. This section outlines the characteristics considered by the CbPD algorithms to identify suspiciously similar citation patterns that may indicate plagiarism.

4.2.1 Bibliographic Coupling Strength

As explained in Section 3.2.2, the Bibliographic Coupling (BC) strength, which is the absolute number or fraction of references that two academic documents have in common, is a well-known similarity characteristic. A high BC strength usually indicates topical similarity in the research described. Because BC is a document-wide similarity measure, it does not allow pinpointing specific areas of highest similarity. Nonetheless, BC is a useful measure for CbPD, since documents sharing no references (BC strength = 0) can be excluded from a citation-based similarity assessment altogether. Therefore, the CbPD algorithms consider BC strength as one of several characteristics.

4.2.2 Probability of Citation Co-occurrence

The probability that two documents share citations depends on multiple factors, which the CbPD algorithms use to quantify the degree to which matching citation patterns are treated as suspicious.

Existing citation counts influence future citation counts. If a document is already highly cited, the likelihood of that document gathering additional citations increases. Merton termed this phenomenon the Matthew effect[15] in science [227]. Current search engines for academic literature, e.g., Google Scholar, increase the Matthew effect, because they use the number of citations a document received as the most important criterion to rank search results, as we demonstrated in [26]. Documents ranked highly by search engines have a higher likelihood of gaining additional citations.

---

[15]   The term refers to the line in the Gospel of Matthew: *"Everyone who has will be given more."* (Matthew 25:29, NIRV).

Imagine two documents C and D, where document C is frequently cited by others, while document D is cited more rarely. Assume 500 documents cite C, but only 5 documents cite D. Now, if two independent documents, A and B both cite C, this indicates some degree of similarity between them. However, if they both cite D, this is a much stronger indicator of similarity between documents A and B, since D is only cited rarely. Thus, higher citation counts indicate a higher probability of co-citation occurrence and this must be taken into account when assessing citation pattern suspiciousness.

Time influences the likelihood of citation co-occurrence because papers tend to receive more citations over time [255, 291]. Increasing citations also increase the probability of documents being co-cited. We ran first experiments on adjusting the CbPD algorithms to compensate this influence on the similarity score, by comparing the expected citations per unit of time if texts *A* and *B* were published at different times.

The topic of research influences the likelihood of two documents sharing citations. Documents addressing the same or very similar topics are more likely to contain citations to identical sources. We derived this assumption from empirical evaluations using co-citation analysis to identify clusters in academic domains [139, 302].

Author ties are another factor increasing the probability of co-citation. Research shows that a document *A* is more likely to be cited by a document *B* if the author(s) of document *B* is/are connected to the author(s) of document *A* [225]. For example, former co-authors, or researchers who know each other personally, tend to cite publications of their colleagues more frequently, a behavior called cronyism [225].

4.2.3 Order and Proximity of Citations

Sharing identical citations in close proximity and/or similar order are intuitive indicators that the text segments containing the respective citations are semantically similar. Therefore, proximity and similar order of citations are the most important characteristics of citation patterns. Certain document sections commonly contain more citations than others. For example, related work sections contain more citations than summaries. Therefore, shared citation patterns in document sections other than in the related work section can be stronger indicators of potentially suspicious similarities.

4.3 Challenges to Citation Pattern Identification

There are several challenges to citation pattern identification, which the citation-based detection algorithms must overcome. Sections 4.3.1–4.3.4 briefly present these factors: unknown pattern constituents, citation transpositions, citation scaling, and insertions and substitutions of citations by the plagiarist as challenges that make accurate citation pattern detection a non-trivial task. Section 4.4 describes how the design of the citation-based detection algorithms addresses these challenges.

4.3.1 Unknown Pattern Constituents

Unlike in string matching, the pattern in a CbPD analysis, i.e. the sub-sequence of citations in a suspicious text, which the detection algorithm must search for within the original text, is initially unknown. Individual citations shared by two documents are comparatively easy to identify. However, it is highly unlikely that all shared citations are attributable to plagiarism. As mentioned earlier in this section, the detection algorithms must consider additional characteristics, including proximity and order of citations, to distinguish potentially suspicious citation patterns from unsuspicious commonly shared citations.

For example, assume the documents A and B share eight citations. A plagiarized text segment contains three of the shared citations "[1,2,3]" and the remaining five shared citations are distributed throughout the document along with non-shared citations and do not represent plagiarism. The citation sequences of the two documents might look like this:

Doc A (Original):   1 2 3 x x x 4 x x 5 x 6 x 7 8
Doc B (Plagiarism):   x x 5 x x x 4 x 3 1 2 x x 7 x 8

The numbers 1–8 represent shared citations and the x represents non-shared citations. Given only the above sequences, it is initially unclear which subsequences represent a potentially suspicious citation pattern. The detection algorithms must consider the proximity and order of the shared citations 1–3 to identify them as potentially suspicious.

4.3.2 Transpositions

The order of citations in the unoriginal text segments may be transposed when compared to the original segment. Causes of citation transpositions are different citation styles, or the rearranging of longer text segments, which is typical in shake & paste plagiarism.

Assume the original sentence:

> *Studies show that <finding1>, <finding2> [3,1,2].*

A second author may express the semantically identical content as:

> *Studies show that <finding1>, <finding2> [1-3].*

4.3.3 Scaling

Scaling denotes the use of the same citation more than once.

Assume the original text:

> *Study X showed <finding1>, <finding2> and <finding3> [1]. Study Y objected <finding1> [2]. Assessment Z proved <finding3> [3].*

A second author may paraphrase the text and scale the citation to study X:

> *Study X showed <finding1> [1], which was objected by study Y [2]. Study X also found <finding2> [1]. Assessment Z was able to prove <finding3> [3], which had already been indicated by study X [1].*

So, in the original text this results in the citation sequence: [1],[2],[3] while in the paraphrase we have the sequence: [1],[2],[1],[3],[1].

4.3.4 Insertions or Substitutions of Citations

Authors may paraphrase text segments and include the citations from other documents, or they may insert additional non-shared citations or substitute the existing citations with semantically similar non-shared citations.

The resulting citation sequences of two documents may equal:

Doc A (Original):   1 2 3 4 5 6 7 8
Doc B (Paraphrase):   1 2 x 3 x x 4 5 x 6 x x 7 x 8

As in the earlier examples, numerals represent shared citations and the letter x denotes non-shared citations. Paraphrasing in such a manner may not constitute plagiarism, yet still represents a similarity between the two documents that may be of interest to a reader, for example, to trace the origin and progression of ideas.

4.4   Design of Citation-based Detection Algorithms

No prior research has examined citation-analyzing algorithms regarding their suitability to detect plagiarism. To fill this empirical knowledge gap, we designed and evaluated algorithms that focus on different factors when it comes to assessing citation-based similarity. We included algorithms that perform global and local similarity assessments[16], as well as algorithms that consider the order of citations and algorithms that ignore the order.

Table 9 displays the categories of similarity assessments, *local* vs. *global* and *order-preserving* vs. *order-neglecting*, according to which we designed the detection algorithms. We first examined whether we could adapt similarity functions from other areas of application. Since citation sequences of documents are equivalent to strings, string processing lent itself to searching for potentially suitable methods. A string refers to any collection of uniquely identifiable elements linked in such a way that each element, except for exactly one leftmost

---

[16] Refer to Figure 3 on page 21 for an explanation of the definition of "global" and "local".

and exactly one rightmost element, has one unique predecessor and one unique successor [305]. From string processing, we selected the longest common subsequence and Greedy String Tiling (GST) algorithms to be adapted for CbPD. Considering the challenges to citation pattern identification outlined in Section 4.3, we designed a new class of similarity assessment algorithms termed Citation Chunking explained in Section 4.4.4. Additionally, we tested Bibliographic Coupling on its suitability as a CbPD algorithm.

Table 9: Categorization of Evaluated Similarity Assessments

	Global Similarity Assessment	Local Similarity Assessment
Order preserving	Longest Common Citation Sequence	Greedy Citation Tiling
Order neglecting	Bibliographic Coupling	Citation Chunking

4.4.1 Bibliographic Coupling (BC)

Bibliographic Coupling is one of the oldest and most widespread citation-based similarity measures for academic texts. The measure, as described in Section 3.2.2, considers the absolute number or fraction of shared references, but ignores order and position of citations for similarity computation. Like all citation-based approaches, Bibliographic Coupling has thus far not been used for plagiarism detection. Thus, we tested its applicability for this use case. However, we expected Bibliographic Coupling alone to be an insufficient plagiarism indicator, since it solely considers global document similarity and does not allow pinpointing the position of plagiarized text segments.

The following three sections present the designed CbPD detection algorithms, which in contrast to Bibliographic Coupling, consider the order in which authors cite sources and the proximity of the citations in the full text to compute document similarity. We hypothesize these approaches to be more suitable for the purpose of plagiarism detection.

4.4.2 Longest Common Citation Sequence (LCCS)

The Longest Common Citation Sequence (LCCS) is a detection algorithm we developed by adapting a traditional similarity measure for text strings. The LCCS is defined as the maximum number of citations that match in both documents in the same order, but can be interrupted by non-matching citations. Each document pair has either exactly one or no LCCS. For instance, the sequence $(3, 4, 5)$ is a sub-sequence of $(2, 3, 1, 4, 6, 8, 5, 9)$ [81].

The following example illustrates the LCCS measure, here with a length of three:

Doc A: 2, 3, 1, 4, 6, 8, 5, 9
Doc B: 3, 8, 9, 4, 10, 11, 5
LCCS: 3, 4, 5

We adapted LCCS to strictly account for the order of citations, unlike Bibliographic Coupling, which is order-ignoring. Intuitively, measuring LCCS yields high similarity scores if a plagiarist uses longer parts of another text without alterations or only minor changes of the source's citations. LCCS is thus suitable for identifying potential plagiarism where text or ideas have been copied in the same order, but also allows for arbitrarily sized gaps of non-matching citations. This may be the case for copy&paste plagiarism concealed using basic rewording, e.g., through synonym replacements. If a plagiarist performed significant reordering within plagiarized text segments (shake & paste plagiarism) or permuted the sequence of citations, the LCCS approach is unsuitable.

4.4.3 Greedy Citation Tiling (GCT)

Greedy Citation Tiling (GCT) is an adaption of a text string similarity function proposed by Wise [367]. Wise designed the original Greedy String Tiling (GST) procedure explicitly for use in PD. Several other researchers successfully applied GST in systems for detecting plagiarism of software source code [5, 267].

GCT identifies all matches of consecutive shared citations in identical order, called citation tiles, in two citation sequences. Tiles are substrings of shared citations in both sequences that are not extendable to the right or left without encountering a citation that both sequences do not share. GCT permanently links the longest individual matches in both sequences and stores them as a tile. A tile is a tuple, $t = (s_1, s_2, l)$, which consists of the starting position of a match in the citation sequence of the first document (s_1), its starting position in the citation sequence of the second document (s_2), and the length of the match sequence, (l). According to this notation, the first tile for the example in Figure 15 is written as I $(1,5,3)$. Matching numbers represent citations to the same work, and extraneous citations are denoted by "x". Roman numerals are used to mark the matching citation tiles, of which there are three in Figure 15.

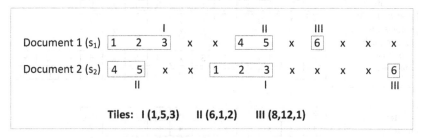

Figure 15: Greedy Citation Tiles

As Figure 15 shows, GCT only identifies substrings of matching citations, i.e. matching citations in exactly the same order, if these matches are longer than a definable minimum length. Yet, the GCT algorithm can cope with transpositions in the order of individual tiles.

To illustrate the GCT approach, Figure 16 shows the application of the algorithm for identifying a citation tile assuming a global minimum match length of 2. For every citation in the citation sequence of document 1 (denoted as s_1 (in the figure), the algorithm iterates through the citations in the citation sequence of document 2 (denoted as s_2 in the figure). GCT strictly identifies longer tiles before shorter tiles by transforming only the longest matches found in the same iteration into tiles. If, for example, a match of length 3 and a match of length 4

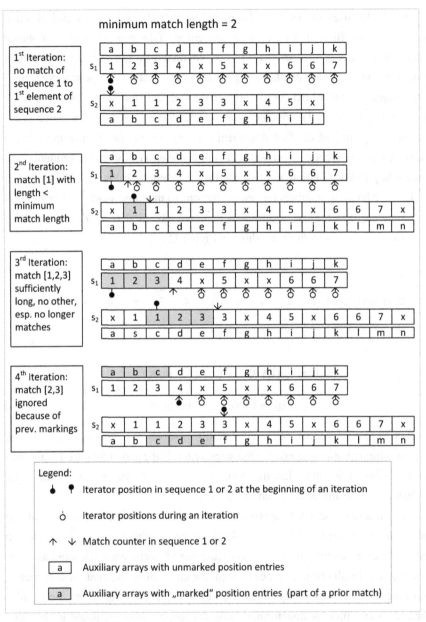

Figure 16: Identification of a Match Using Greedy Citation Tiling

are found in the same iteration, then only the match of length 4 would become a tile for that iteration, even if both matches exceed the global minimum match length. Citations that become part of a tile are inserted into auxiliary arrays, which "marks" them as no longer available for matching, leaving them ignored in future iterations. In this way, matching citations cannot contribute to multiple tiles. For the next iteration, the algorithm reduces the length of the longest match in the previous iteration by one and uses this number as the new maximum match length. The algorithm thus identifies the next-shorter matches to the matches marked in the previous iteration. The iteration continues until no matches longer than or equal to the global minimum match length remain.

Wise proved that the GST algorithm produces the optimal coverage of matching elements with tiles if the minimum match length is one [367]. The worst case complexity of the algorithm is $O(n^3)$. Wise designed the GST algorithm primarily to identify shake & paste plagiarism. Greedy Citation Tiling can serve the same purpose, but in contrast to the text string-matching approach, GCT was developed with the intention to identify paraphrases.

The GCT approach focuses on identical order of citations. Finding such exact matches is a strong indicator for text similarity. GCT is able to deal with transpositions in citation patterns that result from rearranging text segments, which is typical for shake & paste plagiarism. However, the approach is not capable of detecting citation scaling or transpositions of individual citations. To address citation scaling and transpositions, we designed another class of detection algorithms we coined Citation Chunking.

4.4.4 Citation Chunking (Cit-Chunk)

Citation Chunking (Cit-Chunk) is a set of heuristic detection algorithms, which we developed to identify citation patterns regardless of potential citation transpositions and/or scaling. Cit-Chunk owes its name to a strategy of selecting text fragments, so-called "chunks", which character-based fingerprinting algorithms commonly employ [41]. A citation chunk is a substring of a document's citation sequence with a variable size. The main idea of Cit-Chunk is to consider shared citations as textual anchors where local citation patterns are likely to exist. Citation Chunking consists of three steps: formation of chunks, the optional merging of chunks, and the comparison of chunks.

Due to the novelty of CbPD, there is no empirical data on how citations are to be compared for PD purposes. Therefore, we developed and evaluated (see Chapter 6) different variations of the algorithm by implementing multiple approaches for each of the three steps of Citation Chunking. The following sections describe each step of the algorithm in detail.

4.4.4.1   *Formation of Chunks*

In this first step, the Cit.-Chunk. algorithm searches for shared citations as starting points for constructing citation chunks. Beginning at shared citations, the algorithm forms chunks by dynamically increasing the considered substring of the document's citation sequence according to a chunking strategy.

Choosing a suitable chunking strategy to determine the start- and endpoint of a citation chunk is tricky, because no solution fits all plagiarism scenarios. Larger chunks are better suitable to detect global similarities by compensating for transpositions and scaling. Smaller chunks are better suitable to pinpoint local areas of high similarity.

By modeling the behaviors of plagiarists and the typical citation patterns that result, we derived the following three chunking strategies.

Chunking strategy 1 (consecutively shared strategy) – citations must be consecutively shared to form a chunk. Chunking strategy 1 is the most restrictive. It highlights confined text segments with very high citation-based similarities. Strategy 1 is ideal for detecting potential cases of copy & paste plagiarism, which plagiarists may have concealed by rewording or translation.

Doc A: x, 1, 2, 3, x, 4, 5, 3, x, x

Doc B: x, x, 3, 2, 1, x, 5, 3, 4, x

Chunking strategy 2 (prior citations strategy) – citations form a chunk depending on the previous citations. Chunking strategy 2 includes a citation in a chunk if the number of non-shared citations separating it from the last shared citation is smaller than the number of shared and non-shared citations that are already included in the chunk currently under construction.

We denote the number of non-shared citations separating shared citations as n and the number of shared and non-shared citations in the chunk under construction as s. A citation is included in the chunk if $n \leq s$. Therefore, chunking strategy 2 allows for sporadic non-shared citations that plagiarists may have inserted to make their text appear more "genuine". The variable s is a threshold value that determines the sensitivity of the algorithm. The optimal value of s depends on numerous factors comparable to the threshold length for character-based approaches. One factor, for example, is the rate of false positives that is deemed acceptable.

Chunking strategy 2 can detect cases in which plagiarists adopted and disguised longer text segments or logical structures from another text, as well as cases of concealed shake & paste plagiarism from different sources.

Doc A: x, 1, 2, 3, x, x, 4, 5, x, x, x, x, x, x, 6, 7
Doc B: 3, 2, x, 1, x, x, 4, x, x, x, x, x, 5, 6, 7, x

Chunking strategy 3 (distance threshold strategy) – Citations form a chunk if their distance in the text falls below a certain threshold. Chunking strategy 3 defines a textual range in which plagiarism is deemed likely. Studies showed that plagiarism more frequently affects confined text segments, i.e. only one or two paragraphs, rather than extended text passages or the entire document [176, 220, 222, 223, 273]. Building upon this knowledge, chunking strategy 3 only considers citations within a specified range to form chunks (see Figure 17).

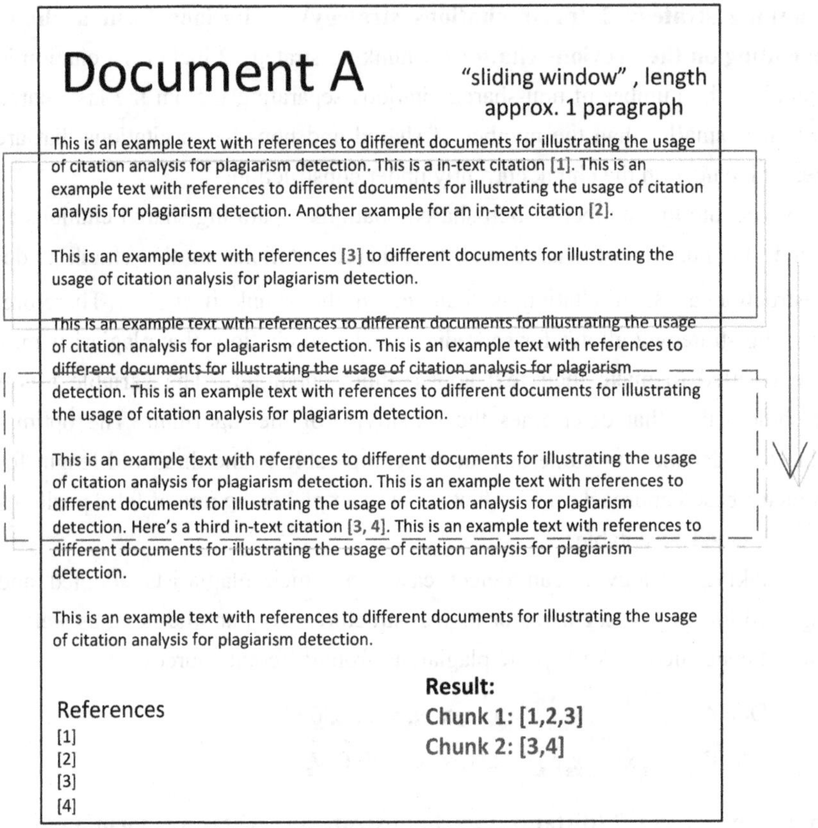

Document A

"sliding window" , length
approx. 1 paragraph

This is an example text with references to different documents for illustrating the usage
of citation analysis for plagiarism detection. This is a in-text citation [1]. This is an
example text with references to different documents for illustrating the usage of citation
analysis for plagiarism detection. Another example for an in-text citation [2].

This is an example text with references [3] to different documents for illustrating the
usage of citation analysis for plagiarism detection.

This is an example text with references to different documents for illustrating the usage
of citation analysis for plagiarism detection. This is an example text with references to
different documents for illustrating the usage of citation analysis for plagiarism
detection. This is an example text with references to different documents for illustrating
the usage of citation analysis for plagiarism detection.

This is an example text with references to different documents for illustrating the usage
of citation analysis for plagiarism detection. This is an example text with references to
different documents for illustrating the usage of citation analysis for plagiarism
detection. Here's a third in-text citation [3, 4]. This is an example text with references to
different documents for illustrating the usage of citation analysis for plagiarism
detection.

This is an example text with references to different documents for illustrating the usage
of citation analysis for plagiarism detection.

References

[1]
[2]
[3]
[4]

Result:

Chunk 1: [1,2,3]
Chunk 2: [3,4]

Figure 17: Illustration of Chunking Strategy 3

Because plagiarists may change the segmentation of plagiarized text, strategy 3 analyzes textual proximity in terms of multiple text units, including characters, words, sentences, and paragraphs. Defining a suitable maximum distance for the proximity of citations in the text is highly dependent on the individual corpus analyzed. If document length is short and individual documents contain fewer sections and paragraphs, altering the text structure is more difficult for a plagiarist. Therefore, a relatively small maximum distance is most suitable to detect plagiarism in short documents with few sections. In contrast, reordering text usually becomes easier the longer the document.

To determine a suitable proximity threshold, we analyzed the average number of hierarchically subordinate text constituents (e.g., characters and words) contained within hierarchically superordinated text constituents (e.g., paragraphs). For example, in one document, a paragraph may on average contain 120 words and 720 characters. If less than 120 words separate one shared citation from another shared citation, chunking strategy 3 would include the second shared citation in the chunk. Using this approach, a CbPD algorithm employing chunking strategy 3 can deal with artificially created paragraph split-ups.

4.4.4.2   *Merging of Chunks*

To assess the impact of larger chunk sizes, we developed a merging step for citation chunks. The merging procedure iterates through all chunks formed according to one of the chunking strategies described in the previous section. The merging combines chunks to outline longer sections of text with shared citations that could point to, for example, idea plagiarism. The merging procedure combines chunks if the number of non-shared citations n is smaller or equal to the number m of shared citations in the previous chunk, $(n \le m)$.

> Iteration 1: XXX, x, XX, x, x, XXX, x, x, x, x, x, x, XX
>
> (merge red and purple? n=1, m=3)
>
> Iteration 2: XXXXX, x, x, XXX, x, x, x, x, x, x, XX
>
> (merge purple and blue? n=2, m=2)
>
> Iteration 3: XXXXXXXX, x, x, x, x, x, x, XX
>
> (merge purple and blue? n=6, m=3)

In the example above, the merging procedure combines all but the chunk furthest to the right, because the distance of XX to the previous chunk is too large. The merging step is optional, i.e. the Citation Chunking algorithms can be applied with or without the merging of chunks after they have been formed according to one of the chunking strategies.

Figure 18 summarizes the formation of chunks according to all three chunking strategies and the optional merging step in a flow chart.

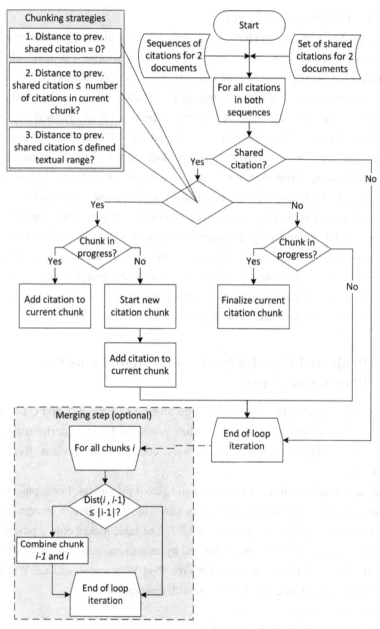

Figure 18: Formation of Citation Chunks

4.4.4.3   *Comparison of Chunks*

Following the formation of chunks, and their optional merging, as described in the previous two sections, the Citation Chunking algorithm compares chunks against each other regardless of the order of citations in the chunks. In this way, the algorithm accounts for potential transpositions and/or scaling. The number of shared citations within the compared chunks is the measure of similarity.

We implemented two strategies for comparing citation chunks. The first strategy compares each chunk of the first document with each chunk of the second. The comparison algorithm stores chunk pairs as matches if these pairs have the highest citation overlap among all pairs. If multiple chunk pairs have an equal overlap, the algorithm stores all combinations with maximum overlap.

The second method only considers the chunks of a single document and compares them to the unaltered citation sequence of the second document. The algorithm "slides" "each chunk of the first document over the entire citation sequence of the second document. The algorithm assigns the chunk to the position in the citation sequence with the maximum citation overlap.

4.5   Projected Suitability of CbPD Algorithms for Plagiarism Forms

This section classifies the three CbPD algorithms – LCCS, GCT and Cit-Chunk – presented in Section 4.4, according to their projected detection performance for the types of citation copying which may occur in the various forms of plagiarism.

Table 10 distinguishes between local and global plagiarism. Local plagiarism primarily affects the sentence level, while global plagiarism encompasses document-wide plagiarism, see Section 2.2.2. The table makes only a projection of algorithm suitability, which we derived by examining a sample of 17 known cases of plagiarism identified using the VroniPlag Wiki and Retraction Watch[17]. The classification should thus be viewed with reservation.

---

[17]   http://retractionwatch.wordpress.com/

Local and global plagiarism can both contain identical, transposed, scaled, or a combination of transposed and scaled citation copying. If, for instance, a plagiarist translates a text verbatim, the order of citations is unlikely to change much. In Table 10, such a case falls in the category "identical". If, however, a plagiarist translates a text freely, possibly altering the arrangement of sentences or paragraphs, this can result in different citation patterns. Such a case would fall in the categories "transposed", "scaled", or a combination thereof.

Table 10: Overview of CbPD Algorithm Detection Performance

	Plagiarism form	*LCCS*	*GCT*	*Cit-Chunk*
Local	Identical (copy & paste, translations)	-	++	+(+)
	Transposed (shake & paste, translations)	-	-	+
	Scaled (shake & paste, paraphrases)	-	-	+
	Transposed & scaled (paraphrases)	-	-	+
Global	Identical (copy & paste, translations)	++	++	+(+)
	Transposed (shake & paste, translations)	+	-	+(+)
	Scaled (shake & paste, paraphrases)	+	-	+(+)
	Transposed & scaled (paraphrases)	+	-	+(+)

Detection rates: ++ good | + fair | - low | (+) performance depends on chunking strategy

The LCCS algorithms best indicate suspicious similarity if a document shares a large fraction of its citations in similar, yet not necessarily identical order, with another document. This algorithm is a global similarity measure, because it represents the single longest sequence of citations that matches in the same order in both documents, when non-matching citations are ignored. Therefore, local forms of plagiarism often do not contain enough copied citations to trigger suspicion in an assessment using LCCS. In cases of extensive global plagiarism, the LCCS approach performs quite well, despite potential local re-arrangements of citations.

Greedy Citation Tiling was designed to detect copy & paste plagiarism and verbatim translations on both the local sentence level and the global document level. Such forms of plagiarism often contain citations copied in identical order, which the exact matching approach of GCT can detect with high accuracy. Greedy Citation Tiles with a length of three or greater are typically indicators of text segments with a semantic similarity worth examining. Even slight alterations in the citation sequences can prevent the formation of longer citation tiles. Therefore, the detection performance of GCT decreases rapidly if text segments are paraphrased, freely translated, or reordered, as in shake & paste plagiarism.

The detection performance of Citation Chunking depends on the chunking strategy, refer to Section 4.4.4, which is why performance indicators are in brackets in Table 10. Chunking procedure 1 includes only consecutive shared citations; chunking procedure 2 includes shared citations in a certain range within the citation sequence. Both chunking procedures perform identically to Greedy Citation Tiling for local or global plagiarism forms containing identically copied citations. The performance of chunking procedure 3, which includes shared citations within a certain range, depends on the split-up of plagiarized text segments in the suspicious document. In general, Citation Chunking is the best approach for detecting plagiarism, even in the presence of citation transposition or scaling, on both the local and global document level. Depending on the plagiarism form, chunking procedures 2 and 3 in particular can detect local and global plagiarism forms that contain transpositions and/or scaling of shared citations.

Since all CbPD algorithms require a minimum amount of citations to reliably calculate a citation-based similarity, the citation-based detection approach is not suitable to identify suspicious similarity for short plagiarized fragments.

Therefore, we consider the CbPD approach as a complement and not as a substitute to the currently used character-based approaches.

4.6 Assessment of Identified Citation Patterns

The citation patterns identified using the CbPD algorithms must subsequently be analyzed and assessed according to their degree of plagiarism suspicion. As described in Section 4.2, two main factors influence the degree of suspicion of matching citation patterns. The first is the probability of the shared citations in the matching patterns co-occurring by chance. The second is the number, proximity, and order of shared citations in the matching patterns, which we summarized using the term "continuity".

In this section, we describe the design of two scores to evaluate the likelihood that the identified citation patterns represent an instance of suspicious similarity, by taking into account these two factors: probability of citation co-occurrence and probability of citation pattern continuity. We termed the scores the *Citing Frequency-Score* and the *Continuity-Score* for a citation pattern.

4.6.1 Citing Frequency-Score (CF-Score)

To incorporate the citation frequencies of documents into the assessment of a citation pattern's degree of suspicion, we devised the *Citing Frequency-Score* heuristic, or *CF-Score*.

The probability of authors citing identical sources independently of each other depends on many factors, including similarity of their research objectives, popularity of the cited source, relationships among the authors, etc. Most of these factors are hard to quantify. However, citation counts can quantify the "popularity" of a source document. Intuitively, two "popular" sources A and B, which both received 100+ citations, are more likely to appear in a matching citation pattern than two sources C and D, which received only three citations each.

Therefore, we consider citation patterns containing highly cited documents to be less likely a result of undue practices, but rather to represent commonly cited standard literature in a field. Contrarily, we regard citation patterns occurring less frequently as a stronger indicator for potentially suspicious document similarity.

One possible method to estimate the probability of co-occurrence of citations is to use retrospective citation information to compute a $n \times n$-matrix for all n citations in a corpus so that each element of the matrix represents the number of times that two citations co-occur in a document of the corpus. However, we decided not to follow this approach, because it is computationally expensive, especially if not only the co-occurrence of citation pairs, but larger citation groups must be considered.

To derive a computationally less expensive estimation of co-occurrence probability, we make the simplified assumption that the occurrence of citations is statistically independent. With this assumption, the probability of a reference r pointing to a source document X equals the count of all references to document X, r_x, in a given corpus divided by the size N of that corpus:

$$P(r_x) = \frac{r_x}{N} \tag{4.1}$$

Because rarely cited documents are more predictive and should receive a higher score, we inverse the ratio of the probability to equal $\frac{N}{r_x}$. We expect that the value of frequently cited sources in predicting uncommon, highly specific content similarities does not decrease in direct proportion to the number of citations these sources gather. Due to a lack of empirical data, we used the square root of the total number of references to a source, $\sqrt{r_x}$, as a starting point for determining a suitable denominator for the score.

The CF-Score for a citation c_i that links to a reference r_j, which represents the source document X, computes as:

$$CF\big(c_i(r_j)\big) = \frac{N}{\sqrt{r_x}} \tag{4.2}$$

To compute a CF-Score for a citation pattern p_k that consists of n citations $c_1 \ldots c_n$ that link to m references r_j, we accumulate the CF-Scores of all citations in the pattern: $CF(p_k) = \sum_1^n CF(c_i(r_j))$.

Analogously, we compute the CF-Score for a pair of documents d_1, d_2 that share q matching citation patterns p_k by accumulating the *CF-Scores* of the matching patterns: $CF(d_1, d_2) = \sum_1^q CF(p_k)$.

To exemplify the computation of *CF-Scores* for citation patterns, we assume a corpus of 1,000 documents. In this corpus four documents A, B, C and D have the following citation counts: $r_A = 100$, $r_B = 50$, $r_C = 10$, $r_D = 5$. Furthermore, we imagine two document pairs X, Y and X, Z that share the following citation patterns: X, Y: (A, B) (A, C) and X, Z: (C, D).

The resulting *CF-Scores* for the document pairs compute as:

$$CF(X,Y) = CF(p_1(A,B)) + CF(p_2(A,C))$$

$$= \left(\frac{1,000}{\sqrt{100}} + \frac{1,000}{\sqrt{50}}\right) + \left(\frac{1,000}{\sqrt{100}} + \frac{1,000}{\sqrt{10}}\right) = 657.65 \qquad (4.3)$$

$$CF(X,Z) = P(p_1(C,D)) = \left(\frac{1,000}{\sqrt{10}} + \frac{1,000}{\sqrt{5}}\right) = 763.44$$

The example shows that although the document pair X, Y shares more citation patterns, the single pattern that document X shares with document Z scores higher, because it consists of rarely cited sources.

4.6.2 Continuity-Score (Cont.-Score)

To include the continuity of a citation pattern, i.e. the number and proximity of matching citations in the pattern, into the assessment of a pattern's degree of suspicion, we devised the *Continuity-Score*.

Within a citation pattern, each matching citation that follows another matching citation, after n or less intermediate non-matching citations should increase the *Cont.-Score* of the pattern. The score increase in this case should be greater than 1 for not reflecting a simple count of matching citations, which we record separately. Furthermore, the score increase should be larger if fewer non-matching citations separate two subsequent matching citations.

Lastly, the score should increase in proportion to the number of previous matching citations that fulfill the criterion of having a maximum of n intermediate, non-matching citations separating them from the preceding matching citation. This characteristic of the equation reflects that the similarity of citation patterns increases progressively with the length of sequences of matching citations in the pattern. Equation 4.4 defines the *Cont.-Score*:

$$Cont.-Score = \sum_{i=1}^{k} max\left\{a - \frac{1}{n+1} \cdot \left(p(c_M^i) - p(c_M^{i-1}) - 1\right), 1\right\}$$

$$(4.4)$$

$$a = \left\{\begin{matrix} 1 \\ a+1 \\ 1 \end{matrix} \middle| \begin{matrix} c_M^1 \\ p(c_M^i) - p(c_M^{i-1}) \le n+1, i > 1 \\ p(c_M^i) - p(c_M^{i-1}) > n+1, i > 1 \end{matrix}\right\}$$

The equation considers a base score a for matching citations. For the first matching citation in the pattern c_M^1 we set the base score equal to 1. We increment the base score for each subsequent matching citation $c_M^i |i > 1$ in the pattern if not more than n non-matching citations separate c_M^i from the previous matching citation c_M^{i-1}. We express this condition in terms of the sequential position $p(c)$ of citations.

To penalize non-matching citations between matching citations, we subtract a penalty value of $1/(n+1)$ for each non-matching citation. If more than n non-matching citations separate two matching citations, the base score is set back to 1. If n intermittent non-matching citations separate the matching citations, the summand would be 0. If more than n non-matching citations exist in between, the summand would be negative. We disallow the *Cont.-Score* of a pattern to become less than the count of matching citations in the pattern through the application of the *max()* operator. This operator ensures that the minimum score increase for each matching citation is 1. We assume that the suitable maximum threshold for the number of non-matching intermittent citations, n, is collection-dependent and identifying this threshold requires a case-by-case consideration. For documents in disciplines that generally cite more references, e.g., the life sciences, the threshold should be set higher than in disciplines that typically cite fewer references, e.g., mathematics.

Figure 19 illustrates the computation of the *Cont.-Score* for two citation patterns assuming an allowed maximum number of intermittent non-matching citations $n = 3$. Arabic numerals represent matching citations and the x denotes non-matching citations. In the figure, both citation patterns contain eight matching citations. This relatively high number of matching citations leads to the *Cont.-Score* of both patterns being greater than the length of the pattern. The *Cont.-Score* of the second pattern equals about 1.7 times the score of the first pattern. In this example, the higher score could signal that the second pattern is more likely to be one long match, and hence more suspicious. The first pattern is likely to represent three smaller matches, which are less suspicious.

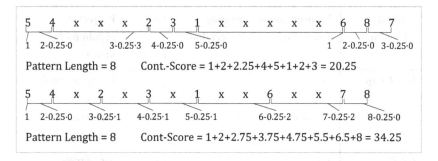

Figure 19: Cont.-Score Computation for Citation Patterns

4.7 Conclusion

The concept of Citation-based Plagiarism Detection for the first time uses the information on semantic relatedness contained in citations as a method to detect plagiarism.

To cover four different plagiarism forms and the unique styles of citation pattern copying which result, we adapted Bibliographic Coupling and developed three algorithms: *Longest Common Citation Sequence*, *Greedy Citation Tiling*, and *Citation Chunking*. The algorithms examine citation patterns regarding three factors as shown in Table 12, transpositions, scaling and global vs. local comparison.

- Transpositions describe whether the order of shared citations must be identical.

- Scaling describes whether shared citations may occur multiple times.

- Global vs. local similarity describes whether the plagiarism occurs document-wide or only locally.

Each algorithm features unique strengths. By combining the four approaches, we intend to address the various forms of local and global plagiarism.

Table 11: Overview CbPD Algorithms

(CbPD) Algorithm	Transpositions detectable?	Scaling detectable?	Global vs. local	Projected capability to detect
Bib. Coup	Yes	yes	global	Likely to produce false positives
LCCS	Partially	no	global	paraphrases, translations
GCT	No	no	local	paraphrases, translations
Cit-Chunk	Yes	depends on chunking strategy	local	strong paraphrases, structural and idea plagiarism

In addition to the CbPD algorithms, we proposed the Citing Frequency-Score, which considers the probability of co-occurrence of identical citations by chance, and the Continuity-Score, which reflects the number and proximity of matching citations in a pattern, to assess the probability that a citation pattern indicates plagiarism. The next chapter presents the implementation of the CbPD algorithms in a prototypical plagiarism detection system.

5 Prototype: CitePlag

This chapter describes the implementation of the Citation-based Plagiarism Detection (CbPD) approach in a first prototype: CitePlag. The prototype has a Java backend and a HTML5 frontend. CitePlag is available under an open source license[18]. Figure 20 illustrates CitePlag's system architecture, which is composed of four components: a document parser, a relational database, a detector, and a web-based frontend.

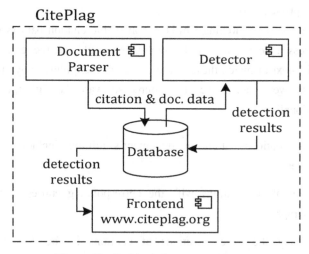

Figure 20: CitePlag's System Architecture

The database stores the document's bibliographic data as extracted by the document parser and stores the results of the CbPD and character-based algorithms, which are implemented in the detector. The web-based frontend retrieves the detection results from the database and visualizes them for human inspection. The following four sections present more details on the components of the CitePlag prototype.

---

[18] The source code is available for download; refer to Appendix C.

5.1 Document Parser

The document parser extracts metadata, citations, and references from the input documents and stores the data in the database. Parsing citation data and matching this data with the references in the bibliography of documents is essential for CbPD. Automatic extraction of citation data is not a trivial task. Hundreds of citation styles exist and the application of these styles is often inconsistent due to inadvertent mistakes when citing. Additionally, technical characteristics of different file formats, for example, different PDF versions, make the extraction process error-prone [195].

When we began researching CbPD, the available citation parsers were only able to process a document's bibliography, but could not recognize citations within the full-text or match these to the entries in the bibliography. To address this weakness, we added to the open source software ParsCit[19] the following crucial functionalities:

- parsing citations within the document's full-text including the footnotes

- matching these citations with the corresponding entries in the bibliography

- identifying the exact positions of citations in the document including chapter, section, paragraph, sentence, word and character count

These improvements and extensions are now part of the official ParsCit release. Currently, we are still working on improving the citation extraction accuracy:

- for different file formats (PDF, PS, etc.) and versions thereof

- for different citation styles

---

[19] http://aye.comp.nus.edu.sg/parsCit/

Figure 21 illustrates the general parsing procedure for PDF files using the adapted version of ParsCit. Citation extraction performs reliably for the most common citation styles. However, in some academic fields citation styles are inconsistent. In the legal field, for example, footnote citations and in-text citations may be used alternatingly. Such discrepancies in citation formatting currently leads to unsatisfactory parsing results. For the discussion on parsing errors and their consequences, refer to Section 6.4.1 on page 141.

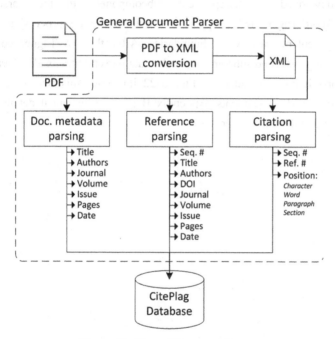

Figure 21: General Document Parser

For the evaluation of the PubMed Central Open Access Subset (PMC OAS) presented in Section 6.4, parsing the references was not necessary, because the National Library of Medicine, which hosts the PMC OAS corpus, offers all documents in a machine-readable XML format. The National Library of Medicine XML format is termed NXML, and includes markup for document metadata, citations and references. For the purpose of CbPD, determining the exact positions of citations within a document's full-text is necessary. We measured the positions of citations in terms of the character, word, sentence, paragraph, and section counts. The parser applies Java text processing methods to acquire character counts and evaluates the corresponding tags in the NXML texts to obtain the paragraph and section position of citations. NXML texts do not provide markup for sentences and words. Thus, identifying the boundaries of these elements requires a pre-processing step.

We developed an independent subcomponent to the parser, the Sentence-Word-Tagger (SW-Tagger), to perform the pre-processing step of identifying sentence and word boundaries. After the SW-Tagger completes pre-processing, a second subcomponent, the data parser, extracts all relevant data and imports it into the database. Figure 22 illustrates this two-stage parsing process for NXML documents. Appendix B presents technical details on the SW-Tagger and the data parser.

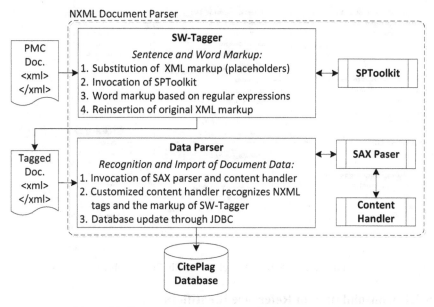

NXML Document Parser

SW-Tagger

Sentence and Word Markup:
1. Substitution of XML markup (placeholders)
2. Invocation of SPToolkit
3. Word markup based on regular expressions
4. Reinsertion of original XML markup

PMC Doc.

SPToolkit

Data Parser

Recognition and Import of Document Data:
1. Invocation of SAX parser and content handler
2. Customized content handler recognizes NXML tags and the markup of SW-Tagger
3. Database update through JDBC

Tagged Doc.

SAX Paser

Content Handler

CitePlag Database

Figure 22: Two-stage Parsing Process for NXML Documents

5.2 Database

We chose the open source software MySQL for database management. Figure 23 depicts CitePlag's data model using the Entity Relationship Model (ERM) notation. Relationship connectors link the attributes that participate in the relationship. Most table and attribute names are self-explanatory. The size of database including all tables is about 530 GB. Appendix B.4 presents a detailed description of the tables and attributes.

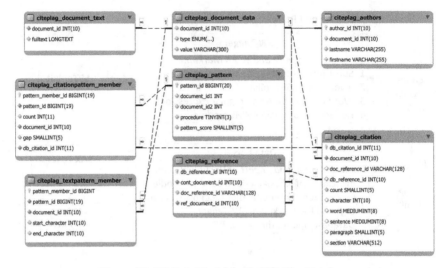

Figure 23: ER Data Model for the CitePlag Database

5.2.1 Consolidation of Reference Identifiers

In the process of creating the database, the consolidation of reference identifiers was a challenge to be overcome. The reference strings in documents contained in the PMC OAS often include different document identifiers, e.g., PubMed IDs (PMID), Medline IDs (MEDID) or Digital Object Identifiers (DOI). PMIDs and MEDIDs are identifiers assigned by the National Library of Medicine to documents in the PubMed database and the Medline index. Digital Document Identifiers are maintained by the DOI Consortium and can be obtained by anybody upon request and payment of an administration fee. In addition to these numerical identifiers, we computed Reference Title Keys (RefTitKeys) and Reference Author Keys (RefAuthKeys), which represent the first 40 ASCII characters of the title or of the author names in a reference. We used a combination of the RefTitKey and the RefAuthKey to identify references that did not have numerical identifiers.

By examining references manually, we found that all document identifiers available in the PMC OAS were subject to error from incorrect assignments by authors or processing by the NLM. For instance, for some references with a

PMID and a DOI, the PMID corresponded neither to the document, nor to the DOI. Furthermore, authors did not use identifiers consistently for citing sources. Some authors stated no identifiers, some used a PMID, and others preferred a DOI.

Accurate identification of matching references is a prerequisite for a CbPD analysis. For this purpose, we consolidated available document identifiers after importing the data into the CitePlag database. Appendix B.3 describes the applied consolidation procedure in detail. The current disambiguation methods of the CbPD prototype are basic. However, we expect that research on informed heuristics and machine learning can improve disambiguation procedures.

5.3 Detector

The detector component of the CitePlag prototype implements the CbPD algorithms as described in Section 4.4. Figure 24 outlines the main components of the detector using a UML class diagram. We implemented each CbPD algorithm as a stand-alone Java class. The class "CitationPatternChecker" is a central hub that instantiates the different analysis classes. CitationPatternChecker also bundles functionality, which all CbPD algorithms require, e.g., determining the set of shared references. The other classes are multithreaded implementations for subtasks related to input and output operations on the CitePlag database. The source code is available for download; refer to Appendix C. To determine and visualize the character-based similarities we used the open souce software Encoplot (see Appendix J).

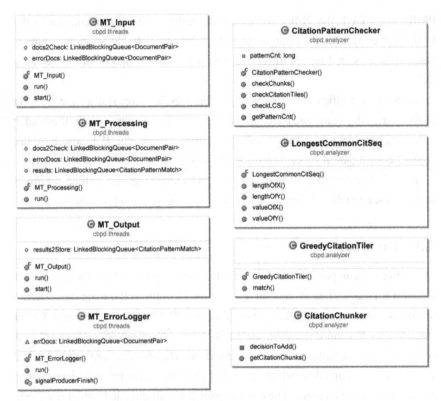

Figure 24: UML Class Diagram for CitePlag Detector

5.4   Frontend

The CitePlag frontend retrieves detection results from the database and visualizes citation-based and character-based similarities for the PDS user.

Current plagiarism detection software solely visualizes character-based similarity. For CbPD, however, citation pattern visualization is crucial to help users discover and navigate the sections in documents potentially featuring strongly disguised plagiarism. We believe that numeric similarity scores without proper visualization are insufficient for both character-based and citation-based PDS. To assist the human examiner, we developed a frontend to visualize the computed similarities.

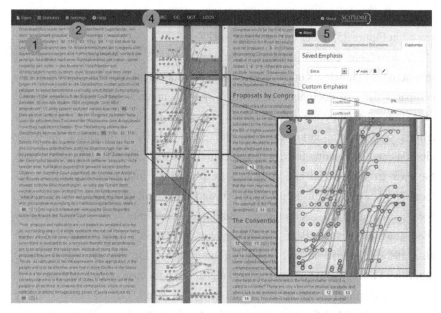

Figure 25: CitePlag's Document Similarity Visualization

The frontend was developed in collaboration with students from the HTW Berlin[20]. Among other features, the CitePlag frontend offers interactive document navigation, highlighting for matching citations and text segments, as well as statistics summarizing identified similarities, refer to Figure 25. A HTML5 compliant browser, such as Chrome, Firefox or Safari, is required.

CitePlag features a customizable side-by-side document visualization, see #1 in Figure 25, to efficiently browse academic documents for text and citation similarities and aid the user in identifying plagiarism. The suspicious document is displayed on the left and the potential source document is displayed on the right. When clicking on highlighted text or citation similarity in either document, the respective section in the other document is retrieved. The visualization of text

[20] I wish to acknowledge the contributions to the frontend by André Gernandt, Leif Timm, Markus Bruns, Markus Föllmer, and Rebecca Böttche from the HTW Berlin – University of Applied Sciences.

and citation similarities is customizable to the user's preferences in the menu bar, see #2 in Figure 25, under the 'settings' tab.

A scrollable central document browser, see #3 in Figure 25, enables interactive and quick document navigation. The document browser schematically compares the two documents selected in the 'documents' tab using the CbPD algorithm selected by the user, see #4 in Figure 25. The higher the text similarity among sections, the darker they are marked in red. By highlighting matching citations and connecting these in the document browser, CitePlag visualizes both the easy to spot global and copy & paste plagiarism instances, as well as the local and heavily disguised plagiarism instances. A collapsible cluster side tab, see #5 in Figure 25, recommends additional documents with high similarity scores, which are selectable for subsequent comparison. The cluster view tab also allows the user to set weighting coefficients for the individual CbPD algorithms thus creating a hybrid CbPD algorithm with customized emphasis.

In the documents tab of the menu bar, documents can be selected using PubMed or PubMed Central IDs or uploaded from the local file system. The menu bar also features a 'help' tab and a document 'statistics' tab. Under the statistics tab, the user can view two graphs summarizing the document being compared. The first graph shows the stacked lengths of text overlap per page for the selected document (see Figure 26 for this graph). A second graph, which the user can select, shows the Bibliographic Coupling strength per page.

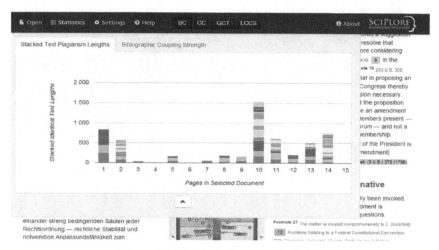

Figure 26: CitePlag's Document Statistics

5.5 Conclusion

The CitePlag prototype described in this chapter is the first implementation of a citation-based approach to plagiarism detection. The CitePlag system architecture consists of a parser, which extracts the required bibliographic data from documents and stores them in the database. The database provides this document data to the detector. The detector runs the CbPD algorithms and stores the results in the database, from where the frontend retrieves the detection results and visualizes them for human inspection. CitePlag is accessible at: http://www.citeplag.org

6 Quantitative and Qualitative Evaluation

This chapter[21] presents the evaluation framework and the evaluation results of the Citation-based Plagiarism Detection (CbPD) approach. By evaluating the performance of CbPD for both known and currently unknown plagiarism cases, this chapter addresses Research Task 5. Employing the commonly used plagiarism evaluation frameworks to gauge the effectiveness of the CbPD approach in identifying disguised plagiarism proved challenging for several reasons:

1. No existing method is capable of detecting strongly disguised plagiarism forms for which the CbPD approach was designed. This makes a meaningful comparison to existing approaches difficult.

2. Due to the covert nature of disguised plagiarism and the lack of reliable methods for detecting it, the true extent of disguised plagiarism present in any non-fabricated collection is unknown, thus a ground-truth can only be approximated.

3. Existing artificially created test collections are unsuitable, since they do not realistically represent the sophisticatedly disguised real-world plagiarism committed by experienced scientists.

For these reasons, a straightforward CbPD performance evaluation is not feasible. The methodology section addresses the requirements of a suitable test collection and the challenge of deriving a ground truth for heavily disguised plagiarism forms. Instead of a single evaluation using only one corpus, we perform multiple evaluations using three distinct test collections. This three-stage evaluation process pursues the following questions:

---

[21] A journal article containing excerpts from this evaluation chapter, with particular focus on the results obtained from the PMC OAS evaluation, has been accepted for publication in the Journal of the American Society for Information Science and Technology [135].

1. How suitable is CbPD for identifying plagiarism, in particular translated plagiarism, in a collection of identified plagiarism instances, where an extensive manual verification has resulted in a reliable ground truth? (Refer to the evaluation using the GuttenPlag Wiki in Section 6.2.)

2. How suitable is CbPD for identifying plagiarism in a collection of identified plagiarism instances from multiple authors featuring diverse plagiarism styles? (Refer to the evaluation using the VroniPlag Wiki in Section 6.3.)

3. How suitable is CbPD for identifying plagiarism in a large collection of scientific publications likely featuring strongly disguised and currently undiscovered plagiarism instances? (Refer to the evaluation using the PubMed Central Open Access Subset in Section 6.4.)

6.1   Methodology

Plagiarism detection systems are specialized information retrieval (IR) systems[22]. The evaluation of IR systems is a mature, empirical research discipline for which methodological standards have been established. According to Manning [209], the standard IR systems evaluation framework comprises four components:

1. a suitable document collection

2. clearly defined information needs

3. relevance judgments, i.e. assessments about which documents fulfill which information needs

4. performance metrics

---

[22] PD is sometimes considered as a Natural Language Processing (NLP) problem.

A single 'suitable document collection', was not readily available for an evaluation of CbPD. The main challenge is that there is no currently existing large-scale test collection of academic plagiarism containing non-artificially created plagiarism, where at the same time all occurrences of plagiarism are known and verified. Therefore, most studies resort to evaluating PDS using artificially created plagiarism (see Section 2.3.1). However, using artificial plagiarism is not an option for evaluating the capability of PDS to detect heavily disguised, realistic plagiarism.

The second component, 'clearly defined information needs', at first seems easily established. Naturally, the goal when using the CbPD approach is to identify instances of strongly paraphrased text, translated plagiarism, structural plagiarism or idea plagiarism. However, upon closer examination, the subjectiveness of human judgment on plagiarism allows no clear definition of what constitutes plagiarism in a given circumstance. Therefore, we uniformly defined the information need for the user study as:

"A retrieved document must fulfill the information need of an examiner in a real plagiarism detection scenario, i.e. the document features similarities, which the examiner would likely find valuable to be made aware of."

The third component, 'reliable relevance judgments', is challenging to obtain, because the level of document similarity that constitutes plagiarism varies widely, especially for disguised forms of plagiarism. Even for the comparatively easy to identify literal text similarities, PDS tend to set varying thresholds, because examiners' opinions differ on the level of textual similarity that constitutes plagiarism (see Section 6.1.2). To increase the reliability of human relevance judgments and increase inter examiner agreement in the user study, we provide a set of uniform guidelines for classifying and rating the retrieved documents.

The fourth component, 'performance metrics', is only feasible if reliable relevance judgments exist for a document collection.

In summary, the rigid four-component evaluation framework applied to IR systems is applicable to the evaluation of CbPD only to a limited extent. Currently, no available framework exists where all components are suitable for the goal of our evaluation. Therefore, we evaluated CbPD using three distinct document collections. Each collection offers unique benefits in terms of the characteristics making it suitable as a test collection for CbPD evaluation. The following section discusses the requirements of an ideal test collection and subsequently describes the three chosen collections.

6.1.1 Test Collection Requirements

To evaluate the effectiveness of CbPD in detecting realistic, strongly disguised academic plagiarism, an ideal test collection should contain:

1. non-fabricated plagiarism – to reflect realistic disguise

2. verified cases of plagiarism – to allow for a ground truth approximation and derive performance indicators

3. academic citations – within readily accessible full-text

4. a variety of documents – many authors, a variety of academic disciplines and different languages

5. optional: machine-readable citations

First, the test collection must contain *non-fabricated cases of plagiarism* to allow a realistic evaluation of CbPD's ability to detect strongly disguised plagiarism. Academic plagiarists are highly motivated to avoid detection and meet the high quality standards of peer-reviewed journals. Therefore, we assume that only real-world cases of paraphrased, translated, or idea plagiarism accurately exemplify the creative disguise tactics employed by plagiarizing scientists in order to deceive both their peers and the public. Most plagiarism in existing test collections lacks a sufficiently sophisticated disguise because it was artificially fabricated. For example, paraphrases were created using automated methods, or texts were machine translated using Google Translate.

To introduce more realistically disguised plagiarism into the evaluation corpora of the PAN competitions 2010-2013, Potthast et al. contracted human writers using the crowdsourcing platforms Amazon Mechanical Turk (PAN 2010 and 2011) and oDesk (PAN 2012 and 2013) [262, 264, 265]. The contractors were provided with a web crawl dataset of approximately 1 billion web pages, a specialized search engine and modified word processing software. The writers' task was to use only the dataset and software tools provided to them to produce plagiarized articles of approximately 5,000 words by paraphrasing web pages in the given dataset. The modified software tools monitored the writers' searches for and use of source documents. This approach produced the most realistic test cases of disguised plagiarism currently available; however, the articles of the PAN collections were unsuitable for an evaluation of CbPD, because they included no citations. Additionally, it remains doubtful whether articles written by contractors without expert knowledge accurately resemble the plagiarism disguise of scientists who often work months or even years on publications.

Second, an ideal test collection should contain *verified cases of plagiarism* to allow the derivation of a ground truth to quantify and compare the detection performance of PD approaches. The true amount of plagiarized content in any non-artificially created collection will most likely never be fully known. However, a thorough manual examination of a document collection can identify a large fraction of plagiarism instances, hence allowing the establishment of a derived ground truth, equivalent to a gold standard data set.

Third, a test collection used for CbPD evaluation must contain *academic citations,* and the full-text of the documents must be available.

Fourth, the test collection should ideally comprise a *variety of academic documents* from different authors, academic disciplines and languages to reflect diverse, real-world plagiarism styles.

Fifth, the presence of *machine-readable citations* is a desirable test collection feature; however, it is not a mandatory prerequisite, since we adapted the open source citation parser ParsCit to parse citations within the full-text according to our needs (see 7.3.1 for more information).

Since artificially created plagiarism cases are not suitable for the intended evaluation, we turned to the use of real plagiarism cases. The unique challenges of using real-world plagiarism are discussed in the following section.

6.1.2 Test Collection Challenges

There are several challenges associated with using real-world test collections for plagiarism detection system evaluations.

The most prominent limitation posed by any real-world collection is the unavailability of a ground truth. While for fabricated test collections, the precise amount of plagiarism is known, the true extent of plagiarism in real-world collections remains unknown. Even the most resource-intensive manual identification efforts are likely to miss some instances of plagiarism in large collections. Thus, calculating precision and recall and comparing the results to the results obtained from other collections provides only a limited insight into the true detection performance of the evaluated PDS.

The second limitation of real-world plagiarism collections arises from the inconsistencies in human judgment regarding plagiarism. Even when assuming all plagiarism instances can be identified for a real-world plagiarism case, expert examiners may disagree on whether plagiarism has taken place. Such discrepancies in opinions could be observed in recent plagiarism investigations involving the dissertations of high-ranking politicians, e.g., the conflicting verdicts reached by plagiarism investigators regarding the dissertation of D. Dähnert, compared to the dissertation of Mrs. Schavan[23]. This limitation in the

---

[23] The German Technical University Cottbus (BTU) refused to rescind the doctorate of D. Dähnert, although investigations by the VroniPlag Wiki identified 44% of total pages in his thesis to contain at least one instance of plagiarism [350]. The BTU Cottbus, however, declared the work to contain only "technical weaknesses" but no "conscious manipulation of data" or other "deceptive practices" [359]. On the other hand, in a plagiarism investigation led by the Heinrich Heine University, the dissertation of Annette Schavan was rescinded despite her thesis containing few literal text overlaps, refer to Section 2.1.3, page 16. Dähnert is a director at the energy company, Vattenfall, which, according to the words of Mr. Kunze is a valuable industry partner of the BTU Cottbus having provided the University with several million euros in third-party funds [258]. Debora Weber-Wulff, professor for Media

inconsistencies in human judgment regarding plagiarism is due in part to three main contributing factors.

1. The definition of plagiarism and what constitutes academic plagiarism under certain circumstances, remains subjective.

2. In evaluations of real-world plagiarism, examiners are susceptible to be swayed by external factors. For example, political, economic, and social ties, as well as the context in which evidence is presented, and the document similarity visualization method used can contribute to volatile human judgment.

3. The extent of similarity that may be regarded as legitimate largely depends on the scientific field and the document type, e.g., case study, literature review, medical standards update, etc.

Additional concerns associated with real-world document collections for use in PD evaluations have been outlined by Potthast and include:

- The distribution of detected real-world plagiarism is skewed towards ease of detectability [262].

- The acquisition of real-world plagiarism is resource intensive, especially in the case of concealed plagiarism [262].

- Publishing real-world cases may require consent of both plagiarists and the original author [262]. If a real-world collection does contain plagiarism, then it has usually not yet been made public or been verified. This is a problem, because once an accusation has been made – be it just or unjust – the

---

and Computing at the HTW Berlin, comments that zu Guttenberg, who was forced to rescind his doctorate, made a mistake in selecting his university, because standards seem to vary [359].

accusation can result in serious negative consequences for the accused.

The next sections introduce the three real-world document collections we identified as promising for an evaluation: the GuttenPlag and VroniPlag Wikis, and the PubMed Central OAS collection.

6.1.3 GuttenPlag Wiki

The GuttenPlag Wiki [147] is the result of a crowd-sourced project aimed to expose all instances of plagiarism in a single work: the doctoral thesis of former German Minister of Defense, Karl-Theodor zu Guttenberg. A law professor happened to detect plagiarized sections in Mr. zu Guttenberg's doctoral thesis by chance [146]. After the popular politician repudiated the accusations as "abstruse", volunteers initiated the GuttenPlag Wiki project [147] to investigate the accusations. The project identified 1,218 plagiarized text fragments from 135 sources[24]. Zu Guttenberg subsequently retracted his initial claim of a flawless thesis; his doctorate was renounced and he eventually stepped down from his political position. In part due to the widespread media attention, zu Guttenberg's thesis represents one of the most thorough plagiarism investigations to date.

As of April 3rd 2011, the joint investigation efforts revealed approximately 64 % of all lines of text in the thesis to be plagiarized. Of the 393 main text pages in the thesis, 371 pages, or almost 95 %, contained plagiarism. The following barcode-representation of the document illustrates the findings.

---

[24] As of 2011-04-03.

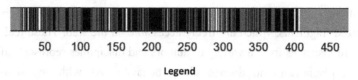

50   100   150   200   250   300   350   400   450

Legend

Red sections – pages with plagiarism from multiple sources
Black sections – pages with plagiarism from one source
White sections – plagiarism-free pages
Blue sections – table of contents and the bibliography

Figure 27: Plagiarized Pages in zu Guttenberg's Thesis

Source: [147]

Although no ground truth exists regarding the total amount of plagiarism present in the thesis, we assume that the thousands of person-hours invested by volunteers and experts at the responsible university led to the identification of a very large fraction of the total plagiarism contained in the document.

In summary, the key advantages of the GuttenPlag Wiki are:

- The analyzed thesis contains real plagiarism, including disguised paraphrases and translations, which were created with a noticeably high motivation to conceal the misconduct.

- The extremely thorough, manual verification of plagiarism instances allows for a ground truth approximation of total plagiarism in the thesis.

- The thesis is a comprehensive academic work with a sufficient number of citations.

6.1.4 VroniPlag Wiki

The VroniPlag Wiki [350] is an ongoing, crowd-sourced project investigating academic plagiarism allegations. Volunteers manually analyzed 23 dissertations[25] of German politicians and scientists and identified ~3,600 plagiarized fragments, which are freely accessible on the web. These real-world plagiarism instances from a variety of authors and disciplines represent different styles of plagiarism and diverse citing behavior. As with any real-world plagiarism collection, examiners may not have identified *all* plagiarized fragments, thus no ground truth exists. However, the carefully verified cases of plagiarism allow for a ground truth approximation.

The key advantages of the VroniPlag Wiki are:

- The large collection of manually examined documents from different authors and disciplines contains real academic plagiarism, representing various forms of plagiarism.

- The thorough verification of plagiarism instances allows for a ground truth approximation of the total amount of plagiarism in the examined documents.

- The documents are comprehensive academic works with suitable amounts of citations.

Both the VroniPlag and the GuttenPlag Wikis are collections of text fragments featuring high character-based similarity, since suspicious text overlap is typically what led to the plagiarism suspicion in the first place. Thus, many plagiarism cases in the VroniPlag and GuttenPlag Wikis could naturally have also been identified using available character-based PDS. This is why we additionally apply CbPD to the large real-world collection PMC OAS, where plagiarism, if present, does not necessarily feature high character-based similarity.

---

[25] The VroniPlag Wiki is an ongoing project and new plagiarism instances are continuously identified. At the time of analysis, 2012-05-10, the collection consisted of 23 works containing 3,345 instances of plagiarism in the *confirmed* category (the category we considered for an evaluation of CbPD). These instances of plagiarism originated from 636 literature sources.

6.1.5 PubMed Central OAS

The PubMed Central Open Access Subset (PMC OAS) is a continuously expanding archive of open access (OA) full-text journal articles from the biomedical and life sciences. The OA Subset is part of the full-text archive PubMed Central (PMC) and contained 234,591 articles by approximately 975,000 authors from 1,972 peer-reviewed journals at the time of evaluation[26]. PMC and the PMC OAS are maintained by the National Center for Biotechnology Information (NCBI), a sub-unit of the National Library of Medicine (NLM).

Given its large size and numerous authors, the PMC OAS is representative of diverse citation styles and potentially many different forms of plagiarism. The mostly reputable journals in the PMC OAS and their thorough peer-review process foster the assumption that yet-undiscovered plagiarism instances will be sparse. However, if present, they may be more strongly disguised, i.e. cleverly paraphrased and modified with less copy & paste or shake & paste plagiarism, given that they have withstood detection.

---

[26] As of 2011-04.

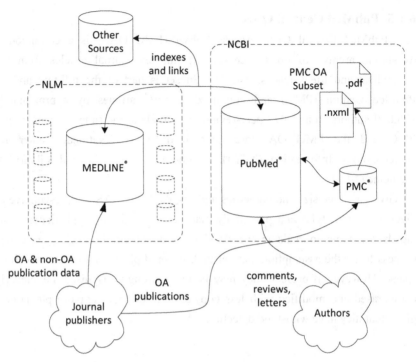

Figure 28: Data Sets and Information Systems Related to the PMC OAS

In summary, the unique advantages of the PMC OAS are:

-   The open-access collection is large and contains scientific articles from many authors.

-   The collection contains peer-reviewed articles from reputable journals, and the articles are freely available as open access full-text.

-   The PMC OAS provides articles in an XML-document format that offers machine-readable markup for metadata and citations.

6.1.6 Summary and Comparison of Test Collections

We found no single test collection suitable for a plagiarism detection evaluation that fulfilled *all five* criteria: non-fabricated plagiarism, verified cases of plagiarism, available academic citations in the full-text, and a diversity of scientific documents (and ideally, but optionally machine-readable citations) as described in Section 6.1.1.

The PAN-PC collection fulfills none of the outlined criteria, except for containing verified cases of plagiarism. The collection contains few academic works, and these not in their entirety, meaning availability of full-texts is missing and citations – if present – are incomplete. Furthermore, most plagiarism in the collection is artificially fabricated and does not reflect realistically disguised plagiarism.

The collection used for the HTW PDS Tests does not fulfill the outlined criteria because most texts are artificially plagiarized essays under 1.5 pages, which contain few or no citations. The few strongly disguised, manually translated plagiarism cases in the collection are not sufficient to compile a test collection of suitable size. A collection of partially plagiarized short answers compiled by Clough et al. [72] is equally unsuitable, because the texts do not contain citations.

Table 12 shows the collection properties and the forms of plagiarism contained in available test collections. No collection on its own is ideally suited for an evaluation of the CbPD approach. However, by combining the unique characteristics of the GuttenPlag Wiki, the VroniPlag Wiki, and the PMC OAS, the performance of CbPD can be evaluated on a combination of the most suitable corpus characteristics.

Table 12: Characteristics of Test Collections for PD Evaluation

	Test Collection	Collection size by # of documents	Real, non-fabricated Plagiarism	Citations avail.	Citations machine extractable	Verified real-world plagiarism	Copy & paste	Shake & paste	Paraphrase	Translation	Idea plagiarism
		Collection Properties					Plagiarism Form	Slightly Disguised		Strongly Disguised	
Fabricated	PAN-PC	26, 939					✓	✓	✓	✓	
	HTW	42			‡		✓	✓	✓	✓	
Real-world	PMC OAS	234,591	✓	✓	✓		✓	✓	✓		?
	GuttenPlag Wiki	1	✓	✓		✓	✓	✓	✓	✓	?
	VroniPlag Wiki[27]	23	✓	✓		✓	✓	✓	✓	✓	?

? unknown

‡insufficient citations available

The GuttenPlag Wiki features strongly disguised plagiarism instances and a very thorough manual investigation that allows for one of the most accurate ground truth approximations of any non-fabricated collection. These characteristics make it ideal for a primary evaluation of the detection performance of CbPD. However, because all the plagiarism of the GuttenPlag Wiki stems from a single author[28], the results of analyzing this collection should not be generalized. We bridge this weakness by including the VroniPlag Wiki plagiarism collection in the CbPD evaluation framework. The VroniPlag Wiki

---

[27] As of 2012-05-10.
[28] According to the claims of Karl-Theodor zu Guttenberg.

contains strongly disguised instances of plagiarism originating from many authors, allowing an evaluation of CbPD for diverse plagiarism styles and academic citing behavior.

Both the GuttenPlag and VroniPlag Wikis contain only verified instances of plagiarism. Therefore, the collections allow the retrieval only of true positives (TP), i.e. the actual plagiarism identified by CbPD in a collection of verified plagiarism. Detecting false positives (FP), i.e. text erroneously flagged as plagiarism, is not possible due to the missing full-texts and the uncertainty as to whether examiners have identified all plagiarized text fragments. Despite the extremely thorough manual examinations, a small fraction of all plagiarism may nonetheless have escaped detection for both collections. Determining the number of false negatives (FN), i.e. plagiarism that remains undetected, and true negatives (TN), i.e. non-plagiarized text rightfully not identified as suspicious, is also not possible for the GuttenPlag and VroniPlag Wikis. Table 13 summarizes the categories into which detection results can fall.

Table 13: Detection Categories for Plagiarism

	Plagiarism	Non-Plagiarism
Identified	True Positive (TP)	False Positive (FP)
Not identified	False Negative (FN)	True Negative (TN)

The absence of FP and TN in the GuttenPlag and VroniPlag Wikis prevents establishing a baseline for citation match occurrences, i.e. the rate of citation matches that may legitimately occur among non-plagiarized documents. To address these limitations, the PMC OAS is a valuable addition to the VroniPlag and GuttenPlag Wiki collections. Using the PMC OAS, we can test the ability of CbPD to identify yet undiscovered plagiarism in a large scientific collection containing diverse document types. This collection also allows for the quantifying of retrieved false positives. The main drawback of the PMC OAS collection is the nonexistence of a ground truth, which must first be established.

6.2   Evaluation using GuttenPlag Wiki

The thorough manual investigation of plagiarism in the GuttenPlag Wiki can serve as a ground truth approximation, which is necessary for a comparative evaluation of available plagiarism detection methods with the CbPD approach. For details on the GuttenPlag Wiki and its suitability as a test collection, please refer to the discussion in Section 6.1.2. Previous evaluations, as presented in Section 2.3.1, show that disguised plagiarism is especially difficult to detect using conventional character-based PDS. In the evaluation of CbPD, we therefore examine the translated plagiarism in the GuttenPlag Wiki, because this form of plagiarism is one of the most difficult to identify and is not present in the largest evaluation collection; refer to Section 6.4.

At the time of investigation[29], the GuttenPlag Wiki identified plagiarized passages on 31 pages within the thesis, which had been translated from English into German. We analyzed[30] these 31 pages for matching citations with their identified sources. To compare CbPD with currently used detection methods, we selected three popular character-based PDS:

Ephorus – ranked among the top three performing systems, featuring 60 % –70 % detection accuracy in the 2010 HTW PDS Test [356].

Ferret (v. 4.0) – a free PDS that, like *Ephorus*, uses fingerprinting [203]. We ran the application with default settings, i.e., Ferret searches for matching word tri-grams.

WCopyFind (v. 3.0) – a free PDS using substring matching [35]. We ran the application with default settings, except for the detection parameters shortest phrase to match, which we decreased to three words, and fewest matches to report, which we decreased to 50 words.

---

[29]   2011-04-10
[30]   This analysis has been published [132].

By choosing these three systems for comparison, we include one of the top scoring systems according to the HTW PDS Test, *Ephorus*, and we include systems employing distinct character-based approaches: fingerprinting and substring matching. *Ephorus* requires payment from its users, while the other two systems are available free of charge. Because *Ferret* and *WCopyFind* depend on local availability of possible source documents, we downloaded all digitally available sources identified by the GuttenPlag Wiki project and provided them to the PDS.

The results we obtained when using character-based PDS on the GuttenPlag Wiki confirmed observations from prior PDS evaluations as discussed in Section 2.3.1. Manually querying search engines, such as Google, yielded high detection rates for copy & paste plagiarism. Depending on the time invested and keywords selected, we could even find paraphrased and translated plagiarism through manual web searches.

The three PDS, especially *Ferret* and *WCopyfind*, which work with local document comparisons, delivered good results for identifying copy & paste plagiarism, given that the sources were available. The performance of *Ephorus* was disappointing. Despite the large fraction of (almost) verbatim plagiarism in the thesis, the system found only 2 % of the text to match the sources of plagiarism. Given the online availability of 77 sources from which text sections were plagiarized, and with only 63 sources not being available for free online [147], this result is unsatisfactory.

As expected, all three systems failed to identify 90 % or more of more creatively paraphrased sections and could not detect a single instance of translated plagiarism. Table 14 gives an overview.

Table 14: Comparison of Detection Results

Plagiarism form	Character-based	Citation-based
Copy & paste	~70 % Good results even for short fragments	Unsuitable Short fragments cannot be detected
Disguised plagiarism	< 10 %	Depends on fragment length ~30 %
Idea/structural plagiarism	0 %	Some cases could be identified
Translated plagiarism	< 5 %	~80 % 13 out of 16 fragments could be identified

The results should be treated with reservation, since it is uncertain whether the GuttenPlag Wiki examiners identified *all* plagiarized fragments (see the related discussion in Section 6.1.2). The detection rates stated may therefore be too high, especially for the more difficult to detect idea plagiarism.

Figure 29 shows the citation patterns of all translated plagiarism fragments in the thesis of zu Guttenberg as identified by the GuttenPlag Wiki project. The depicted patterns are the results of applying Citation Chunking according to strategy two (see Section 4.4.4) or LCCS (see Section 4.4.2) to individual fragments. Except for pages 44, 226 and 300, all pages that contained translated plagiarism shared identical citations in a similar order with the source documents of the respective plagiarism. This becomes especially clear after cleaning the citation sequences by removing unshared citations in both documents in their corresponding positions. The last row of Figure 29 exemplifies this 'cleaning' of citation sequences for the pages 242–244.

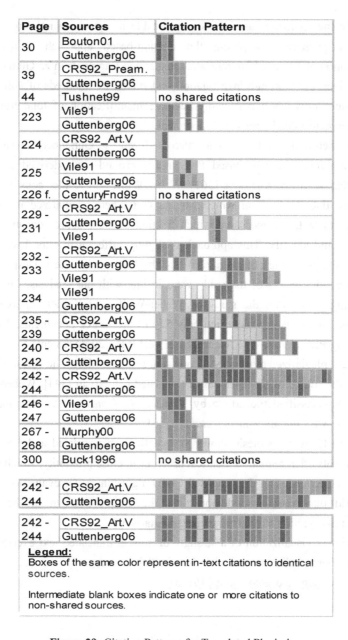

Page	Sources	Citation Pattern
30	Bouton01	
	Guttenberg06	
39	CRS92_Pream.	
	Guttenberg06	
44	Tushnet99	no shared citations
223	Vile91	
	Guttenberg06	
224	CRS92_Art.V	
	Guttenberg06	
225	Vile91	
	Guttenberg06	
226 f.	CenturyFnd99	no shared citations
229 -	CRS92_Art.V	
231	Guttenberg06	
	Vile91	
232 -	CRS92_Art.V	
233	Guttenberg06	
	Vile91	
234	Vile91	
	Guttenberg06	
235 -	CRS92_Art.V	
239	Guttenberg06	
240 -	CRS92_Art.V	
242	Guttenberg06	
242 -	CRS92_Art.V	
244	Guttenberg06	
246 -	Vile91	
247	Guttenberg06	
267 -	Murphy00	
268	Guttenberg06	
300	Buck1996	no shared citations

242 -	CRS92_Art.V	
244	Guttenberg06	

242 -	CRS92_Art.V	
244	Guttenberg06	

Legend:
Boxes of the same color represent in-text citations to identical sources.

Intermediate blank boxes indicate one or more citations to non-shared sources.

Figure 29: Citation Patterns for Translated Plagiarism

While the character-based PDS were unable to detect a single instance of translated plagiarism, applying the citation-based approach allowed the identification of 13 out of 16 translated plagiarized fragments in zu Guttenberg's thesis. Given the thorough investigation undertaken by hundreds of volunteers, this number provides a reasonably accurate quantification of total translated plagiarism detectable by the CbPD approach.

D. Weber-Wulff and K. Köhler also analyzed the Guttenberg thesis using five commercial character-based PDS and a ground truth derived from the GuttenPlag Wiki investigations [361]. Weber-Wulff and Köhler considered the 20 source documents from which Mr. zu Guttenberg plagiarized the largest quantities of text, and measured which fraction of those source documents the systems could identify. This approach is slightly different to ours, because we recorded the percentage of plagiarism that the PDS could detect. Despite these differences, the results of the study were in line with our analysis. The worst performing systems in the study of Weber-Wulff and Köhler, *Ephorus* and *PlagScan*, both of which identified only 5 % of the source documents. The best performing PDS, *iThenticate*, identified 23 %. Of the 20 documents from which Guttenberg plagiarized most heavily, one source authored by Vile was in English and was the source of six instances of translated plagiarism [344]. Weber-Wulff and Köhler classified the article by Vile as *"[...] maschinell unauffindbar"*, meaning it was *"not machine detectable"* [361].

The zu Guttenberg thesis shows that citations in translated and rearranged text segments often remain in identical order, or in close proximity, which allows for their detection using the proposed CbPD algorithms. Our evaluation of this real-world plagiarism case demonstrates the unique strength of the CbPD approach in detecting strongly disguised plagiarism.

To view a visualization of a strongly disguised, translated text excerpt from the Guttenberg plagiarism case visit the CitePlag prototype: http://www.citeplag.org/compare/6861131

6.3 Evaluation using VroniPlag Wiki

The VroniPlag Wiki collection of plagiarism served to evaluate the performance of the CbPD approach for confirmed plagiarism cases from a variety of authors [350]. For an overview of the characteristics that make the VroniPlag Wiki a suitable test collection refer to Section 6.1.4.

In the VroniPlag Wiki, examiners either categorized plagiarized fragments as "confirmed" or as "suspicious" instances. For the purpose of the evaluations in Sections 6.3.1 and 6.3.2, we only considered the text fragments[31] labeled "confirmed", approximately 92 % of total fragments in the collection, with the assumption that these instances generated no controversy about the presence of plagiarism.

We[32] performed three distinct evaluations using the VroniPlag Wiki. The first examined what fraction of plagiarism the CbPD approach could identify out of a random sample of plagiarized fragments containing different plagiarism forms, see Section 6.3.1. The second evaluation tested the ability of CbPD to detect translated plagiarism, see Section 6.3.2, and the third examined a single plagiarism case to test whether sufficient citation-based similarity remains for CbPD to be effective for academic texts containing more creatively paraphrased or heavily disguised plagiarism, see Section 6.3.3. The results obtained using the VroniPlag Wiki collection are available for review and download as an Excel file. See Appendix C for access details.

6.3.1 Evaluation: Random Sample of Sources

The first evaluation using the VroniPlag Wiki tested the ability of CbPD to identify confirmed instances of plagiarism regardless of the plagiarism form, i.e.

---

[31] At the time of analysis: 2012-05-10. The VroniPlag Wiki project is ongoing and new plagiarism instances are continuously added.

[32] I would like to acknowledge the contributions of all VroniPlag Wiki volunteers and the help of Corinna Breitinger and Norman Meuschke in analyzing the corpus of the VroniPlag Wiki.

copy & paste, shake & paste, paraphrasing, or translated plagiarism. The following question was addressed:

How capable is the CbPD approach in identifying plagiarized documents out of a collection containing known plagiarism?

To select a random sample of plagiarism regardless of type, we considered the 636 literature sources from which authors were known to have plagiarized[31]. For the analysis, we only included the 198 source documents from which authors plagiarized at least five text fragments. These slightly more extensive instances of plagiarism are more likely to contain citations. Yet, the fragments may stem from any location in the text, e.g., the introduction may contain two plagiarism instances, while the other three instances occur in the conclusion.

Shorter instances of plagiarism are less likely to adopt the citations of the source document, which makes them difficult, if not impossible, to detect using CbPD. However, we do not see this as a threat to the value demonstrated by CbPD, because plagiarism spanning more than a few sentences is likely to contain citations and thus be exposed using CbPD. Since existing systems already perform well in identifying short copy & paste plagiarism, being able to identify more serious yet disguised plagiarism forms is of importance.

From the 198 qualifying source documents from which at least five text fragments were plagiarized, we took a random sample of 25 sources. For each of the 25 sources, we compared the citation patterns in the source to the citation pattern in the respective fragments that plagiarized from the source.

This citation pattern analysis was performed manually. The following barriers prevented an automatic extraction of citations. First, documents in the VroniPlag Wiki collection are from diverse disciplines, e.g., law, medicine, philosophy, and engineering. Each discipline has its own unique citation styles, making automatic citation extraction error-prone. Second, the full-texts for most source documents are not digitally available, making automatic citation extraction laborious, because the documents would have to be scanned and converted into machine-readable text. Third, some citations contain errors, for example, misspelled author names or incorrectly cited publication dates, which can more easily be corrected manually. For real-world document collections, the presence of some errors in citation information is unavoidable.

By choosing manual citation extraction over an automated extraction approach, we could achieve a higher accuracy and minimize extraction errors. The citation information in the VroniPlag Wiki collection is at times incomplete, since plagiarized fragments are presented as short excerpts taken from the full-text (some only 1 to 3 lines). Additionally, we cannot be certain that all investigators consistently include citations when preparing the excerpts for inclusion in the collection. Whenever a document's full-text was available online, we accessed it to confirm the citations in the plagiarized fragments and in the source. Yet, most full-texts were unavailable to us, which represents a source of error in this evaluation.

6.3.1.1 *Results*

We split the results into three categories, as shown in Table 15. The first category contains sources with five or more matching citations[33] in close proximity, which is a strong indicator of plagiarism. The second category includes sources with three to four matching citations in close proximity, which is a potential indicator of plagiarism. The third category contains sources with two or fewer matching citations, which is an insufficient indicator for potential plagiarism. Of the 25 randomly selected sources, nine sources shared clearly suspicious citation matches with seven dissertations that plagiarized from these sources. The documents contained between six and 97 matching citations in close proximity to each other. The dissertations from the authors with initials Dv, Awb, Bds, Mh, Ub, each contained suspicious citation matches with one source, while the works of Lm and Pes contained suspicious citation matches with two sources.

In addition to identifying seven dissertations as highly likely to contain plagiarism, CbPD also identified two dissertations, the works of the authors with

---

[33] We use the term "matching citations" for citations of identical sources, which a plagiarized document shares with the source document.

initials Ah and Bds, with three or four matching citations, as possible plagiarism candidates. The dissertations of another seven authors contained no citations, or featured insufficient citation pattern similarities to be identified as plagiarism using the CbPD approach.

It is interesting to note that the plagiarist with initials Mh translated the text from LeBaron 2005 [188] (highlighted in gray in Table 15) from English to German. Being a translation, this example of plagiarism shares no literal text overlap with its source aside from a copied quote. Despite the low character-based similarity in the plagiarized fragments, 18 citations are similarly arranged, allowing the CbPD approach to reliably detecting such cases of translated plagiarism.

In summary, we found the CbPD approach capable of reliably identifying a significant fraction of plagiarism. Of the 15 authors who plagiarized from the random sample of 25 sources, the CbPD approach could identify the theses of seven authors (~47 %) as likely to have been plagiarized (green in Table 15).

Table 15: Citation Matches between Plagiarism and Source Fragments in the VroniPlag Wiki

Rand. Sample #ID	Source Document (Author, Year)	Initials of respective Plagiarist	# fragments Plagiarized from Source (≥ 5)	Citation Pattern Matches
9	Randelzhofer 1991b	Dv	31	97
18	Vahl 1995	Awb	24	93
17	Stelkens 1998	Pes	10	24
1	Nork 1992	Bds	41	21
6	Schurig 1981	Lm	9	21
25	LeBaron 2005	Mh	6	18
14	Roeser 1988	Ub	17	14
13	Kropholler 1997	Lm	14	6
23	Hoppe 1970	Pes	5	6
21	Martens 1995	Ah	9	4
4	Hüffer 1995	Ah	6	4
5	Kuehn Becker 1999	Bds	5	3
3	Krause 1998	Gc	17	1
19	Lehmann 1984	Mw	7	1
10	Tavlas 1993	Skm	5	1
7	Mathiopoulos 1983	Mm	5	1
22	Stadtentwicklung 1991*	Sh	71	0
15	Veit 1969	Skm	10	0
8	Puhle 1983*	Mm	8	0
2	IZMF (web)*	Vs	7	0
11	Stadtumbau (web)*	Jg	7	0
12	Hartje 1990	Bds	7	0
16	Harpprecht 1982	Mm	7	0
20	Mathiopoulos 1982	Mm	7	0
24	Huber 2001	Bds	6	0

* no citations present in source document

Green: 5 or more citation order matches – very strong indication of plagiarism

Orange: 3-5 citation order matches – likely indication of plagiarism

Red: 2 or fewer citation order matches – insufficient indication of plagiarism

6.3.2 Evaluation: Translated Plagiarism

The second evaluation using the VroniPlag Wiki collection tested the performance of CbPD on instances of translated plagiarism. The following question was addressed:

> *How many of the seven dissertations containing translated plagiarism can the CbPD approach identify?*

Discovering strongly disguised forms of plagiarism containing little or no character similarity is the strength of the CbPD approach. Thus, an evaluation of real-world, heavily disguised plagiarism cases is central to assessing the performance of CbPD. VroniPlag Wiki investigators found seven of the 23 authors[34] to have engaged in translation plagiarism. These seven dissertations contained a total of 146 translated fragments, of which 95 fragments (65 %) featured citation information. For the evaluation, we recorded the similarities in citations between these 95 citation-containing translated plagiarism fragments and their sources.

6.3.2.1 *Results*

We split the results into three groups according to the success in identifying the plagiarized document using CbPD. The first group contains plagiarism with five or more citation pattern matches with their sources (a strong indicator of plagiarism). The second category contains plagiarism with three to four citation pattern matches with their sources (a likely indicator of plagiarism) and the third category contains plagiarism with two or fewer citation pattern matches (an insufficient indicator of plagiarism).

Of the seven dissertations containing translated plagiarism, the dissertations of five authors showed a suspicious overlap in their citation order compared with the confirmed sources from which they plagiarized. The translated plagiarism cases of the authors with initials Mm (two sources contained suspicious citation overlap), Mh (four sources contained suspicious overlap), and Gc, Awb and Skm

---

[34]   As of 2012-05-10.

showed between four and 24 matching citations in close proximity or in the identical order as their source documents. Table 16 summarizes the findings.

Of the 28 sources from which authors plagiarized, about one-third of sources (nine) contained three or more citations in an order similar to their respective plagiarized text. As pointed out in Section 6.3.1, we classified such similarity as a likely indicator of plagiarism. The two dissertations the CbPD approach was unable to identify as suspicious (red in Table 16) featured only five and seven citation-containing plagiarized fragments, while three of the four dissertations that were identified as highly suspicious featured 20 or more citation-containing fragments.

Table 16: Citation Matches for Translated Plagiarism in VroniPlag Wiki

| Plag-iarist Initials | Fragments analyzed | fragment-based overview | | source-based overview | | Highest citation order match from a single source |
		Fragments containing citations	Fragments containing at least 1 matching cit. with source	Sources from which plagiarist transl. plagiarized	Sources with 3 or more matching citations	
Mm	33	26	18	4	2	33
Mh	30	23	19	7	4	17
Gc	24	20	6	3	1	10
Awb	12	4	3	1	1	6
Skm	30	10	4	6	1	4
Dv	12	7	4	5	0	2
Cs	5	5	1	2	0	1
Totals	146	95	55	28	9	-

Green: 5 or more citation order matches – very strong indication of plagiarism (LCCS match)
Orange: 3-5 citation order matches – likely indication of plagiarism (LCCS match)
Red: 2 or fewer citation order matches – insufficient indication of plagiarism

Figure 30 visualizes the citation patterns of three translated plagiarism instances compared with their source. Aside from a few insertions (white bars) and some minor transpositions in citation order, the citation patterns extending over several pages were suspiciously similar.

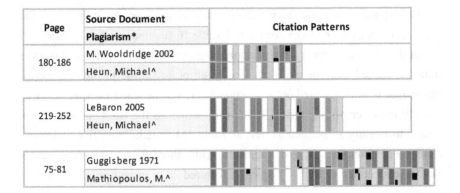

Page	Source Document Plagiarism*	Citation Patterns
180-186	M. Wooldridge 2002 Heun, Michael^	
219-252	LeBaron 2005 Heun, Michael^	
75-81	Guggisberg 1971 Mathiopoulos, M.^	

^ full text unavailable. Not all citations outside of plagiarized fragement sections are known.

* Citation patterns were analyzed on a fragment-source basis. Due to full text unavailability, the citation pattern for the sum of fragments given in VroniPlag may slightly differ from the complete citation pattern in the full text.

Legend

Lines of identical color represent in-text citations to the same sources.

White lines indicate one or more citations of non-shared sources.

Diagonally stripped lines are inserted spaceholders. They do not represent citations, and only serve to better visually align the matching citations.

Figure 30: Citation Patterns for Translated Plagiarism in the VroniPlag Wiki

In conclusion, the CbPD approach could identify five of the seven theses containing translated plagiarism as likely plagiarism, given their suspicious citation pattern matches. The results show that the copying of citations, if present in the source, was common behavior among five of the seven plagiarists, even when the plagiarized text was translated. This observation of plagiarism behavior in VroniPlag Wiki indicates that the CbPD approach is promising for detecting strongly disguised translated plagiarism in real-world plagiarism settings.

6.3.3 Evaluation: Plagiarism Case Heun

Investigations of Michael Heun's dissertation [156] by VroniPlag Wiki examiners found that the author plagiarized 56 text fragments[35] from a single source authored by Matthias Unser [337]. Most of these fragments are extensive and run more than a paragraph in length. The unique characteristic of Heun's plagiarism from Unser is that it gives a realistic example of extensive plagiarism, in which the plagiarist invested much effort into disguising the plagiarism, e.g., masking copied text through synonym replacements or paraphrasing, while at the same time copying citations. Both documents were available as full-text.

An examination of Heun's plagiarism from the source document, tested the performance of CbPD in identifying extensive, yet disguised academic plagiarism. The evaluation addressed the following question:

Are fewer citations copied, or is the citation order transposed in such a way that CbPD may not be effective in a case where an author copies extensively, yet makes an effort to paraphrase and disguise plagiarism?

We randomly selected 15 pages of Heun's thesis for comparison against the source document by looking up the first entry in the reference list of Heun's dissertation (Aarts H.B.) and beginning the extraction of the 15-page excerpt on the page where this source was first cited, on page 140 [156].

6.3.3.1 *Results*

The resulting consecutive 15-page excerpt of Heun's dissertation contained 301 citations. Of these, 192 citations matched the respective citations in the source document in identical or only slightly transposed order. This represented a 63.8 % citation overlap in a 15-page excerpt. Such high citation overlap is very

---

[35] At the time of analysis: 2012-06-10. The Frankfurt School of Finance and Management retracted the doctorate of Michael Heun as of 2012-10-17, refer to http://de.vroniplag.wikia.com/wiki/Mh.

suspicious and would be a strong indicator of potential plagiarism even in the absence of character-based similarity.

Figure 31 visualizes a 2-page excerpt from the 15-page citation pattern analysis. The figure shows the citation patterns for pages 145–146 of Heun's thesis on the left and the arrangement of citations in the source document by M. Unser on the right. Identical colors represent the individual matching citations or entire matching citation groups. Black lines in the figure separate the citation groups. A citation group is defined as a collection of several references contained in a single in-text citation, for example, [author A, author B, author C] is a citation group of size three. Note that for the full 2-page excerpt visualized in Figure 31, no non-shared citations were present.

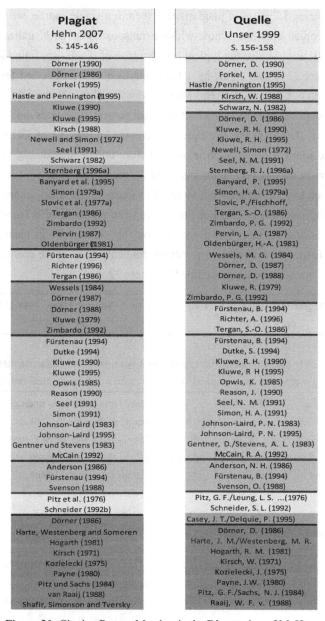

Plagiat Hehn 2007 S. 145-146	Quelle Unser 1999 S. 156-158
Dörner (1990)	Dörner, D. (1990)
Dörner (1986)	Forkel, M. (1995)
Forkel (1995)	Hastie /Pennington (1995)
Hastie and Pennington (1995)	Kirsch, W. (1988)
Kluwe (1990)	Schwarz, N. (1982)
Kluwe (1995)	Dörner, D. (1986)
Kirsch (1988)	Kluwe, R. H. (1990)
Newell and Simon (1972)	Kluwe, R. H. (1995)
Seel (1991)	Newell, Simon (1972)
Schwarz (1982)	Seel, N. M. (1991)
Sternberg (1996a)	Sternberg, R. J. (1996a)
Banyard et al. (1995)	Banyard, P. (1995)
Simon (1979a)	Simon, H. A. (1979a)
Slovic et al. (1977a)	Slovic, P./Fischhoff,
Tergan (1986)	Tergan, S.-O. (1986)
Zimbardo (1992)	Zimbardo, P. G. (1992)
Pervin (1987)	Pervin, L. A. (1987)
Oldenbürger (1981)	Oldenbürger, H.-A. (1981)
Fürstenau (1994)	Wessels, M. G. (1984)
Richter (1996)	Dörner, D. (1987)
Tergan (1986)	Dörner, D. (1988)
Wessels (1984)	Kluwe, R. (1979)
Dörner (1987)	Zimbardo, P. G. (1992)
Dörner (1988)	Fürstenau, B. (1994)
Kluwe (1979)	Richter, A. (1996)
Zimbardo (1992)	Tergan, S.-O. (1986)
Fürstenau (1994)	Fürstenau, B. (1994)
Dutke (1994)	Dutke, S. (1994)
Kluwe (1990)	Kluwe, R. H. (1990)
Kluwe (1995)	Kluwe, R H (1995)
Opwis (1985)	Opwis, K. (1985)
Reason (1990)	Reason, J. (1990)
Seel (1991)	Seel, N. M. (1991)
Simon (1991)	Simon, H. A. (1991)
Johnson-Laird (1983)	Johnson-Laird, P. N. (1983)
Johnson-Laird (1995)	Johnson-Laird, P. N. (1995)
Gentner und Stevens (1983)	Gentner, D./Stevens, A. L. (1983)
McCain (1992)	McCain, R. A. (1992)
Anderson (1986)	Anderson, N. H. (1986)
Fürstenau (1994)	Fürstenau, B. (1994)
Svenson (1988)	Svenson, O. (1988)
Pitz et al. (1976)	Pitz, G. F./Leung, L. S. ...(1976)
Schneider (1992b)	Schneider, S. L. (1992)
Dörner (1986)	Casey, J. T./Delquie, P. (1995)
Harte, Westenberg and Someren	Dörner, D. (1986)
Hogarth (1981)	Harte, J. M./Westenberg, M. R.
Kirsch (1971)	Hogarth, R. M. (1981)
Kozielecki (1975)	Kirsch, W. (1971)
Payne (1980)	Kozielecki, J. (1975)
Pitz und Sachs (1984)	Payne, J.W. (1980)
van Raaij (1988)	Pitz, G. F./Sachs, N. J. (1984)
Shafir, Simonson and Tversky	Raaij, W. F. v. (1988)

Figure 31: Citation Pattern Matches in the Dissertation of M. Heun

In analyzing 15 pages of plagiarized text from a single source, we found that M. Heun copied citations almost without transpositions. To visualize not only citation patterns, but also the typical text disguise of plagiarism found in Heun's thesis, Figure 32 shows a side-by-side comparison of a plagiarized text excerpt and the source. Citations are renumbered from one through seven in both texts, such that identical numbers represent identical sources with lines drawn between the matches. Although the texts are in German, knowledge of German is not required to see that sentence structure and word choice are notably different in the plagiarism and source. Heun meticulously paraphrased the copied sentences and replaced key words with synonyms. In Figure 32, identical colors highlight semantically identical text sections that have been paraphrased. Character-based similarity is limited. Only one fragment contains four words in identical order and three fragments contain two words in identical order. These character-based similarities are additionally underlined in Figure 32.

Plagiarism: Heun 2007 [156] pp. 139-140	Source: Unser 1999 [337] pp. 152-153
Legend Colored Text = semantic similarity (paraphrases/synonym word replacements) Underlined = character-based similarity (two or more words in identical order)	
Aus dem Blickwinkel der Entscheidungstheorie werden diese Daumenregeln (rules of thumb) oft als irrational interpretiert [1]. Hingegen betonen Vertreter ... Bewältigung der Komplexität der Umwelt [2]. Untersuchungen zeigen, dass die Verwendung von Heuristiken in dynamischen Situation oft effizienter sind als die statische klassische Entscheidungstheorie [3].	Diese Daumenregeln können zwar auch zu einer zielkonformen Entscheidung führen, bieten aber keine Gewähr für die Optimalität der gefundenen bzw. für die Existenz irgendeiner Lösung. Während aus entscheidungstheoretischer Sicht eher die „Irrationalität" dieser Regeln betont wird, [1] stellen Vertreter ... Bewältigung der Umweltkomplexität in den Vordergrund [2]. Ferner ist zu beachten, daß die klassische Entscheidungstheorie statisch ist und die be-obachteten Heuristiken in dynamischen Situationen oftmals sehr effizient sind. [3]

Als Folgen dieser simplifizierten Selektionsregeln können die folgenden Punkte identfiziert werden: [4] ..	Die Anwendung dieser vereinfachten Auswahl-prinzipien führt jedoch auch dazu, daß [4] ... Vorhandene Informationen werden zugunsten dieser Alternative interpretiert und widers-prüchliche Informationen vernachlässig [5]. Ferner führen in der Vergangenheit gemachte Erfahrungen bzw. gewohnheitsmäßige Verhaltensweisen dazu, daß entscheidungsrelevante Informationen nicht im erforderlichen Umfang aufgenommen und suboptimal verarbeitet werden [6]. Der Grad der subjektiven Wichtigkeit der Information bestimmt außerdem, welche Informationen in welcher Reihenfolge aufgenommen werden [7]
Dazu gehören insbesondere die Uminterpretation bzw. Vernachlässigung von nicht passend erscheinenden Informationen [5], das nicht vollständige Aufnehmen und suboptimale Verarbeiten von Informationen aufgrund vergangener Erfahrungen bzw. Gewohnheitsmäßiger Verhaltensweisen [6] sowie die Reihenfolge der Informationsaufnahme gemäß dem subjektiven Grad der Wichtigkeit [7].	

References	References
[1] Vgl. Kahneman, Slovic und Tversky (1982).	[1] Vgl. Kahneman, D./Slovic, P./Tversky, A. (1982)
[2] Vgl. Anderson (1986), S. 83-88; Berens (1992); Groner, Groner und Bischof (1983); Hogarth (1981); Lopes (1991); Pitz und Sachs (1984), S. 140; van Raaij (1988), S. 79; Schaefer (1979), S. 398 sowie Tversky und Kahneman (1974). Die Anwendung von Heuristiken führt in (Simulations-) Experimenten häufig zu nahezu optimalen Ergebnissen; vgl. Cason (1994); Gigerenzer und Goldstein (1996), S. 666; Thorn-gate (1980) sowie Schoemaker und Hershey (1996), S. 199.	[2] Vgl. Anderson, N. H. (1986) S. 83-88; Berens, W. (1992); Groner, R./Groner, M./Bischof, W. F. (1983); Hogarth, R. M. (1981); Lopes, L. L. (1991); Pitz, G. F./Sachs, N. J. (1984) S. 140; Raaij, W. F. v. (1988) S. 79; Schaefer, R. E. (1979) S. 398; Tversky, A./Kahneman, D. (1974). In (Simulations-) Experimenten konnte darüber hinaus gezeigt werden, daß die Anwendung von Heuristiken häufig zu nahezu optimalen Ergebnissen führt; Cason, T. N. (1994); Gigerenzer, G./ Goldstein, D. G. (1996) S. 666; Thomgate, W. S. (1980); Schoemaker, P.

J. H./Hershey, J. C. (1996) S. 199.	
[3] Vgl. etwa Einhorn und Hogarth (1981) sowie Klein (1983).	[3] Vgl. Einhorn, H.J./Hogarth, R.M. (1981); Klein, N.M. (1983).
[4] Vgl. Aschenbrenner, Böckenholt, Albert und Schmalhofer (1986), S. 68; Grunert (1982), S. 38-41 und S. 105; Tyszka (1986), S. 159; Payne (1976), S. 384; Unser (1999), S. 152 sowie Wedeil und Senter (1997), S. 61.	[4] Vgl. Aschenbrenner, K. M./Bökenholt, U./Albert, D./Schmalhofer, F. (1986) S. 68; Grunert, K. G. (1982) S. 38-41, 105; Tyszka, T. (1986) S. 159; Payne, J. W. (1976) S. 384; Wedell, D. H./Senter, S. M. (1997) S. 61
[5] Vgl. Russo et al. (1996), S. 107; Gilad et al. (1987), S. 67; Gilovich (Hrsg.) (1991), S. 62 sowie Hofacker (1985), S. 47.	[5] Vgl. Russo, J. E./Husted Medvec, V./Meloy, M. G. (1996) S.107; Gilad, B./Kaish, S./Loeb, P. D. (1987) S.67; Gilovic, T. (1991) S. 62; Hofacker, T. (1985) S. 46.
[6] Vgl. Aarts, Verplanken und van Knippenberg (1997).	[6] Vgl. Aarts, H./Verplanken, B./Knippenberg, A. v. (1997)
[7] Vgl. Ben Zur und Breznitz (1981), S. 102; Kuß (1991), S. 58 sowie Hofacker (1985), S. 47.	[7] Vgl. Ben Zur, H./Breznitz, S. J. (1981) S. 102; Kuß, A. (1991) S. 58, Hofacker, T. (1985) S. 47.

Figure 32: Strongly Disguised Plagiarism in the Dissertation of M. Heun

Several sections of Heun's plagiarized text contain insufficient character-based similarity to reasonably arouse suspicion using character-based PDS. Character-based systems generally require at least 15 % of n-grams, each commonly spanning three to four words, to match in the analyzed text [85]. Heun's dissertation thus provides examples where character-based PDS would fail to identify plagiarism instances that CbPD can detect, e.g., the seven citations in identical order from the short text excerpt in Figure 32 would be a strong indicator of plagiarism.

Heun's real-world plagiarism case gives insight into our question of whether citation order may be transposed by a plagiarist in such a way that CbPD becomes unsuitable when an effort to paraphrase and disguise plagiarism is made. We found no evidence in this examined case of noticeably changed citing behavior in an effort to conceal plagiarism, despite the author having made an effort to disguise character-based similarity. This observation is in line with the evaluations of the GuttenPlag and VroniPlag Wiki collections, confirming that it is common behavior among plagiarists to copy citations with little or no modification. The CbPD approach thus shows promise in identifying even cases of heavily disguised academic plagiarism.

6.3.4 Conclusion VroniPlag Wiki

In conclusion, all three VroniPlag Wiki evaluations confirmed a high tendency of plagiarists to copy citations, whenever these are present in the source document.

The first evaluation demonstrated the ability of the citation-based plagiarism detection approach in identifying a significant percentage of academic plagiarism from a collection of known plagiarism. Of 15 authors who plagiarized from a random sample of 25 source documents, using the CbPD approach alone identified seven theses as likely cases of plagiarism. The second evaluation demonstrated that citation copying is common behavior among plagiarists even when text is translated. The CbPD approach identified five of the seven theses containing translated plagiarism as likely cases of plagiarism, solely because of their suspicious citation pattern matches. The third evaluation examined the citation-copying behavior of a single plagiarist who invested considerable effort into disguising his misconduct. Observations collected over a 15-page excerpt confirmed that despite a high degree of textual disguise, citations were not substituted or transposed sufficiently to render the CbPD algorithms ineffective.

In examining the 23 dissertations in the VroniPlag Wiki we found that only the plagiarized fragments contained in two doctoral theses, [149] and [280], did not feature a single copied citation from a least one source document from which they had plagiarized. However, since the VroniPlag Wiki collection of plagiarism is fragment based, it is possible that even these theses share some citations with the sources from which they copied at some location within their full-texts.

We believe one reason why the real-world plagiarism cases of the VroniPlag Wiki, including the Heun plagiarism case, feature no substitutions, or only very few substitutions of plagiarized citations, is partly due to the individual reasons why authors choose to cite sources. The reasons for choosing certain citations are very specific and replacing them requires considerable effort, and in some cases is impossible. See Section 4.1, for a discussion on author citation motivations and a list of common motivations.

6.4   Evaluation using PubMed Central OAS[36]

This section presents an evaluation of the CbPD approach, using the PubMed Central Open Access Subset (PMC OAS). This third and final evaluation assesses the practicability, usability, and computational efficiency of the CbPD algorithms in detecting unknown instances of plagiarism in a large, real-world document collection.

The two previously presented evaluations using the GuttenPlag and the VroniPlag Wikis provided the following insights. Relying on the plagiarism identified in the GuttenPlag Wiki as a ground truth approximation, the CbPD approach capably identified translated plagiarism. In the case of the VroniPlag Wiki, the CbPD approach also demonstrated good detection performance in a multiple author setting.

However, for both test collections, the number of documents available for analysis was relatively small and the instances of plagiarism had already been detected. The known plagiarism containment of the GuttenPlag and VroniPlag Wikis was used as a baseline against which we compared CbPD performance. While practical for evaluation purposes, the characteristic of known plagiarism occurrence is non-representative of the typical use case for PDS. The final evaluation using the PMC OAS collection is thus the most representative of a

---

[36]   A summary of this evaluation of CbPD using the PMC OAS collection has been accepted for publication in the Journal of the American Society for Information Science and Technology [135].

realistic plagiarism detection setting in that it checks for plagiarism on a large-scale in a collection of scientific publications where the true manifestation of plagiarism is unknown.

Most importantly, the PMC OAS collection is suitable for assessing the effectiveness and efficiency of CbPD in detecting plagiarism forms that have remained undetected using available approaches, such as skillful paraphrases or structural and idea plagiarism, which are plagiarism forms potentially present in the PMC OAS. The PMC OAS consists of 234,591 peer-reviewed articles[37], by approximately 975,000 authors. Given that the articles in the PMC OAS appeared in reputable medical journals and passed the peer-review process, still undiscovered instances of plagiarism are likely to be sparse. If present, however, we hypothesize that some instances of plagiarism will be more heavily disguised. A large collection is also more likely to offer a high diversity of academic writing styles and various plagiarism forms. Additionally, the large collection size allows testing the algorithms for their computational efficiency.

The evaluation approach pursued for the PMC OAS collection will target the most pressing limitations of current PDS:

1. Detection effectiveness for the diverse plagiarism forms – current approaches are unable to reliably identify heavily disguised plagiarism.

2. The time and resource intensiveness of manual plagiarism verification – current approaches only visualize character-based similarity, not semantic similarity, which leads to an incomplete document representation for human examiners who must judge potential plagiarism.

3. Computational efficiency of document comparisons – current approaches cannot perform exhaustive n:n comparisons of very large collections. They must limit collection size in an initial

---

[37] As of 2011-04-15.

heuristic retrieval step, which typically decreases detection accuracy; refer to Section 2.2.1.

To address these challenges, the following objectives are pursued using the PMC OAS collection.

Objective 1: Assess the *effectiveness* of CbPD in the two stages of plagiarism analysis: the automatic detection phase, which includes heuristic retrieval, detailed analysis, and knowledge-based processing of the results (refer to Section 2.2.1); and the manual verification stage. A user study provides the ground truth for document suspiciousness and serves to measure user utility.

CbPD effectiveness is measured in:

a. *Detection performance* – comparative performance evaluation of CbPD and character-based algorithms *(automatic detection stage)*. This evaluation is twofold. First, we analyzed documents in an *n:n fashion* and gauged the ability of detection methods to rank highly the document pairs that users identified as most suspicious for each of the various plagiarism forms. In a secondary, smaller *1:n* evaluation, we analyzed the precision and recall performance of the detection methods that performed best in the *n:n* evaluation.

b. *User utility* – usefulness and potential time-savings of CbPD for the examiner *(manual verification stage)*.

Objective 2: Examine the computational efficiency of CbPD and compare its average case time complexity in theory and in practice with currently used character-based approaches.

We do not use the term plagiarism for any documents containing instances of potentially suspicious similarity unless the documents have been officially confirmed by the earlier authors, or have already been retracted by the responsible authorities. The following Sections 6.4.1 and 6.4.2 respectively present the evaluation methodology for the PMC OAS collection and the CbPD evaluation results.

6.4.1 Methodology

This section describes the methodology for the evaluation of CbPD using the PMC OAS corpus. At the core of the methodology is a four-step approach, as shown in Figure 33. The first three steps of the evaluation methodology will be presented in this section, while the final comparison of algorithm rankings to the user-study-derived ground truth will be presented in the results, see Section 6.4.2.

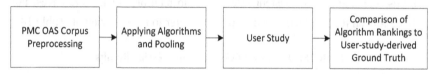

Figure 33: PMC OAS Four-step Evaluation Methodology

6.4.1.1 *Corpus Preprocessing*

This section describes the composition of the PubMed Central Open Access Subset and the preparation of the corpus for the evaluation of CbPD. We excluded 13,371 documents for being either unprocessable, non-relevant, i.e. non-scientific or duplicates. Such cases included documents missing a text body, (e.g., scanned articles in image file formats) documents with multiple text bodies, (e.g., summaries of all articles in conference proceedings) and duplicate files. See Table 17.

Table 17: Excluded Documents

Criterion	Documents
Files in PMC OAS	234,591
No text body	12,783
Multiple text bodies	117
Duplicate files	471
Processable documents	221,220

After parsing, we removed an additional 36,050 documents from the set of processable documents for containing incomplete or erroneous citations, e.g., citations referring to non-existent references, no citations, or no references. For more details on the results of the data parsing; refer to the overview in Table 18.

Table 18: Overview of Corpus Preprocessing Results

Criterion	Documents	Citations	References
Processable documents	221,220	10,976,338	6,921,249
Containing no references	35,369	0	-
Containing no citations	35,980	-	6,447
Inconsistent citation count	68	11,405	4,722
References without citations	16,866	-	65,588
Non-unique references	10,746	-	32,122
Citations without references	59	474	-
Test collection	185,170	10,964,933	6,910,080

Samples indicated that documents without citations and/or references are typically short comments, letters, reviews or editorial notes that do not cite any other documents, or give references without in-text citations. Documents with inconsistent citation counts are texts in which the document's internal numbering of citations, according to their sequential position in the text, is not strictly increasing. Errors in stating the abbreviated numeric citations in the source documents are the main cause for this inconsistency.

An additional 16,866 documents contained citations and/or references that we could not fully acquire. The reason for this was typically that citations were not marked up properly in the XML source file, for instance, because the original text states citations in figures or figure captions. We retained such documents in the test collection, because retaining as well as excluding them can cause false negatives, i.e. undetected documents with potentially suspicious similarities. However, the likelihood of false negatives is higher when documents with incomplete citations or references are excluded entirely instead of retaining the documents, and hence including at least the citation information that could be acquired.

We also retained 10,746 documents that listed the same reference multiple times in their bibliography. Because non-unique references may cause false positives, we checked all documents with high citation-based similarities for non-unique references, and if applicable, determined the influence these references had on the similarity assessment.

An initial concern was that errors in the automated parsing and disambiguation of references and citations might lead to insufficient data quality to apply the citation-based approach. However, at least in the case of the examined dataset, the error margin for incorrectly parsed and/or disambiguated references and citations was approximately 14 %[38]. We tolerated this error rate, because comparatively small numbers of erroneously parsed citations are not as critical for CbPD as for other IR tasks. To understand why, let us consider the two scenarios that arise from erroneously parsed citations.

The first scenario is when parsing errors affect one or both citations which do not match in reality. Most likely, the extraction procedure would distort the bibliographic data of the two cited documents differently. In this case, the error would have no effect because the detection algorithm would still not recognize

---

[38] Error of margin was calculated for a random sample of 100 manually examined citations from the PMC OAS collection.

the incorrectly parsed citations as a match. In the other, very unlikely, but theoretically possible case in which the extraction procedure distorts two non-identical citations in such a way that the detection procedure considers them identical, the procedure could report a false positive. However, extraction errors of this sort are extremely rare and even if they do occur, reporting a false positive is unlikely, because a single matching citation is not sufficient to trigger suspicion.

The second scenario occurs when parsing errors affect one or both citations, which match in reality. In this case, there is the chance of a false negative, i.e. the detection algorithm does not recognize the match. However, the CbPD detection algorithms require that several matching citations exist to trigger suspicion. Furthermore, a user can lower the suspiciousness threshold to prevent erroneous citations from causing false negatives.

The final test collection included 185,170 documents. The analyzed test collection represents only a small subset of the approximately 2.5 million full-text documents available in PMC and an even smaller fraction of the 22 million documents available in PubMed. The National Library of Medicine, which hosts PMC and PubMed, allows bulk processing of full-texts only for the documents included in the PMC OAS. The restrained accessibility of full-texts is a limitation of our evaluation, because we can only detect plagiarism within documents included in the PMC OAS and originating from other documents in the PMC OAS. Yet, for the similarity assessment, the CbPD algorithms analyzed all identifiable citations and references within the documents. That is, if two documents being compared have cited identical sources outside the PMC OAS, the CbPD algorithms consider these citations.

6.4.1.2   Preliminary Corpus Analysis

A comprehensive preliminary analysis of the PMC OAS corpus was performed. While this was a crucial first step in gauging the composition of the corpus to effectively design the subsequent evaluation approach, it is not directly related to the methodology described in the remainder of this chapter. Nevertheless, for a deeper technical understanding the reader is encouraged to read the detailed preliminary analysis in Appendix A, pages 266–294. No discontinuity occurs if reading is resumed in the following section.

6.4.1.3 *Applying Detection Algorithms and Pooling*

We used the two character-based methods Encoplot[39] (ENCO) and Sherlock[40] (Sher) as a baseline against which we compared the following seven citation-based detection methods:

1. Absolute Bibliographic Coupling strength (BC abs.)

2. Relative Bibliographic Coupling strength (BC rel.)

3. Longest Common Citation Sequence (LCCS)

4. Longest Common Sequence of distinct citations (LCCS dist.)

5. Longest Greedy Citation Tile (Max. GCT)

6. Longest Citation Chunk – both documents chunked, considering consecutive shared citations only, no merging step (CC bcn)

7. Longest Citation Chunk – both documents chunked, considering shared citations depending on predecessor, no merging step (CC bpn)

Due to limited resources available in the user study, we evaluated the citation patterns analysis algorithms, but not the scoring procedures for ranking the suspiciousness of patterns, i.e. CF-Score and Cont.-Score introduced in Section 4.6. Evaluating the influence of CF-Score and Cont.-Score on the results of each detection algorithm would have required collecting significantly more examiner judgments. Because the number of user study participants and the feasible workload for each participant were limited (see the section *User Study Design*, page 149 ff.), performing additional judgments would have required a reduction

---

[39] Encoplot received the most satisfactory score in the PAN 2009 competition, see Appendix A.6.

[40] Sherlock is a popular open source PD software, see Appendix A.5.

of the number of judgments per algorithm, and hence decreased the significance of the results for the individual algorithms. For this reason, we limited the current evaluation to the detection algorithms, and evaluated the influence of CF-Score and Cont.-Score in a subsequent study.

The evaluation corpus comprised 185,170 documents from the PMC OAS as described in the subsection *Corpus Preprocessing*, page 139.

The lack of known disguised plagiarism cases in the PMC OAS required analyzing the collection in an *n:n* fashion to identify suspicious documents. Character-based detection methods, such as Encoplot and Sherlock, do not allow limiting the number of document pairs to be analyzed without decreasing detection accuracy. For optimal accuracy, Encoplot and Sherlock have to compare each document with every other document in the collection, which equals $\binom{n}{2}$ comparisons with n being the number of documents in the collection. Analyzing the entire PMC OAS with Encoplot or Sherlock therefore requires $\binom{185170}{2} = 17,143,871,865$ comparisons, which are practically infeasible to perform. Refer to *Comparison of Computational Efficiency* in the results section, page 176, for an estimation of processing times.

To our knowledge, no PDS capable of analyzing a collection in the size range of the PMC OAS is publicly available. By drastically limiting the number of analyzed documents, some proprietary commercial PDS may be capable of checking very large collections in an *n:n*-fashion. To reduce the retrieval space, these systems typically compare heuristically selected text fragments and impose minimum amount of shared text as explained in Section 2.2.3. However, applying such heuristics has the inherent disadvantage of decreasing detection accuracy.

Citation-based detection methods allow limiting the document collection to be analyzed without compromising detection accuracy. Because documents that do not share references, i.e. are bibliographically coupled, cannot possess citation-based similarities, such documents can be excluded. The PMC OAS contained 39,463,660 document pairs sharing at least one reference, meaning this was the number of document pairs requiring analysis. Refer to Figure 57 in

Appendix A.1 for a graph of the number of document pairs in the PMC OAS that share 1, 2, 3, ..., etc. references.

Due to the practical infeasibility of a full character-based $n{:}n$ analysis, we applied Encoplot and Sherlock only to those 6,219,504 document pairs with a Bibliographic Coupling strength > 1. To our knowledge, Bibliographic Coupling strength has thus far not been used as a criterion for limiting the document collection for plagiarism detection. Although this limitation may lead to the exclusion of some true positives, we consider this approach to be an acceptable trade-off given the current infeasibility of a collection-wide character-based $n{:}n$ analysis for such a large collection.

We hypothesize that the loss of detection performance in the $n{:}n$ setting is minimal, given the strong positive correlation between character-based and citation-based similarity. Figure 34 shows this positive correlation between the BC strength of documents in the PMC OAS corpus compared to their character-based Encoplot similarity score. For each Bibliographic Coupling strength, the Encoplot scores of 20 randomly selected document pairs are plotted on the vertical axis. The smallest dots represent single occurrences and the largest dots represent up to 20 occurrences.

Figure 57 in Appendix A.1, on page 267, shows the total number of documents in the PMC OAS for the various coupling strengths.

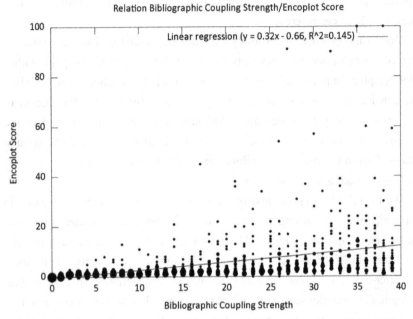

Figure 34: Correlation between BC Strength and Enco Score in the PMC OAS

Alternatively, we could have limited the number of documents for the *n:n* comparison using Encoplot and Sherlock by first applying character-based heuristics like fingerprinting, keyword-based clustering, or VSM retrieval. This approach may have eliminated fewer true positives than citation-based filtering, but would have required additional implementation effort. Conceptually, both the character-based and the citation-based filtering approaches are heuristics, and thus the results are collection-specific and hardly predictable.

To substantiate our hypothesis that Bibliographic Coupling strength and Encoplot score strongly correlate for suspicious documents, we additionally performed an ex post *n:n* analysis of the top-20 most suspicious documents as identified in the user study (see Section 6.4.2 on page 168). Since we did not filter for Coupling Strength it took several weeks on a quad-core system to compute the Encoplot scores for these 20 documents with all other documents in the PMC OAS corpus. The results supported our hypothesis; the sample did not contain a single publication pair with a high Encoplot score that was not bibliographically coupled.

To establish a ground truth for the main $n{:}n$ evaluation, we pooled the top-30 ranked document pairs returned by each of the nine detection algorithms and presented the pooled results to human examiners for relevance judgment on document suspiciousness. Pooling is a common approach for the collection of relevance judgments [209], e.g., applied in IR systems comparisons such as TREC, NTCIR, or CLEF [49], because judging all retrieval results is practically infeasible for most IR tasks.

Figure 35 illustrates the described document selection procedure for the main $n{:}n$ evaluation. The methodology is described in detail in the subsection *User Study Design* on page 149.

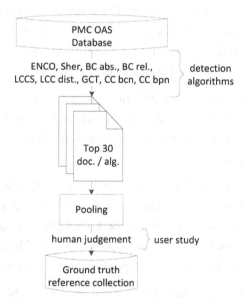

Figure 35: Applying Detection Algorithms and Pooling for $n{:}n$ Evaluation

For the subsequent, smaller $1{:}n$ evaluation, we did not limit the comparisons to documents with a BC strength > 1, because the processing time for comparing the chosen query documents to the collection was only two weeks. For this $1{:}n$

evaluation we pooled for each form of plagiarism, the five document pairs users rated most suspicious in the *n:n* evaluation. The subsection *Precision-Recall Curve for Best Performing Approach*, page 168, presents details on the methodology and results of this analysis.

6.4.1.4   *Addressing False Positives*

The retrieval of false positives (FP) is a universal problem for PDS. In this section we explain the pre-user study false positive reduction strategy that addresses the collection-specific documents prone to being retrieved as false positives. In the evaluation of the PMC OAS, two additional factors contributed to FP retrieval.

- The first pooling process was carried out as an *n:n* document comparison, while the typical PD use case is a *1:n* comparison. A *n:n* comparison of a large collection the size of the PMC OAS (~200,000 documents) naturally also results in the retrieval of a high number of legitimate document similarities.

- The peer-review of publications in the PMC OAS yields a relatively low expected ratio of plagiarism, which makes the retrieval of a high number of legitimate document similarities more likely.

In pooling the top-30 retrieval results of each detection method for user inspection, we found that character-based detection methods in particular flagged many documents legitimately sharing text similarity as suspicious. Documents with very high similarity, which happened to be considered as *legitimate text reuse* in the PMC OAS, were most typically *editorials* and *updates*.

- *editorials* – texts written by journal editors or publishers, which provide publishing guidelines, state the policies of journals on such matters as publishing fees or open access, etc., are commonly "recycled" among journals without citing the source. Our definition of *editorial* false positives exclusively contained articles of non-scientific nature.

– **updates** – corrections, annual medical standards updates, or best practices updates for certain fields and medical conditions. The same panel or medical association, e.g., American Diabetes Association, often publishes annual updates.

To avoid punishing character-based algorithms, and to a lesser extent citation-based algorithms, in the performance evaluation for correctly detecting these documents, we manually excluded editorials and updates before presenting document pairs to user study participants for rating.

In addition to the two excluded document types named above, documents citing each other – given the citation style was machine-identifiable – were excluded from analysis. This exclusion reduced the number of FP that correctly referenced the source. Articles with shared author sets were also filtered and excluded to reduce the number of FP resulting from legitimate author collaboration. For the purpose of the evaluation, this means potential self-plagiarism was not examined.

Despite applying a strategy for false positive reduction as described, additional false positives were identified in the user study. These user-classified false positives were caused by different reasons than the ones filtered for here, and are presented in detail in the subsection *Retrieved False Positives* on page 179.

6.4.1.5   *User Study Design*

The user study addresses the first evaluation objective, the *identification* and *verification* of document suspiciousness using the CbPD prototype.

Pooling the top-30 results of the nine evaluated detection methods resulted in 270 document pairs, as described in the subsection *Applying Detection Algorithms and Pooling*, page 143, of which 181 were unique. We randomized and presented the unique pairs to 26 user study participants for a blind, web-based evaluation using the CitePlag prototype. Table 19 gives an overview of the numbers pertaining to the design of the user study.

Table 19: User Study Statistics

Participants	
Group 1: Undergraduates	11
Group 2: Graduate students	10
Group 3: Medical experts	5
Total study participants	*26*
Documents	
Examined documents	181
Duplicates[41]	89
Total top-30 documents	*270*
Time	
Avg. time participant spent / document pair	6.32 min.
Avg. time participant spent for evaluation	~2.2 hours
Total time spent by all examiners	*~57 hours*

Study participants had three levels of background knowledge in medicine. The first group comprised 11 undergraduate students from non-medical majors, the second group comprised 10 graduate students, and the final group comprised five experts from the medical field. This three-group approach allowed observing the potential influence of expertise on document suspiciousness-rating, visualization preference, or time needed to arrive at a conclusion on document suspiciousness. Rather than labeling documents as plagiarism or non-plagiarism,

---

[41] Some document pairs were among the top-30 results for more than one approach. Duplicate pairs were rated only once.

we asked participants to conduct the examination of documents with the following objective in mind:

> *"Consider viewing a retrieved document pair as relevant if similarities exist that an examiner in a real check for plagiarism would likely find valuable to be made aware of."*

This criterion is in line with what we deem to be an examiner's information need in a real plagiarism detection scenario. For each document pair – if examiners deemed the result to fulfill the above criterion – participants were asked to provide the following:

- suspiciousness rating (see Table 20, right column)

- potential plagiarism form (see Table 20, left column)

- similarity visualization method perceived to be most suitable (rated by a sub-group of participants)

Additionally, we tracked the time participants required to submit each rating. To ensure consistent human judgment, as far as consistency can be expected in a subjective human rating task, an online submission form provided uniform guidelines. The guidelines included the definitions of plagiarism forms[42] and the rating criteria for document suspiciousness, as shown in Table 20. Note that these guidelines are only intended to categorize the level of document similarity, which may potentially point to suspiciousness.

No guidelines can provide a straightforward formula by which a document can be classified as plagiarism. For the definition of plagiarism used in the thesis, as well as in this evaluation, refer to Section 2.1.1.

---

[42] Refer to Section 2.1.2 for the full list of plagiarism forms and their definitions. Table 20 gives an abridged version of plagiarism form definitions, as presented to user study participants, with the definitions tailored to the characteristics of the PMC OAS.

Table 20: Guidelines as Presented to User Study Participants

Potential plagiarism form – definition guidelines	Document suspiciousness – rating guidelines
Consider viewing a retrieved document pair as relevant if similarities exist that an examiner in a real check for plagiarism would likely find valuable to be made aware of.	
Please refer to the following definitions to categorize the prevailing form of similarity: *copy & paste* – verbatim copying, with little or no re-writing or restructuring *shake & paste* – verbatim copying, with some re-writing, e.g., inserting or deleting words, rearranging text, or restructuring *paraphrase* – copying is disguised by synonym replacements, use of own style and terminology, or careful rewriting and change of syntax *structural and/or idea plagiarism*[43] – document structure shows similarity or inspiration derived from the earlier article, e.g., many citations are presented in the same/similar order, author may not have independently researched all sources and copied citations instead. Authors may have received inspiration from ideas,	Please refer to the following guideline to rate document suspiciousness: 1 interesting similarities in some document sections – likely to have read the older article 2 strong similarities in some sections of document – likely to have read and been inspired by the older article 3 suspiciously strong similarities in the document – extremely likely to not only have read, but also copied some text, citations, ideas or graphs and figures 4 very suspicious similarities with certain signs pointing to plagiarism, i.e. high text overlap, copying of long citation patterns; ideas, graphs or figures appear copied 5 extremely suspicious similarities with obvious plagiarism intent

---

[43] Instances of shake & paste plagiarism and paraphrases can also simultaneously contain structural and idea plagiarism. However, for the purpose of this user study, we reserved structural and/or idea plagiarism specifically for documents without highly suspicious text overlap. Refer to Section 2.1.2 for more definitions of plagiarism forms.

arguments, document methodology, results, conclusions, or reviews of literature without giving credit. ***non-plagiarism (FP)*** – document pair shows no notable, or no interesting similarity that could point to unoriginal content. If content is shared, it is correctly cited	present, i.e. clearly unoriginal text, ideas, methodology, graphs and figures or citations and literature reviews, etc. **0** false positives, e.g., document pair is genuinely non-similar, unrecognized shared authors, or duplicate publications[44]

Note that documents retrieved by the algorithms, or classified in the user study, will only be termed plagiarism if they have been officially reviewed and confirmed by either PubMed or the issuing journal.

To guarantee identical document representation for all study participants, the CitePlag display settings for document representation were set as follows: (1) show text highlights, (2) highlight citations, (3) show connections between matching citations, (4) show document browser, and (5) minimum character-match length to be highlighted was set to the value 16.

---

[44] Some instances of document pairs with shared authors, including duplicate publications, were falsely retrieved as plagiarism, despite our effort to preprocess the dataset and eliminate shared author sets; refer to *Corpus Preprocessing* on page 139. We asked users to flag these cases and subsequently inspected false positives manually to identify why they failed to be excluded in the preprocessing step and if future improvements may prevent this. We excluded false positives attributable to preprocessing errors from the results so as not to unjustly skew detection performance, see *Addressing False Positives* on page 148. The objective is to determine the quality of the detection algorithms, not the quality of the preprocessing procedure.

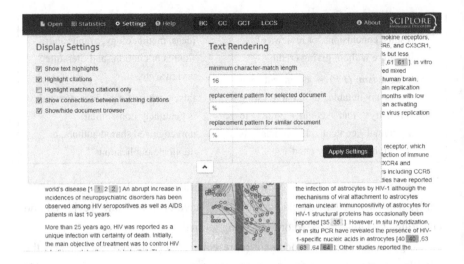

Figure 36: CitePlag Document Visualization for User Study

In addition to categorizing the form of document similarity and submitting a suspiciousness rating, users were also asked to indicate whether they viewed text similarity visualization or citation-visualization as more suitable for arriving at a conclusion regarding suspiciousness for each of the four forms of potential plagiarism. A subset of examiners participated in a small-scale evaluation of user utility for the citation visualization approach, in which we recorded the time examiners spent for document examination, from URL-retrieval in the CitePlag prototype to submission of the first identified document similarities.

Examiners had the opportunity to provide comments on notable document characteristics or the level of confidence in their judgments. The user study concluded by questioning participants on how useful they perceived the citation-based approach. See Appendix F for a selection of responses.

Perceptions of plagiarism and its severity vary, especially for disguised plagiarism (refer to Section 6.1.2). Therefore, we regarded deriving a binary ground truth, which categorized documents as either plagiarized or non-plagiarized, as unsuitable for a quantitative analysis of detection rates. Instead, we adopted the following evaluation procedure:

1. We selected all documents that were assigned a suspiciousness score, $s > 0$, by at least one user study participant.

2. These documents were grouped by plagiarism form, as indicated by the expert judge, for each document pair.

3. For each document pair, the weighted average of the scores assigned by the three groups was calculated as: $\bar{s} = (s_u + 1.25s_g + 1.5s_e)/3.75$, where s_u denotes the score assigned by undergraduate students, s_g the score assigned by medical graduate students, and s_e the score assigned by medical experts. The number of scores assigned for each document pair was three (one score from each group).

4. For each group of the same plagiarism form, we ordered the documents by decreasing $\bar{s}$.

5. To obtain the user-study-derived ground truth, we selected the 10 top-ranked documents.

6.4.1.6 Limitations of PMC OAS Evaluation

This section describes the specific challenges unique to the PMC OAS document collection and the limitations inherent to the user study approach. For an overview of general challenges to PD evaluations, e.g., establishment of a ground truth and the inconsistency of human judgment regarding plagiarism, as well as the limitations associated with the use of real-world document collections, refer to Section 6.1.2.

PMC OAS Collection-Specific Limitations

An inherent challenge of the PMC OAS collection for PD evaluations is its assumed low level of plagiarized content. The publications originate predominantly from peer-reviewed medical journals. Previous studies on the number of duplicate publications in select medical journals found low rates of duplicate text ranging from ~0.7 % [95] to ~2 % [66]. Errami et al. found only

0.04 % of a sample of abstracts from different authors in Medline to show high text similarity [104]. If we assume a similar rate of duplicate text in the PMC OAS, we can estimate the PMC OAS to contain ~120 cases of duplicated text, of which only a fraction thereof may be attributable to plagiarism[45] [104]. This leads to the assumption that detecting yet undiscovered plagiarism will be more challenging than, for example, detecting plagiarism in a collection of student assignments.

To gauge the validity of this assumption, we searched the PubMed database for publications that had been retracted for plagiarism, but were still available online. We identified 28 such retraction notices. Of these, only five provided the PMCIDs of the sources from which had been plagiarized. None of the sources, however, were included in the PMC OAS, which means we found no instances of known plagiarism for which *both* document pairs would have been available in the Open Access Subset. While we identified only this sparse number of retractions due to plagiarism and no cases of retracted plagiarism that were self-contained in the PMC OAS, it is likely that older retractions remain available online only for a limited time, or that not all retraction notices are published online.

Plagiarism content in the PMC OAS may also have been reduced by earlier detection using character-based PDS, or as a result of earlier examinations of the PMC OAS corpus, for example, the experiments carried out by a team of the Garner Lab [202, 321]. Especially non-disguised plagiarism forms are more likely to have been detected and removed, e.g., employing character-based PDS in the journals' submission process. With character-based PDS likely to have prevented instances of plagiarism with high character-based similarity from entering the collection in the first place, the results of this evaluation are only representative of other collections to a limited extent.

---

[45] *Addressing False Positives* on page 148 explains why high textual overlap among publications in the PMC OAS does not necessarily indicate plagiarism.

User Study Limitations

A limitation inherent to the user study is the potential for data presentation bias, since human judgment on plagiarism can vary depending on the visual representation of a document's similarity, for example, red vs. green text highlights, or bold vs. weak lines connecting matching citations.

That user study participants come from different backgrounds introduces another bias. The diversity of examiners, however, is representative of real plagiarism investigations. In the plagiarism investigation of Annette Schavan, for example, the members from the faculty council who decided the case included three student representatives, and not solely experts in pedagogy, the field in which Ms. Schavan had received her doctorate [152, 153].

Due to the challenges of judging whether text similarities truly represent undue text use, see Section 6.1.2, we refrain from classifying documents as plagiarism if the responsible authorities have not yet confirmed the suspicion. Publications in the review process will be referred to only in an anonymized form in which the first and last digits of the unique PMCIDs have been removed. Evaluation results are made available online on a password-protected website[46], where we encourage interested individuals to arrive at their own judgments.

6.4.2 Results

The data collected in the user study and the analysis presented in this section is available for download; refer to Appendix C.

6.4.2.1 *Comparison of Effectiveness*

This section addresses Evaluation Objective 1, as explained in Section 6.4. The retrieval results of the seven citation-based and the two character-based detection methods are evaluated, and their effectiveness in identifying the different forms of plagiarism is compared against a user-study-derived ground truth.

---

[46] Refer to Appendix C for access details.

Overview of Retrieval and Ranking Performance

In the evaluation using the GuttenPlag Wiki in Section 6.2, we observed citation-based methods to achieve higher detection rates for disguised plagiarism in comparison to character-based detection methods. Evaluating the effectiveness of the CbPD algorithms using the PMC OAS presents the first evaluation assessing whether this observation also holds for a large-scale, realistic plagiarism detection setting.

Ranking and presenting documents in decreasing order according to their suspiciousness is crucial to the usefulness of PDS. In the typical use case, a manual inspection is feasible only for the highest ranked documents. Therefore, we consider the rank at which a detection method retrieves a suspicious document pair as the critical measure of effectiveness. To compare the effectiveness of detection methods in this ranked retrieval task, we derived a ground truth by means of a user study, as described in Section 6.4.1.

The analysis of detection effectiveness gauged the precision of each detection method in identifying and ranking the different plagiarism forms: (1) copy & paste, (2) shake & paste, (3) paraphrased and (4) structural and/or idea plagiarism. For this purpose, we grouped document pairs by their potential plagiarism forms as determined in the user study. From each group, we selected the set of ten document pairs with the highest combined user-assigned suspiciousness scores ignoring order.

To confirm the presence of agreement regarding document suspiciousness among examiners above the agreement rate that could be expected by chance we calculated Fleiss' Kappa (k):

$$k = \frac{\bar{P} - \bar{P}_e}{1 - \bar{P}_e} \tag{6.1}$$

In Equation 6.1, $\bar{P}$ presents the observed agreement, while $\bar{P}_e$ presents the hypothetical probability of chance agreement. Thus, $\bar{P} - \bar{P}_e$ represents the degree of agreement actually achieved above chance and $1 - \bar{P}_e$ represents the degree of agreement that is attainable above chance. Inter-rater agreement for all plagiarism forms was calculated as 0.65, indicating the presence of substantial agreement among examiners on the degree of document suspiciousness. Kappa was highest for copy & paste, $k = 0.73$, and lowest for structural and idea plagiarism, $k = 0.59$. This observation is in line with the larger discrepancies in human judgment for the more challenging task of judging disguised plagiarism forms.

For each of the ten document pairs, we determined if, and at which rank, the individual detection method identified the pair. If detection methods assigned the same score and therefore the same rank i to multiple documents, the mid rank $\bar{r}_i$, was calculated as $\bar{r}_i = r_{i-1} + (|d_i| - 1)/2$ and assigned to all documents d_i with initial rank i.

The four box plots on the following pages show the distributions of ranks; one plot is given for each form of plagiarism. Each box plot includes a data table showing the values for the minimum rank (Min.), the first quartile (Q1), the median, the third quartile (Q3), the maximum rank (Max.) and the mean of the distribution.

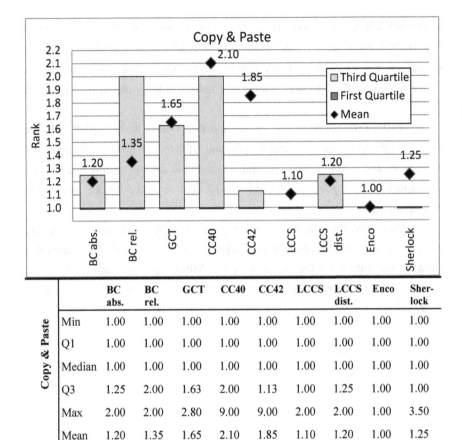

		BC abs.	BC rel.	GCT	CC40	CC42	LCCS	LCCS dist.	Enco	Sher-lock
	Min	1.00	1.00	1.00	1.00	1.00	1.00	1.00	1.00	1.00
Copy & Paste	Q1	1.00	1.00	1.00	1.00	1.00	1.00	1.00	1.00	1.00
	Median	1.00	1.00	1.00	1.00	1.00	1.00	1.00	1.00	1.00
	Q3	1.25	2.00	1.63	2.00	1.13	1.00	1.25	1.00	1.00
	Max	2.00	2.00	2.80	9.00	9.00	2.00	2.00	1.00	3.50
	Mean	1.20	1.35	1.65	2.10	1.85	1.10	1.20	1.00	1.25

Figure 37: Distribution of Ranks for Top-10 Document Pairs for Copy & Paste

Figure 37 shows the distribution of ranks for copy & paste. The character-based detection method Encoplot performed best in highly ranking copy & paste, followed by the citation-based LCCS algorithm and the character-based PDS Sherlock. The upper quartile of these three best performing methods equals one, i.e. for at least 75 % of the examined top-10 document pairs, the methods retrieved the source document at rank one.

The average rank and the third quartile of ranks at which the other citation-based methods retrieved potentially suspicious document pairs are higher than for the three best-performing methods. The good performance of character-based detection methods for copy & paste is in line with the previous findings using the GuttenPlag Wiki, as well as findings from other studies, such as the PAN competitions and the HTW PDS comparisons (see Section 2.3.1). Character-based methods are better able to detect literal text matches than CbPD. Yet, the citation-based methods, and especially LCCS, performed better than expected in the analysis of the PMC OAS. The reason is that many of the literal text overlaps in the analyzed document pairs are extensive and include many shared citations in similar order.

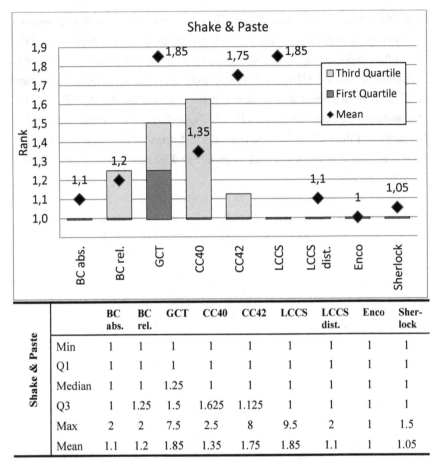

Figure 38: Distribution of Ranks for Top-10 Document Pairs for Shake & Paste

Figure 38 shows the distribution of ranks for shake & paste similarities. Encoplot performed best in retrieving shake & paste similarities at prominent ranks, followed by Sherlock and the citation-based measures LCCS distinct, LCCS and BC absolute. The third quartiles of all five highest performing methods equal one. The remaining citation-based methods demonstrated slightly lower retrieval performances, yet could identify the source document for each of the user classified top-10 document pairs. No third quartile of any citation-based method exceeded rank two; see Q3 in Figure 38.

The good performance of Encoplot and Sherlock in identifying shake & paste similarities is no surprise, given that many of the identified instances have high verbatim text overlap. The citation-based measures performed better than expected, which was mainly due to most shake & paste similarities being concentrated in the introduction and background sections, which also included a high number of shared citations.

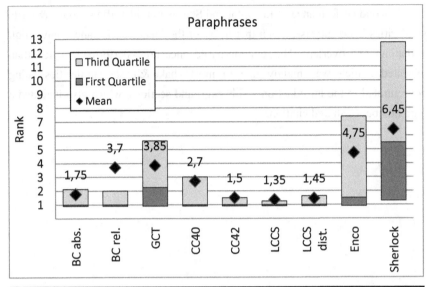

	BC abs.	BC rel.	GCT	CC40	CC42	LCCS	LCCS dist.	Enco	Sher-lock
Min	1	1	1	1	1	1	1	1	1
Q1	1	1	1	1	1	1	1	1	1.375
Media	1	1	2.25	1	1	1	1	1.5	5.5
Q3	2.125	2	5.625	3	1.5	1.25	1.625	7.375	12.75
Max	6	26	13	14	4	3.5	4	18	14.5
Mean	1.75	3.7	3.85	2.7	1.5	1.35	1.45	4.75	6.45

(Paraphrases)

Figure 39: Distribution of Ranks for Top-10 Document Pairs for Paraphrases

Figure 39 shows the distributions of ranks for paraphrases. Citation-based methods significantly outperformed character-based methods in retrieving paraphrases at prominent ranks. The two variations of Longest Common Citation Sequence (LCCS and LCCS dist.), and Citation Chunking (CC42) performed best. The results support our hypothesis that citation-based methods are more suitable for identifying paraphrases than character-based methods.

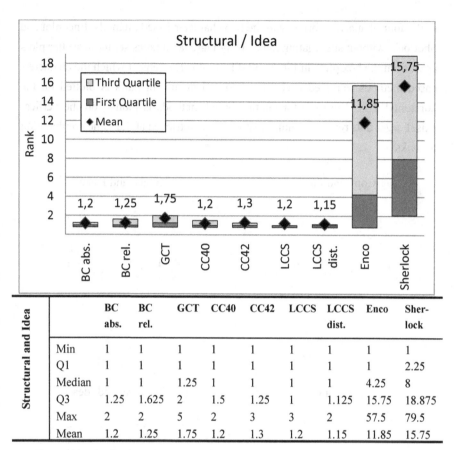

Structural and Idea		BC abs.	BC rel.	GCT	CC40	CC42	LCCS	LCCS dist.	Enco	Sherlock
	Min	1	1	1	1	1	1	1	1	1
	Q1	1	1	1	1	1	1	1	1	2.25
	Median	1	1	1.25	1	1	1	1	4.25	8
	Q3	1.25	1.625	2	1.5	1.25	1	1.125	15.75	18.875
	Max	2	2	5	2	3	3	2	57.5	79.5
	Mean	1.2	1.25	1.75	1.2	1.3	1.2	1.15	11.85	15.75

Figure 40: Distribution of Ranks for Top-10 Document Pairs for Structural and Idea Plagiarism

Figure 40 shows the distribution of ranks for documents featuring structural and/or idea plagiarism forms. Citation-based methods, especially the two variations of the LCCS (LCCS and LCCS dist.) outperformed character-based methods in prominently ranking structural and/or idea plagiarism.

Detailed Comparison of Retrieval and Ranking Performance

The ranking performance is presented in detail using 16 scatter plots in Figure 41. The plots compare the two best performing citation-based methods for each of the four plagiarism forms with the two character-based methods, Encoplot and Sherlock, without aggregating ranks. Non-aggregated ranks set these scatter plots apart from the box plots in Figure 37–Figure 40. The rank at which the character-based methods retrieved each of the top-10 document pairs is plotted on the horizontal axis. The rank for citation-based methods is plotted on the vertical axis. Larger dots represent multiple documents retrieved at the same combination of ranks.

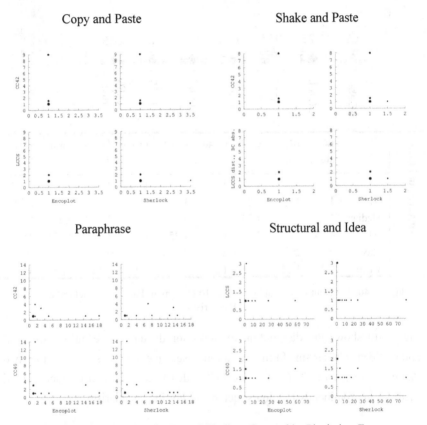

Figure 41: Scatter Plots for Top-10 Findings Grouped by Plagiarism Form

The scatter plots for copy & paste and shake & paste plagiarism forms show that the character-based and even the best performing citation-based methods prominently ranked these forms of similarities. Of the ten document pairs in the copy & paste category, Encoplot identified all at rank one, LCCS and Sherlock retrieved nine at rank one. Similarly, Encoplot identified all ten document pairs in the shake & paste category at rank one, Sherlock and the two LCCS measures each identified nine pairs at rank one. The results confirm that current detection methods also have no difficulty in identifying verbatim text overlap in real-world collections.

The scatter plots for paraphrases and structural and idea plagiarism show that the CbPD algorithms outperform character-based approaches in identifying these forms of plagiarism, which typically have very little or no notable text overlap. For paraphrases, the CbPD algorithms CC40 and CC42, identified seven and eight of the ten document pairs at rank one and ranked none of the document pairs lower than rank four. Encoplot and Sherlock identified six and eight of the document pairs below the top rank of one. The lowest ranks at which the two character-based approaches retrieved one of the top-10 document pairs were at rank 18 for Encoplot and at rank 14.5 for Sherlock. For structural idea plagiarism, the advantage of CbPD in ranking effectiveness is even stronger. The CbPD algorithms CC42 and CC40 identified eight and seven document pairs at rank one and the remaining document pairs no lower than rank 3. Encoplot and Sherlock ranked six and nine document pairs at rank four or at lower ranks. The lowest ranks at which Encoplot and Sherlock retrieved the document pairs were at rank 57.5 for Encoplot, and rank 79.5 for Sherlock.

The scatter plots reflect the complementary strengths of character-based and citation-based approaches. While the plots show dots mostly on vertical lines for copy & paste and shake & paste, they show dots mostly on horizontal lines for paraphrases and for structural and idea plagiarism. These results show that character-based approaches excel in identifying copy & paste and shake & paste plagiarism, while the CbPD approach more effectively detects semantic document similarities with little or no textual overlap.

Precision-Recall Curve for Best Performing Approach

The previous evaluation measured the performance of detection approaches in prominently ranking a single, already identified document that human examiners rated as suspicious and subsequently categorized as containing one of the potential forms of plagiarism. In a realistic PD scenario, however, the documents to be retrieved are unknown. A detection approach will receive an input document for which the algorithm must identify all documents with relevant similarities. To assess the detection performance of character-based and citation-based approaches in such a *1:n* setting, we performed an additional evaluation.

Due to the high human effort necessary to judge results in a *1:n* evaluation, we only compared the performance of Encoplot, LCCS distinct and Bibliographic Coupling. We chose Encoplot and LCCS, because they are the character-based and the citation-based method that performed best overall in the previous evaluation. Bibliographic Coupling was included as a baseline measure.

To derive a ground truth for this *1:n* evaluation, we applied the following pooling procedure. For each of the four plagiarism forms, we selected the five document pairs rated highest by users in the previous *n:n* comparison. We used the more recent publication from each of these 20 document pairs as the query document. For each query document, we collected the documents that each of the nine tested detection methods identified as most similar, yet not more than six documents per method to limit the effort necessary for manual inspection.

The resulting document collection contained 160 unique documents, which we presented to six study participants for relevance judgment. Due to the high level of effort associated with this evaluation, each document pair was only rated by one study participant, in contrast to the *n:n* evaluation, where one participant from each of the three groups judged each document pair. Study participants were asked to classify a document as relevant if it fulfilled the following information need:

"The documents feature similarities, which an examiner in a check for plagiarism would find valuable to be made aware of."

To compare retrieval performance, we plotted the 11-point precision-recall curve ([209], pp. 158-159) using interpolated average precision and relative recall for each of the three methods (see Figure 42). We average the precision achieved by detection methods for each of the 20 query documents and interpolate precision if no measured values exist for any of the 11 predefined recall levels. We consider *relative recall* [70], because determining recall as traditionally defined in IR requires collecting relevance judgments for *all* possible retrieval results, i.e. all documents in the PMC OAS. This is unfeasible. Therefore, our evaluation is similar to search engine evaluations, in which the set of possible retrieval results is often unbounded or larger than a human can possibly judge [6]. Pooling results and then collecting relevance judgments only for the pooled results is a common approach to dealing with this restriction, e.g., applied in TREC [49]. We adopted this pooling approach and calculated relative recall, i.e. the fraction of retrieved relevant documents over the number of documents judged relevant among the pooled documents.

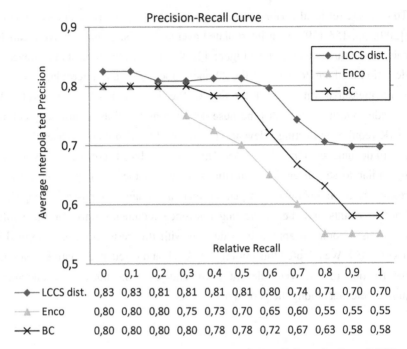

	0	0,1	0,2	0,3	0,4	0,5	0,6	0,7	0,8	0,9	1
LCCS dist.	0,83	0,83	0,81	0,81	0,81	0,81	0,80	0,74	0,71	0,70	0,70
Enco	0,80	0,80	0,80	0,75	0,73	0,70	0,65	0,60	0,55	0,55	0,55
BC	0,80	0,80	0,80	0,80	0,78	0,78	0,72	0,67	0,63	0,58	0,58

Figure 42: 11-Point Interpolated Avg. Precision – Rel. Recall Curve for Enco, LCCS
Dist. and BC

LCCS distinct performed best in this evaluation, i.e. LCCS dist. consistently identified more relevant documents among its top-6 results than BC or Encoplot. With a value of 0.8, the average precision of BC and Encoplot is identical for recall levels ≤ 0.2. For recall levels > 0.2, average precision drops more strongly for Encoplot than for BC.

The finding that the crude BC measure performed better than Encoplot may be surprising. We assume this to be attributable to the document selection procedure. Since only five of the 20 query documents were of the copy & paste form, the majority of cases contained disguised forms of plagiarism. Encoplot, LCCS distinct, and BC rank copy & paste plagiarism at similarly high ranks (compare Figure 37). However, in cases of disguised plagiarism forms, LCCS distinct and BC yield significantly higher rankings than Encoplot. For structural and or idea plagiarism, the average ranks of BC and LCCS dist. were 1.2, compared to the average rank of Encoplot, which was 11.84 (see Figure 40).

The results in Figure 42 show a sample that contains equal shares of all four forms of plagiarism. While such a distribution may be typical for submissions to reputable journals, it is unlikely to reflect the distribution of plagiarism forms in other settings, for example, among assignments written by undergraduates, where copy & paste plagiarism was shown to be dominant [220]. Therefore, the results obtained from this evaluation using the PMC OAS can only be generalized to a limited extent.

User Utility

This section presents the user-perceived and measured effectiveness of the CbPD approach in comparison to traditional character-based approaches.

We used CitePlag to assess user utility in the following areas:

1. *Subjective*: Which approach, i.e. method of document similarity visualization, text and/or citation visualization, did users identify as most suitable for identifying the various forms of plagiarism?

2. *Objective*: Does citation visualization decrease user effort by reducing the time required for manual document inspection and verification? If so, what are the mean time-savings for the various forms of plagiarism?

3. Open-ended comments from users on the perceived utility of the CbPD approach are summarized in Table 31 in Appendix F.

User-Perceived Suitability of Approaches

The responses regarding the perceived suitability of the individual approaches for verifying various forms or plagiarism are visualized in Figure 43. The figure shows the aggregation of 461 document pair judgments collected for all three examiner groups. Similarity visualization preferences among expert and non-expert groups did not differ significantly. Traditional text-highlights were identified as the most suitable document similarity visualization method for copy & paste plagiarism. For disguised forms of plagiarism, the large majority of examiners considered the visualization of citation patterns, or a combination of text-highlights and citation visualization to be most suitable.

Since the PMC OAS only contains publications in English, we additionally asked 13 study participants[47] to examine the Guttenberg thesis and indicate the suitability of visualization methods for translated plagiarism. Given that opinions for translated plagiarism were collected only for a single document, the results cannot be generalized. Similarly, the user-reported suitability of the visualization approaches may not be representative for other collections.

---

[47] A sub-group of total user study participants.

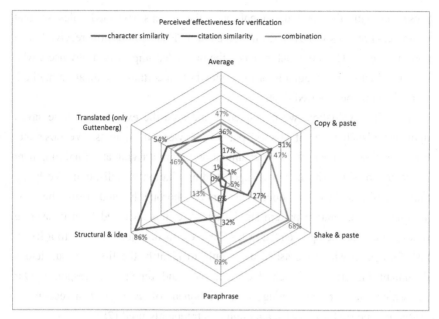

Figure 43: Perceived Effectiveness for Verification by Plagiarism Form

Measured Time-Savings of the Approaches

Eight study participants[48] judged documents on their potential suspiciousness using CitePlag, once with text similarity visualized and once with both text and citation pattern similarity visualized. We recorded the time examiners needed to identify the first two instances of suspiciousness in the documents in both cases. Each participant rated 25 document pairs[49], six document pairs for each of the assigned forms of plagiarism, except for translated plagiarism for which only one document, the Guttenberg thesis, was examined.

We formed two groups of four examiners, whom we showed the same document pairs either with or without citation pattern visualization to assure that no documents were viewed by the same examiner using both methods. When

---

[48] A sub-group of total user study participants.
[49] A randomly selected sample of the top-30 documents for each of the four forms of plagiarism yielded by the pooling approach.

presented with the next document pair, the groups switched roles so that examiners previously shown no citation pattern visualizations now received them and vice versa. This approach reduced the one-sided impact of a few users who responded either more quickly or more slowly to a certain visualization method, from skewing the reported time.

In a first evaluation, we attempted to measure the examination time saved upon the visualization of citation patterns between documents. We observed, however, that the mean time for examination before arriving at a final judgment on document similarity increased upon adding citation visualization. We found that examiners browsed documents more thoroughly and read the text surrounding the citation pattern similarities. We thus switched from measuring time-savings for the open-ended task – "arrive at a final judgment" – to a fixed-task format, in which we asked users only to identify the first two suspicious document instances for each document pair and timed their response. Our assessment of user time-savings is a component of *user effort*, a recognized evaluation metric for IR tasks, although less frequently used [78].

We observed a significant difference in the mean times needed to identify the first two instances of similarity among the groups, depending on whether they were presented with citation pattern visualization or not.

Figure 44 plots the recorded mean times for all plagiarism forms. The difference in the mean times between the groups was highest for the Guttenberg translation[50] at 49 %, and for structural and idea similarities at 42 %. A slight reduction in recorded mean times was also observed for paraphrases, 22 %, and shake & paste, 11 %.

These measured time-savings were in line with the response from users that the citation pattern visualization of the CbPD approach was the single most useful aid in the manual verification of structural & idea plagiarism forms. For plagiarism forms with very high textual similarity, e.g., copy & paste, citation pattern visualization provided no measurable time-savings, and actually had a

---

[50] This result cannot be generalized, having presented examiners only with a single translated plagiarism case.

negative effect, due to some examiners clicking through the sections with high citation pattern similarity more thoroughly and thus taking longer to report the first two instances of similarity. We found, however, that examiners took little notice of the potentially higher user effort, given that they commented that citation visualization was also useful for copy & paste, since connecting lines between citations allowed a quick visualization of the potentially most similar sections. A more in depth overview of comments and feedback collected during the study is available in Appendix F.

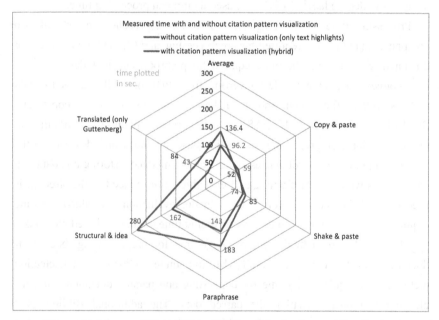

Figure 44: Measured Time With and Without Citation Pattern Visualization

This evaluation of user utility and user effort reduction as measured by time-savings was small-scale and future evaluations will be needed to assess the relevance of the results. However, in the setting described, CbPD demonstrated a measurable increase in user utility, both user-reported and objectively measured, when compared to the traditional text-only document similarity visualization method.

6.4.2.2   *Comparison of Computational Efficiency*

By comparing the run-time behavior of character-based and citation-based detection methods for the average-case scenario, this section addresses Evaluation Objective 2, as outlined in Section 6.4. We compared the two character-based methods, Encoplot and Sherlock, with the seven citation-based detection methods, as described in in the subsection *Applying Detection Algorithms and Pooling*, page 143. The seven citation-based algorithms have similar run time behaviors. Therefore, we summarized all seven citation-based measures under the label "CbPD" and used their mean processing time.

Processing time for all plagiarism detection approaches consists of two components (1) the time required for preprocessing, and (2) the time required for document comparison. The time required for preprocessing includes document type conversions, for example converting from PDF or XML format to plain text, as well as file system and/or database operations. To use Encoplot and Sherlock, we converted PMC OAS's NXML format to plain text. In addition to text conversions, preprocessing for citation-based methods includes parsing the text to acquire citations, references and document metadata, storing this data in a database, as well as data cleaning and disambiguation. Since the BC strength is used to limit the scope of comparisons in our evaluation, we added the time required for computing BC to the preprocessing time of citation-based methods.

Character-based methods require $O(n)$ time for preprocessing, because n documents must be converted from NXML to plain text. Citation-based detection methods also require $O(n)$ time for converting and parsing documents and for cleaning and disambiguating the parsed data. The additional Bibliographic Coupling calculation requires $O(n \cdot log(n))$ time when using an index that allows comparing the references in documents in $O(log(n))$ time. Table 21 lists the preprocessing times for a 3.40GHz quad core processor with 16GB RAM for the three detection approaches used in our evaluation.

Table 21: Average Time for Preprocessing and Comparison per Document

Operation performed	Encoplot[51]	Sherlock	CbPD
Conversion of NXML documents to plain texts	13 ms	13 ms	13 ms
Parsing and storing of citation data (XML)	Not required	Not required	29 ms
Parsing and storing of citation data (PDF)	Not required	Not required	246 ms
Computing Bibliographic Coupling	optional	optional	34 ms
Document comparison (time per document pair)	153 ms	259 ms	2 ms

The time required for document comparisons depends foremost on the number of comparisons necessary. This number differs significantly for character-based compared to citation-based detection methods, with 17,143,871,865 comparisons needed for character-based approaches, and only 39,463,660 comparisons needed for citation-based approaches. This means analyzing the PMC OAS using the CbPD approach requires only 0.23 % of the comparisons necessary for a character-based analysis. Refer to *Applying Detection Algorithms and Pooling*, page 143, for more details. The last row in Table 21 shows the required average time to compare a single document pair with each of the evaluated detection approaches.

---

[51] The required processing time is dependent on the document collection and computing hardware used [142].

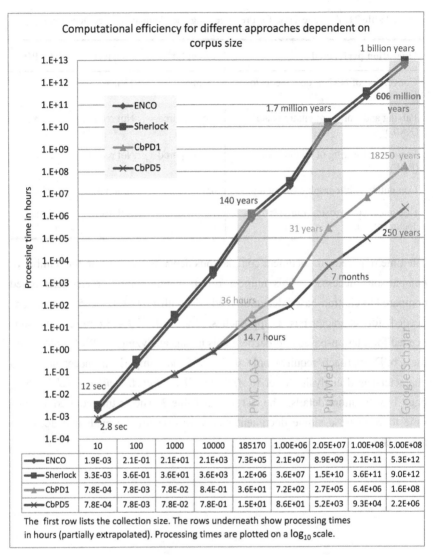

The first row lists the collection size. The rows underneath show processing times
in hours (partially extrapolated). Processing times are plotted on a $\log_{10}$ scale.

Figure 45: Computational Efficiency of PD Approaches for an *n:n* Comparison

Figure 45 shows an extrapolated comparison[52] of processing times on a logarithmic scale for the evaluated plagiarism detection methods dependent on corpus size. The horizontal axis shows different corpora sizes where the gray shaded regions indicate the size ranges of the PMC OAS, PubMed and Google Scholar document collections. The vertical axis shows the processing time in hours using a logarithmic scale with base 10. The table below the figure shows the processing time in hours. If only one document pair (*1:1*) is analyzed, the character-based methods are comparatively less expensive than the citation-based approaches. The reason for this is that citation parsing is initially more expensive than fingerprint creation for the character-based approaches. However, the break-even point, which depends predominantly on document length and number of citations, is usually reached at about five documents. Beyond this size, the character-based approaches are more expensive, given that they require $\binom{n}{2}$ comparisons, while the citation-based approaches only perform a comparison if a document pair is at all bibliographically coupled or if it has a BC above a specified strength.

Figure 45 shows that at a collection size range comparable to that of the PMC OAS, the CbPD5 algorithm[53] requires a total processing time of 14.7 hours, while Sherlock would require 140 years.

6.4.2.3 *Retrieved False Positives*
This section describes the causes for the retrieval of false positives (FP). We distinguished between:

1. Non-scientific or collection-specific FP

---

[52] Processing times for the character-based approaches were measured for sample sizes of 10, 100, and 1,000; the processing times for all values larger than this are extrapolated due to the unrealistic time requirement. The values for the citation based-approaches were calculated up to the size of the PMC OAS dataset; the processing times for the larger collections were extrapolated.

[53] CbPD5 represents any citation-based approach that uses a min. coupling strength of five for comparisons.

2.   True FP

The first class of FP represented non-scientific or PMC OAS collection-specific false positives. These included *editorials* and *updates*, as described in *Addressing False Positives*, page 148. This class of FP was excluded to prevent influencing the algorithm performance evaluation. The second class of FP represented scientific documents retrieved for their similarity characteristics, but viewed as non-suspicious upon manual examination in the user study. This class of FP was retained and allowed to influence detection performance.

Non-scientific and collection-specific false positives

As described in *Addressing False Positives,* non-scientific or collection-specific FP were manually excluded prior to presenting the top-ranked results to user study participants. This step was necessary for a meaningful performance comparison of the approaches, because without these exclusions the character-based approaches – in particular Encoplot – would have retrieved among its top ranks almost exclusively such legitimately similar documents. This would have resulted in an unwarranted high rate of false positives for the character-based approaches, only due to the chosen test collection's properties.

Figure 46 shows the percentage of non-scientific or collection-specific FP retrieved for each evaluated detection method. For each method, we screened the retrieved results ordered by decreasing score and excluded FP caused by editorials, updates and parsing errors until 30 true positives remained[54]. The number of documents examined to retain 30 true positives varied significantly for each method and is indicated as the denominator over the stacked bars in Figure 46.

---

[54] For an explanation of the categories *editorials* and *updates,* see *Addressing False Positives* on page 148. The category *other* contains document pairs for which author overlap or citation relations that should have caused the exclusion of the document pair were not recognized due to parsing errors.

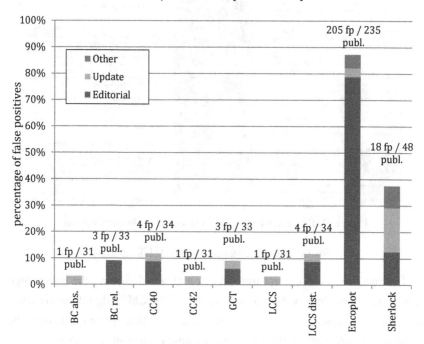

Figure 46: Non-Scientific / Collection-Specific FP Excluded Prior to User Study

31 publications were screened for BC abs., CC42, and LCCS, while 235 publications had to be examined for Encoplot. Encoplot and Sherlock retrieved far more non-scientific FP, mainly of the *editorial* type, when compared to the citation-based approaches. The reason for this is that some editorials re-use text from previously published editorials in other journals, while inserting unique citations that are relevant to their specific field.

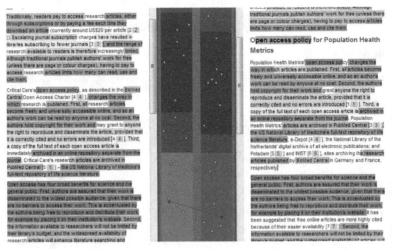

Figure 47: Editorial with High Text Overlap but Unique Citations

Source: http://citeplag.org/compare/43170/120039

Figure 47 shows an excerpt from an editorial, which features the typical high text similarity but low citation-based similarity. The CbPD algorithms retrieved no editorials among false positives, since citation patterns tended be unsuspicious, pointing to differences in semantic content of individual journals, even when text building blocks were borrowed.

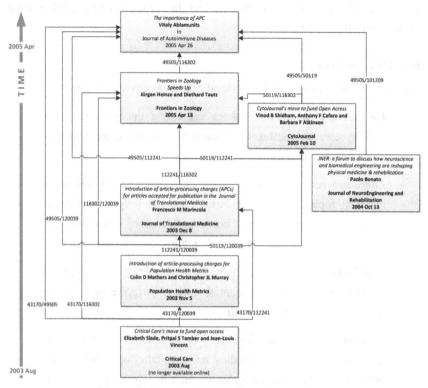

Figure 48: Text Recycled by Journals over Time

Figure 48 shows the common practice of "recycling" text building blocks between journals over the years. The number pair on the connecting lines, e.g., "49505/101209", are the document identifiers to be entered at the end of the prototype's URL to visualize the given document pair, e.g., http://citeplag.org/compare/49505/101209.

In summary, character-based approaches have the inherent problem of retrieving documents with almost identical texts at the highest ranks. Yet, such documents are not always the most interesting or relevant results for a user in a plagiarism detection setting. In many cases, there are underlying reasons that legitimize exceptionally high text overlap. Such reasons are filterable with added effort, yet are highly collection-specific and thus require complete information on the composition of the corpus.

True false positives

The most common causes for the retrieval of true false positives were:

- *Unsuspicious articles* – articles addressing the same topic, or similar research questions but featuring genuine content and no suspicious similarity.

- *Literature reviews* – articles reviewing literature on similar or identical topics, often over 30+ pages, naturally shared many citations. This led to high, but unproblematic, citation pattern overlap and repetition of key words within certain review articles.

- *Legitimate paraphrases* – articles with paraphrases, where author contribution was so significant that classifying the new text as 'suspicious' was not warranted

- *Citation lists* – articles with long in-text citation lists, for example referencing all relevant studies on a certain topic ordered by publication year, are examples of legitimately shared citations patterns.

The user study participants[55] rated 22 of the 181 examined document pairs as true false positives. Figure 49 shows the percentage of total true false positives each evaluated detection method retrieved, classified according to the cause of false positive retrieval, as listed above.

---

[55]   For the description of *User Study Design*, refer to page 149.

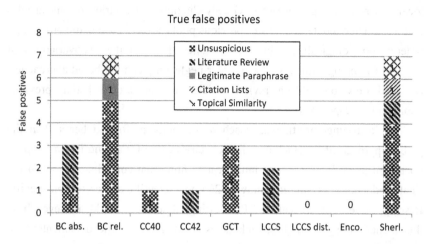

Figure 49: True False Positives Identified by User Study Participants

Figure 49 indicates a systematic weakness shared by global citation-based approaches that neglect citation order (the two variations of Bibliographic Coupling), and of the global character-based approach Sherlock. These approaches retrieved significantly more FP than the other methods. Articles in the life sciences tend to cite more sources than articles in other disciplines [291]. Therefore, longer articles and especially reviews can legitimately share many citations, causing the two BC approaches to rank them highly. Sherlock, the global character-based PDS, tended to flag document pairs as suspicious if they legitimately shared many subject-specific phrases and standardized terminology. Typical examples of such documents included medical case studies, which legitimately described medical history and patient diagnoses using boilerplate text.

Order-observing, global and local citation-based methods yielded fewer false positives. Although the two Longest Common Citation Sequence approaches also represent global citation-based measures, their consideration of the order of citations largely prevents these methods from retrieving false positives. LCCS distinct, which counts multiple citations of the same source only once to be included in the LCCS, retrieved no FP among its top-30 document pairs. The local, order-observing approach of Greedy Citation Tiling retrieved some articles that legitimately contained lists of previous publications in a specific order, e.g., ordered chronologically or by author names. Each of the two variations of Citation Chunking, which are local, order-neglecting, citation-based approaches, retrieved only one FP, a review article, and an article listing previous publications, respectively.

The local fingerprinting approach of Encoplot performed better than the global approach of Sherlock and did not retrieve true FP among its final top-30 document pairs. However, one must bear in mind that compiling the set of the final 30 documents required removing 205 non-scientific and collection-specific false positives. In a realistic PD setting, Encoplot would retrieve these documents among its highest ranked results if non-scientific documents were among the query documents, e.g., if a journal checked one of its issues against the collection.

Table 22: Examples of Most Common FP Types in PMC OAS

Type	Older article	Newer article	CitePlag Link
Non-scientific / collection-specific false positives – excluded prior to user study			
Editorials[56]	[217]	[1]	http://citeplag.org/compare/49505/120039
Updates	[11]	[12]	http://citeplag.org/compare/56236/56684
True false positives – identified by user study participants			
Unsuspicious articles	[101]	[181]	http://citeplag.org/compare/4586/43805
Long literature reviews	[110]	[340]	http://citeplag.org/compare/44315/48342
Legitimate paraphrases	[237]	[331]	http://citeplag.org/compare/21031/34941
Citation lists	[73]	[296]	http://citeplag.org/compare/50197/50325
Case studies	[325]	[112]	http://citeplag.org/compare/13278/92969

Table 22 provides examples for each of the document types prone to false positive classification, both collection-specific FP and true FP. The complete dataset of findings is available for download; refer to Appendix C.

In conclusion, false positives are a problem for character-based as well as citation-based methods. However, our evaluation showed that in the case of the PMC OAS, the two approaches retrieved different types of false positives with different frequencies. In the case of the PMC OAS, the character-based methods yielded significantly more false positives, due to the collection containing many editorials, updates, and case studies that share standardized wording or boilerplate text.

---

[56] Editorials represented the bulk of pre-user study false positives retrieved by the character-based algorithms. An illustration of the common "recycling" of text by journal editors over the years is shown by Figure 48 on page 183.

We hypothesize that combining more than one metric can increase the explanatory power of suspiciousness scores and help in reducing false positives. The citation-based approach adds an additional layer of semantic document uniqueness beyond text, which can give clarity especially for publications on niche topics, or narrowly targeted research, where repeated use of the same terminology, coined expressions or formulas may be justified. As the retrieved false positives demonstrated, evaluating the presence and severity of plagiarism using numerical scores alone remains insufficient without the addition of human judgment.

Future strategies to reduce the number of FP could include targeted heuristics to prevent premature classification of editorials, updates, long review articles on identical topics or articles with matching citation lists, especially when citation lists occur in the background sections. Additionally, a fuzzy author-name-matching method could help avoid minor discrepancies in spelling from contributing to FP.

6.4.2.4 *Examples of CbPD-identified Cases*

Accusations of plagiarism can have serious consequences. To avoid unjust accusations, we publish no unconfirmed plagiarism cases in this thesis. Since PubMed has only brought two[57] retraction procedures to closure thus far, this section presents the publications confirmed as plagiarism by the earlier authors only in anonymized form. The unconfirmed suspicious cases are available through a password-protected website. For access information, please refer to Appendix C.

Examples of Strong Disguise

The CbPD approach identified similarities among publications when the character-based approach detected no notable similarities. Figure 50 shows one such example. The visualization in CitePlag shows a paraphrase rewritten in the

---

[57] Only one retraction procedure was initiated by our contact to earlier authors. Both publications were retrieved by the CbPD algorithms.

author's own words and parallel lines connecting a sequence of matching citations at the location where the paraphrase occurs. This example can be examined using the prototype at: http://citeplag.org/compare/110389/136117. To spot the paraphrase, refer to the paragraph beginning *"The inflammatory cascade... [121]"*.

entering into CNS release various pro-inflammatory, inflammatory cytokines, reactive oxygen, and other biomolecules with high neurotoxic potential. These mediators individually, additively, or synergistically disrupt normal functioning of cells of CNS by inducing neurotoxicity. This may cause alterations in neurotransmitter action and causes leukoencephalopathy resulting in neuronal apoptosis.[64 64 65 65] TNF-?, platelet activating factor (PAF), nitric oxide (NO), and quinolinic acid (QUIN) also behave like neurotoxicant and cause neurotoxicity NO is produced by microvascular endothelial cells, macrophages, and neurons which may result in N-methyl-D-aspartate (NMDA) type glutamate-associated neurotoxicity. Elevated levels of NO synthase has been reported in the brain of HAD patients, while a 40-fold increase in expression of NO synthase in neurons of drug addict HIV patients [66 66 67 67] TNF-? is produced by macrophages and microglia and it mainly affects oligodendrocytes [68 68] An elevated level of TNF-? mRNA has been reported in HIV patients with neurological complications.[69 69] TNF-? causes damage to BBB and facilitates entry of peripheral blood cells.[70 70] Pro-inflammatory cytokines like TNF-?, IL-1, and IFN-? are found to be present in elevated level in AIDS patients.[71 71 72 72]

and ultimately neuronal apoptosis [111 111 ,112 112]. Some of these neurotoxins include TNF-?, arachidonic acid, platelet activating factors (PAF), nitric oxide (NO), and quinolinic acid (QUIN). NO is synthesized by endothelial cells, macrophages and neurons and might be associated with the NMDA type glutamate associated neurotoxicity. A high level of inducible NO synthase has been found in the brain of HAD patients [113 113]. In HIV-1 patients who also are/were drug addicted (e.g. cocaine, heroine), a 40-fold increase in expression of NO synthase in neurons of temporal lobes was reported [114 114]. TNF-? is released by HIV-1 infected macrophage microglia and particularly affects oligodendrocytes [115 115]. It has been shown that TNF-? mRNA level in the subcortical regions of HAD patients' CNS are higher than in AIDS patients without neurological symptoms [116 116]. In addition, TNF-? can damage the BBB, as shown in an in-vivo model, which could facilitate entry into the brain of HIV-1 protein(s) and cytokines secreted in the periphery [117 117] Not only the level of pro-inflammatory cytokines, such as TNF-?, IL-1 and IFN-?, anti-inflammatory cytokines including TGF-? and IL-6, and soluble cytokine receptors is elevated in AIDS patients but the cytokine production is correlated with the gravity of the

Figure 50: Example of CbPD-detected Paraphrase

Source: http://citeplag.org/compare/110389/136117

Figure 51 displays two figures where the placement of cell components and the alignment of arrows between the components are noticeably similar. Despite instances of paraphrasing and similarities among figures, the articles share insufficient text overlap to be retrieved using character-based methods.

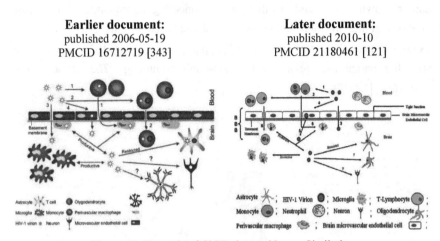

Figure 51: Example of CbPD-detected Image Similarity

Although the author of this thesis does not categorize the similarities in these particular documents as plagiarism, the more subtle similarities, such as those presented in Figure 50 and Figure 51 can be of relevance to examiners when evaluating scientific documents. For example, a reviewer evaluating the merits of a grant proposal may likely be interested in what could be termed "mild forms of unoriginality", i.e. instances of similarity shared with other proposals, patents or published ideas, to cross check the level of uniqueness and originality of the individual proposals. Given this potential use case, one can see that the definition of what constitutes a "relevant" retrieval varies.

Example of High Textual Similarity but low Semantic Similarity

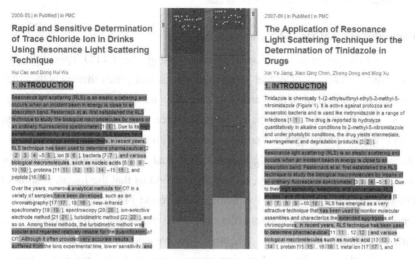

Figure 52: Document with High Character-based but Low Semantic Similarity

Source: http://citeplag.org/compare/49670/49628

The articles PMCID 1920590 and PMCID 2396213, which are shown side-by-side in Figure 52, represent an example of a document pair that shares significant similarity in structure and wording, yet shares no notable citation-based similarity.

The authors of the earlier article judged the similarities as follows:

"Although, there are some similarity for these two papers; however, the research subject, material and data are different from each other. I do not think it is plagiarism."

It seems that the authors of the later article read the earlier article and partially used it as a template for writing their own article. Whether this constitutes plagiarism is controversial. The example illustrates the complementary strength of the character-based and citation-based detection approach. While the character-based approach correctly identified the significant textual overlap, the low citation-based score correctly indicated the absence of a significant semantic similarity in this case.

Examples of Confirmed Plagiarism Cases

This section presents cases we identified using the CbPD approach. We contacted the authors of earlier published articles and asked them whether they considered the later published article to have plagiarized their work.

So far, PubMed has officially retracted three cases [165, 281]. One case [281] was retracted upon our correspondence with the earlier authors, while the other case identified by the algorithms [165], had already been retracted at the time of analysis. Most recently, an author informed us that the Indian Journal of Urology, which had published a medical case report [148] that plagiarized his report plans to release a retraction notice in the next issue. The authors of the earlier publications confirmed plagiarism in five additional cases. This thesis presents author-confirmed plagiarism cases – those which have not yet been retracted – only anonymously to avoid the possibility of false accusation. The direct links to the earlier publications, i.e. the original sources from which the later publications plagiarized are publically available on the http://citeplag.org/ website. However, we refrain from citing the original sources here. We want to avoid linking any researcher's name by citation to a work on the topic of plagiarism detection, which alone can possibly negatively affect an author's academic standing.

Table 23 lists the five author confirmed plagiarism cases, along with the three officially retracted publications. The PMC IDs of the not yet officially retracted publications (both the earlier and later publications) are only given in anonymized form, where "X" replaces the last two digits of the PMC IDs. The not yet officially retracted cases are available upon request, however, only through a password-protected website, as described in C. We will continuously update http://citeplag.org, where the cases will be published once they have been officially retracted.

Table 23: Author Confirmed or Retracted Plagiarism Cases

Case ID	Earlier publication	Later publication	Date authors contacted	Date author-confirmed
1	PMC27651XX	PMC29000XX	2013-05-06	2013-05-06
2	PMC20398XX	PMC27228XX	2013-05-06	2013-05-09
3	PMC22283XX	PMC28819XX	2013-05-06	2013-05-09
4	PMC11494XX	PMC28595XX	2013-05-06	2013-05-07
5	PMC28574XX	PMC26498XX	2013-05-06	2013-05-06
I	PMC1065018	PMC2772258	2012-09-03	retracted[58]
II	PMC514558	PMC2807707	n/a	retracted[59]
III	PMC2740512	PMC2978450	2013-05-06	retracted[60]

Verifying and proving structural and idea plagiarism is considerably more difficult than the verification of copy & paste plagiarism (see Section 2.1.2 and *User Utility* on page 171). While in cases of literal plagiarism a much lower risk of false accusations exists and verification can be done quickly, it is often nearly impossible to prove if someone "stole" or "copied" an idea or lines of argument. This makes *proving* plagiarism extremely difficult, especially if the work bears no close resemblance, such as copied words, to prove it[61].

---

[58] http://citeplag.org/compare/4727/43777
[59] http://citeplag.org/compare/5583/117324
[60] http://citeplag.org/compare/18399/13772
[61] The author is not aware of any publications that were retracted solely on the basis of stolen ideas.

Even in cases where it seems very likely that plagiarism is present, many authors are not willing to initiate a retraction process. For instance, one contacted author confirmed plagiarism but also wrote:

> *"We are not willing to do this job ourselves because this will lead*
> *to great conflict with the author of the second paper who is living*
> *in the same country, even though we do not know him personally."*

(Refer to Appendix G for additional author reactions.)

Moreover, heavily disguised plagiarism, such as paraphrases and the hard to prove structural and idea plagiarism, are often considered "less critical" forms of plagiarism. It is therefore not surprising that the author confirmed and the retracted cases contain extensive plagiarism, most prominently of the copy & paste and shake & paste type. Figure 53 shows the citation pattern visualization for six cases of plagiarism from Table 23 using the CitePlag prototype.

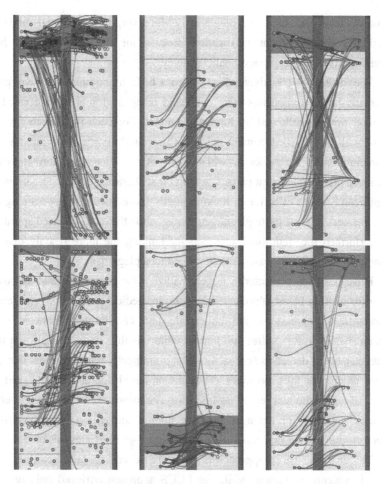

Figure 53: Citation Pattern Visualization of Confirmed Plagiarism

6.4.3 Conclusion of PMC OAS Evaluation

The evaluation using the PubMed Central Open Access Subset (PMC OAS) presented the third and final evaluation of both practicability and detection performance of the CbPD algorithms. Utilizing this large-scale, non-fabricated scientific collection presented a realistic plagiarism detection setting. The CbPD algorithms capably detected currently unidentified scientific plagiarism and outperformed the tested character-based approaches in detecting instances of strongly disguised forms of plagiarism. Moreover, it was shown that CbPD facilitates the document verification process for the examiner and has a significantly higher computational efficiency.

The detection effectiveness of seven CbPD algorithms and two proven character-based approaches were evaluated using a ground truth derived in a pooling process followed by human judgment. For each plagiarism form, we compared the top-10 document pairs that user study participants rated as most suspicious with the ranks at which each of the nine detection approaches retrieved the ten document pairs. We found that character-based approaches were significantly more effective in ranking highly those documents containing copy & paste and shake & paste plagiarism forms, while the citation-based approaches outperformed the traditional approach for ranking the more heavily disguised forms, including paraphrases, structural and idea plagiarism.

False positives presented a larger challenge for character-based approaches than for citation-based approaches, because in medical publications the reuse of standardized expressions and boilerplate text can be legitimate in certain circumstances. Case studies and journal editorials thus posed a challenge to the character-based detection approach, which prominently retrieved these document types among its false positives. The citation-based approaches retrieved such cases of legitimate text reuse less frequently, because they featured either unique citation patterns, for example, in case studies and editorials, or insufficient citations due to their non-scientific nature. Figure 46 illustrates this observation.

The character-based approach Encoplot retrieved 205 false positives out of 235 documents examined, while the LCCS approach retrieved only one false positive out of 31 documents examined. These results may not be applicable to other corpora, since every corpus contains diverse document types from different disciplines, and the reuse of citations or text may be considered legitimate by some disciplines or for certain document types, e.g., medical case studies.

The evaluation of user utility in the verification process of potential plagiarism showed that the citation-based approach offers distinct advantages. Examiners rated the citation-based approach as the single most effective visualization method for assisting in the verification of structural and idea plagiarism. They perceived a combined visualization approach of text and citations as most effective for detecting paraphrases and shake & paste plagiarism. In examining user effort, we recorded a notable reduction in the mean times required to identify suspicious similarity once citation patterns were visualized. User time-savings were highest for structural and idea plagiarism, paraphrases and translated plagiarism forms.

Computational efficiency is crucial for PDS, since performing exhaustive $n:n$ comparisons for large document collections quickly becomes unfeasible using currently available PDS. Character-based approaches require pairwise document comparisons for the entire collection to prevent a reduction in detection performance. The exhaustive $n:n$ examination of the PMC OAS collection could not have been carried out using any of currently and freely available methods, due to the unfeasible runtime requirement. Whether a similar high quality, yet computationally efficient approach is offered by any proprietary systems remains uncertain. The CbPD approach requires fewer resources, since only the documents with Bibliographic Coupling strength greater or equal to one require further analysis. A comparison of computational efficiency of the Encoplot and Sherlock character-based approaches with the CbPD algorithms, using a minimum threshold coupling strength of five, showed that for a collection in the PMC OAS size range, character-based approaches would require approximately 100 years of processing, while the CbPD5 algorithm requires only one day on a current model quad-core system.

Using a non-artificially created corpus allowed the comparison of effectiveness of character-based and citation-based detection approaches in identifying currently unidentified real-world plagiarism cases, some of which showed sophisticated plagiarism disguise. The CbPD approach identified several instances that could not be detected by the two baseline approaches that are representative of today's detection approaches.

As a result of our contact with authors, one plagiarized medical study and a plagiarized case report have already been retracted by the issuing journal.

Furthermore, five publications have been author-confirmed as plagiarism, and several additional publications are currently under examination[62].

6.5   Conclusion of Evaluations

The evaluation of Citation-based Plagiarism Detection (CbPD) algorithms for their practicability, detection effectiveness, user utility, and computational efficiency demonstrated promising results. The single largest benefit of CbPD was its potential to identify heavily disguised plagiarism, such as paraphrases, translated plagiarism, and structural and idea plagiarism. Even for heavily disguised plagiarism, we often observed similarities remaining in the citation patterns. The character-based methods currently in use rely on textual similarity alone for plagiarism detection and are thus unable to detect strongly disguised forms of plagiarism.

An obstacle to the evaluation was the nonexistence of a suitable test collection. Test collections used in previous plagiarism detection evaluations were unsuitable for evaluating the performance of CbPD in detecting strongly disguised plagiarism, because previously used collections were either artificially created or had no ground truth regarding the presence of disguised forms of plagiarism. Methods for artificially creating disguised plagiarism include using crowdsourcing services, e.g., Amazon's Mechanical Turk [262] or oDesk [265], for contracting writers that perform the task. Asking humans to paraphrase text produces more realistic disguise than employing random text alterations. Nonetheless, such services cannot reproduce the sophisticated disguises integrated into publications that scientists worked on, often over years, with the goal of publishing in a reputable journal.

The creation of an *ideal* test collection would require extensive secret monitoring of scientists' work, e.g., a Trojan horse, to study which sources they access and how they attribute the work of others. Only such a study would allow tracing instances of realistic idea plagiarism with acceptable confidence.

---

[62]   As of 2013-05-08.

However, the creation of such an ideal test collection would be extremely resource intensive, not to mention infeasible for ethical reasons. Since no single ideal test collection exists, or can reasonably be created, we combined three real-world document collections of various sizes and characteristics – the GuttenPlag Wiki, the VroniPlag Wiki and the PMC OAS – to mitigate limitations of the individual corpora.

First, we used the GuttenPlag Wiki to compare the CbPD approach to traditional character-based PDS in detecting the translated plagiarism present in the doctoral thesis of K.-T. zu Guttenberg. It can be assumed that the extensive crowd-sourced analysis of this real-word plagiarism case identified a very large portion of all plagiarism instances in the thesis. This serves as a ground truth for performance comparisons. The CbPD algorithms identified 13 of the 16 instances of translated plagiarism in the thesis, while the character-based PDS we tested could not identify any.

Second, we used the VroniPlag Wiki. This collection featured confirmed plagiarism instances from multiple authors, allowing an evaluation of CbPD on various writing and plagiarism styles. In an analysis of randomly chosen plagiarized fragments from 15 theses, citation analysis alone could identify seven of the 15 theses as clearly suspicious. Analyzing translated plagiarism in particular, the CbPD approach identified four of the seven theses that contained translated plagiarism as clearly suspicious and another thesis as likely suspicious.

Third, we demonstrated CbPD's potential to detect plagiarism in the ~234,000 publications of the biomedical collection, PubMed Central Open Access Subset. Some plagiarism cases would have remained undetected using current approaches. Since no ground truth exists, we used a pooling approach in combination with human judgment collected in a user study to create a test collection.

Resulting from our contact with authors, one plagiarized medical study and a plagiarized case report have already been retracted by the issuing journal.

Additionally, five publications have been author-confirmed as plagiarism, and several other publications are currently under examination[63].

A comparison of detection effectiveness against the baselines Encoplot and Sherlock, two proven character based approaches, confirmed our hypothesis that CbPD and character-based approaches complement each other. Character-based approaches are ideal for identifying undisguised local forms of plagiarism, while the citation-based approaches are ideal for detecting disguised global forms.

The complementary strengths of the character-based and citation-based approaches were also reflected in the reports of user utility. While character-based methods were rated as most helpful in manual verification of copy & paste plagiarism, study participants stated the citation visualizations of the CbPD approach as the single most useful aid for verifying structural and idea plagiarism, and as a valuable addition for paraphrases and shake & paste plagiarism. CbPD also reduced user effort, measured in time required to identify suspicious instances, for Guttenberg's translated plagiarism.

The computational efficiency of the citation-based approach was shown to be suitable for the analysis of large corpora and for filtering large datasets prior to applying the computationally more expensive character-based approaches. The worst-case complexity of performing an $n{:}n$ comparison is $O(n^2)$ for both character-based and citation-based approaches. However, in an average case, a CbPD analysis in an $n{:}n$ fashion requires only a small fraction of the comparisons necessary for a character-based analysis. The reason is that CbPD algorithms only need to analyze documents that are bibliographically coupled. In the case of the PMC OAS, the BC requirement reduced the number of document pairs to be analyzed by 99.77 %, from approximately 17 billion to approximately 39 million. Reducing the number of documents to compare is essential when analyzing a collection the size of PMC OAS with character-based approaches. Aside from excluding documents that are not bibliographically coupled as we did, character-based heuristics, like fingerprinting or keyword-based clustering, could be used to limit collection size. However, to our knowledge, we found no

---

[63]   As of 2013-05-08.

publically available character-based PDS that allowed analyzing a collection of several hundred thousand documents in a feasible amount of time.

In conclusion, the multiple-collection evaluation of CbPD uniformly showed that citation-based plagiarism detection and character-based plagiarism detection have complementary strengths and weaknesses. Character-based approaches excel at detecting unmodified and local forms of plagiarism, including short passages copied verbatim and only moderately paraphrased text. They fail, however, when it comes to detecting strongly paraphrased text or translated plagiarism, which we showed to be the strength of the CbPD approach.

The reader is encouraged to explore the citation visualization of the CitePlag prototype and view examples at: http://www.citeplag.org/thesis

7 Summary & Future Work

This chapter summarizes the thesis in Section 7.1, reviews the contributions of the research presented in Section 7.2, and gives an outlook on future work in Section 7.3.

7.1 Summary

This doctoral thesis proposed a novel approach to plagiarism detection, thereby addressing an information retrieval problem that has so far not been satisfactorily solved – the machine-detection of strongly disguised and translated academic plagiarism. State-of-the-art plagiarism detection systems (PDS) employ character-based text comparisons, which reliably detect copy & paste plagiarism and, to varying degrees, slightly modified plagiarism. Current PDS are unable to detect strongly disguised forms of plagiarism, such as paraphrases, translated plagiarism, and idea plagiarism. The concluding remark in the 2012 Collusion Detection System Test performed by the HTW Berlin University of Applied Science states

> *"[...] for translations or heavily edited material, the systems are powerless [...]"* [360].

To address the weakness of current systems, this thesis introduced *Citation-based Plagiarism Detection (CbPD)*, a fundamentally different approach to plagiarism detection. Compared to existing approaches, CbPD does not make use of character-based similarity, but rather analyzes the citation patterns within documents to form a language-independent fingerprint representing semantic similarity between documents. To cover the different forms of plagiarism and the resulting citation pattern characteristics, three classes of CbPD algorithms were introduced: *Longest Common Citation Sequence, Greedy Citation Tiling* and *Citation Chunking*. The algorithms are capable of handling transpositions and scaling of citations. Additionally, the algorithms take into account the probability of co-occurrence of identical citations by chance, as well as the number and proximity of matching citations in a pattern.

As a proof of concept, and to evaluate the detection performance of the CbPD approach in a real plagiarism detection setting, we developed the prototype CitePlag. CitePlag is composed of a document parser, a relational database, a detector component, and a frontend. CitePlag produces interactive visualizations of both citation and text similarities between documents to aid the human examiner in arriving at a conclusion on potential plagiarism. The CitePlag frontend is web-based and accessible at: http://www.citeplag.org

Figure 54: CitePlag Plagiarism Detection Prototype

Source: http://citeplag.org/compare/6861131

We performed a comprehensive evaluation of the CbPD approach using the CitePlag prototype to collect human judgment as a ground truth. Three unique document collections were used for evaluation purposes, since no single collection fulfilled all necessary test-collection criteria:

- must contain scientific publications with citations

- must contain real-world plagiarism cases (non-fabricated)

- the extent of plagiarism must be known (ground truth exists)

We chose the GuttenPlag Wiki because it represents one of the most thoroughly examined cases of plagiarism. This makes the collection unique in that it allows for a realistic ground truth approximation. The CbPD algorithms identified 13 of the 16 translated plagiarism instances contained in the thesis, while the three tested PDS could not identify a single instance.

We chose the VroniPlag Wiki collection because it contains thoroughly examined academic plagiarism from various authors, thus covering a wider range of citation styles and plagiarism forms. Side-by-side comparisons of plagiarized text excerpts from the VroniPlag Wiki showed that the copying of citations – if present in the source – is common behavior among plagiarists. Even when translating text, or otherwise attempting to disguise textual similarity, authors made little to no effort to disguise the order in which they copied citations. Our observation of plagiarism behavior indicates that the CbPD approach is suitable for detecting strongly disguised forms of plagiarism in real-world settings. Relying only upon a comparison of citation patterns, CbPD could identify five of the seven translated plagiarism cases in the VroniPlag Wiki.

We chose the PubMed Central Open Access Subset (PMC OAS) to access more strongly disguised scientific plagiarism, which has not yet been identified. Limiting our evaluation to identified plagiarism cases would be insufficient. Identified cases tend to feature higher instances of textual similarity, given that these cases were detected either using currently available PDS, or because high similarity sparked suspicion among human reviewers. The PMC OAS collection contains almost no examples of identified plagiarism cases. This allows an evaluation of the practicability of CbPD in a realistic setting and on a large scale, using a test collection of 185,170 medical publications. Comparison of detection performance against two state-of-the-art PDS showed that CbPD was the only approach capable of revealing heavily disguised instances of plagiarism. As a result of our investigation, PubMed has already retracted one plagiarized medical study and one plagiarized case report. Moreover, the evaluation showed that plagiarists usually do not substitute citations when disguising the origin of plagiarized text, which makes citations suitable language-independent markers for forming a disguise-resistant semantic fingerprint of a publication.

Table 24: Capabilities of Current PD Approaches and CbPD

This table expands on Table 8.

Detection Approach	Application				Form of plagiarism						References
	Extrinsic PD	Intrinsic PD	Mono-lingual PD	Cross-lingual PD	Copies	Near copies	Shake & Paste	Undue Paraphrase	Translated	Idea	
Character-based (Char.)	X		X								
Exact String Matching											[19, 137, 175, 232]
Approximate String Matching											[285, 370]
Fingerprinting											[57, 142, 245, 293,
Vector Space Models											[24, 238, 252, 328,
Semantic Enhancements											[22, 190, 252, 333]
Cross-language (CLPD)	X			X							[172, 239, 263, 371]
Stylometry (Style)		X	X								[97, 238, 319, 322]
Citation-based (CbPD)	X		X	X							[127, 129, 132]

Hybrid: Character-based and citation-based combined

Hybrid (Char./CLPD/Style/CbPD)	X		X	X							[127, 129, 132]

Detection rate: Good   Fair   Poor   Unfit

The strengths and limitations of the different plagiarism detection approaches are summarized in Table 24. The table shows that both the character-based and the citation-based approaches have their own unique strengths. While the character-based approach capably identifies local forms of plagiarism, such as copy & paste, the CbPD approach excels in detecting global forms of strong paraphrases, translated plagiarism, and idea plagiarism. A hybrid approach that combines CbPD with existing character-based detection approaches significantly improves the detection rates for all forms of plagiarism, as is shown in the final row in Table 24.

Addressing academic plagiarism by technical means alone remains an insufficient solution in the long-run, since plagiarism is a societal problem and must also be addressed with societal solutions, i.e. providing education, guidelines, and policies to prevent plagiarism. At the same time, when prevention fails, employing technical means for plagiarism detection is a promising complementary approach. Advances in plagiarism detection software can significantly increase the likelihood of discovery and thus decrease the benefits of plagiarizing as perceived by the plagiarist. The CbPD approach contributes to making scientific plagiarism less "worthwhile", by forcing the plagiarist to substitute citations, which requires time and subject expertise.

Additionally, CbPD increases the likelihood of machine-identifying even heavily disguised plagiarism, including translated plagiarism. In many cases, disguising plagiarism until it contains neither character-based nor citation-based similarities requires such effort that acquiring content through plagiarism may no longer be an attractive option to a plagiarist over creating genuine content.

7.2 Contributions

This section summarizes the contributions of this thesis for each of the research tasks presented in Section 1.3.

Task 1:   *Perform a comprehensive analysis of the individual strengths and weaknesses of state-of-the-art plagiarism detection approaches and systems.*

We reviewed the literature and tested available detection approaches and systems. We found that state-of-the-art systems for plagiarism detection are capable of detecting copied or slightly disguised cases of plagiarism, but fail to detect the more heavily disguised forms of plagiarism, such as paraphrases, translated, and idea plagiarism.

Task 2:   *Develop a plagiarism detection concept that addresses the identified weaknesses of current plagiarism detection approaches.*

To overcome the deficiency of the current plagiarism detection approaches a novel concept, Citation-based Plagiarism Detection (CbPD), was proposed. Unlike currently used detection approaches, which focus solely on textual overlap, CbPD uses the placement of in-text citations as a language-independent marker for modeling semantic similarity between documents.

Task 3:   *Design detection algorithms that employ the theoretical concept introduced and are fitted to detect the plagiarism forms currently not machine-detectable.*

To enable effective and efficient detection of the different plagiarism forms, we designed and implemented three classes of detection algorithms: *Longest Common Citation Sequence, Greedy Citation Tiling* and *Citation Chunking*. Each class considers the citation pattern characteristics unique to the various plagiarism forms. The Longest Common Citation Sequence algorithm ignores non-matching citations between matching citations. This algorithm is especially suitable to identify document-wide disguised plagiarism, as well as local instances of plagiarism if sufficient citations are given. The Greedy Citation Tiling algorithm identifies only identical citation patterns, an approach especially suitable for detecting shake & paste plagiarism. The variations of the Citation Chunking algorithm check patterns for potential transpositions or scaling of citations, which is useful in detecting locally confined instances of disguised plagiarism. Additionally, citation patterns are evaluated taking into account (1) the probability that the shared citations in the matching patterns co-occur by chance, and (2) the number, proximity, and order of shared citations in the matching patterns.

Task 4:   *Implement a prototype of a plagiarism detection system that employs the developed algorithms to demonstrate the applicability of the approach in real-world scientific document collections.*

To evaluate and demonstrate the proposed concept in real-world conditions we developed *CitePlag,* a plagiarism detection system prototype capable of applying the CbPD approach to a large scientific corpus. The system consists of a relational database, a parser, a detector, and a web-based user-interface at the frontend. The database stores the bibliographic document data as extracted by the parser and stores the results of the CbPD algorithms as implemented in the detector component. The web-based frontend retrieves the detection results from the database and visualizes the suspicious document in an interactive side-by-side display for human inspection.

The frontend[64] is accessible at: http://www.citeplag.org

Task 5:   *Evaluate the proposed concept in identifying strongly disguised plagiarism forms by comparing detection performance, user utility, and computational efficiency to state-of-the-art systems. As proof of concept, identify unknown and currently non-machine-detectable plagiarism instances.*

---

[64] The frontend was developed in collaboration with students from the HTW Berlin. See Section 5.4 for details.

To validate the effectiveness and efficiency of the CbPD approach, we performed three distinct evaluations using real-world document collections.

- An analysis of the doctoral thesis of zu Guttenberg showed that CbPD is considerably more suitable for identifying translated plagiarism than currently used approaches. Of the 16 translated plagiarism fragments in the thesis, the CbPD approach identified 13, while the tested PDS were unable to identify a single fragment.

- An analysis of the VroniPlag Wiki, which contains plagiarism from a diverse group of authors, showed promising results regarding CbPD's ability to detect plagiarism and in particular translated plagiarism.

- An analysis of the PMC OAS corpus, containing ~200,000 medical publications, showed that the CbPD approach is capable of identifying cases of plagiarism, which remain undetected by current plagiarism detection approaches.

In addition to demonstrating the practical suitability of CbPD for three distinct test collections, the comprehensive evaluation led to the following conclusions:

- A high (relative) Bibliographic Coupling strength alone is not a sufficient indicator for plagiarism, since it results in many false positives. Analyzing the citation patterns in regard to factors, such as order and proximity of citations, significantly improves detection performance.

- The presented approach is computationally more efficient than most currently used character-based approaches. This makes it applicable also to large document collections. While an $n{:}n$ comparison of the complete PMC OAS corpus using a character-based PDS, e.g. Encoplot, would have required ~100 years, performing the CbPD computations required only 14.7 hours on a current quad-core processor system.

Evaluating the CbPD approach necessitated the creation of a suitable test collection due to the shortcomings of currently available collections. The collection created using the PMC OAS contains 185,170 scientific publications and a user study derived ground truth for 181 unique publications retrieved by nine tested detection algorithms among their top-30 ranks. This dataset currently represents the only scientific document collection suitable for evaluating structural and idea plagiarism on a large scale. The collection is available upon request. See Appendix C for access details.

The dataset includes:

- the full texts of the PMC OAS collection cleaned of duplicates and converted to plain text.

- extracted data of citations including their positions within the PMC OAS full-texts.

- extracted, disambiguated data of references in the PMC OAS.

- pre-computed similarity scores for documents in the PMC OAS using three character-based similarity measures, Encoplot, Sherlock and Lucene, as well as 21 citation-based measures, including Longest Common Citation Sequence, Greedy Citation Tiling, Citation Chunking, Bibliographic Coupling, Co-Citation.

- user-identified suspicious fragments and confirmed cases of plagiarism in the PMC OAS corpus.

7.3 Future Work

The development and evaluation of a citation-based approach to plagiarism detection (PD) introduced several ideas for future applications and improvements to today's PD technology. This section on future work gives an outlook on the general research needed in Section 7.3.1, and proposes strategies to improve CbPD detection accuracy in Section 7.3.2. Additional applications of the CbPD and the Sequential Pattern Analysis approach are presented in Section 7.3.3, and the need for further evaluations is explained in Section 7.3.4.

7.3.1 General Research Need

7.3.1.1 Defining Newly Detectable Plagiarism Forms

The CbPD approach opens up a discussion on the current definition of plagiarism and the levels of structural similarity in documents that adequately represent critical thresholds. Disguised plagiarism forms have not been addressed as thoroughly in plagiarism research as the more easily detectable and verifiable non-disguised plagiarism forms. No consensus exists on thresholds of similarity that should be interpreted as disguised plagiarism, or how these more subtle forms of similarity should be dealt with.

An example of the type of questions that could arise is if copying numerous carefully selected citations listed in a table constitutes plagiarism. The judgment might depend on factors such as the percentage of identical citations, whether citations have been inserted or deleted, whether the copied citations are highly co-cited, or whether the order of copied citations is identical. However, even an identical order can be legitimate if, for example, both authors cite papers chronologically or alphabetically by author names. Such a plagiarism form, for which a fitting term could be *citation composition plagiarism*, has thus far not been considered. Thus, a discussion of suitable criteria and similarity thresholds for plagiarism forms newly identifiable with the CbPD approach is of importance. Such a discussion, however, lies beyond the scope of this thesis.

7.3.2 Improvements to Detection Accuracy

7.3.2.1 *Considering Document Sections for Citation Occurrences*
When analyzing the PMC OAS document collection for plagiarism, we found that high textual and citation similarity often occurs in the introduction and related work sections. When talking to the authors of the original work, we found that they often do not consider such similarity as plagiarism.

> *"...The basic problem is that there are only a limited number of ways to provide the information common to both introductions (mostly the list of genes responsible for inherited cataracts), and if the authors had not listed them in the order taken from our previous manuscript, they would simply have had to shuffle the order a bit, which seems a little silly... "*[65]

A previous plagiarism investigation of articles in PubMed gathered similar feedback from authors [202]. Authors stated that the repetition of highly similar text in their own manuscripts or the manuscripts of collaborators is a common practice and in most cases not considered a violation of academic principles within their field. Repeating similar or identical text is especially common in introductory sections, for describing experimental settings, or as part of review articles [114, 202].

We agree that mild forms of "plagiarism" are less serious if they occur in certain document sections, such as in the introduction or in the related work section, than if they occur, for example, in the results section. To reduce false positives, the detection algorithms should take into consideration document section when calculating the CbPD score. Additional empirical research will be necessary to determine reasonable weightings for citation matches depending on their placement in the publication.

---

[65] Quoted from an email exchange with an author who wished to remain anonymous.

7.3.2.2   Accounting for Citation Substitution

If CbPD finds widespread use, plagiarists may deliberately substitute references with topically similar references. The CbPD detection algorithms could counteract such obfuscation attempts by also considering related citations as part of the similarity assessment. In order to analyze related citations, the detection algorithms would require a set of references viewed as 'interchangeable'. Character- and citation-based similarity measures, such as Co-citation Proximity Analysis [126], could be employed to compute the set of related citations.

Including related citations in the analysis will potentially lead to more false positives and a higher computational effort. However, we hypothesize that including these additional checks will have a strong deterrent effect. If authors must sift through large amounts of related literature to re-order all references in a unique coherent way, only to avoid detection, the task becomes so time consuming that producing original work becomes the more attractive option.

The counter-measure to citation shuffling and substitution could additionally be to analyze not only the order of these markers, but also their proximities. In this way, the character distance fingerprint would remain similar even if all markers in a document were replaced. So far, however, we have not researched the effectiveness of these counter measures.

7.3.2.3   Reducing False Positives Using Co-citation Proximity Analysis

False positives are a common problem of PDS. To aid in reducing false positives, we are assessing the possibility of using CPA (see Section 3.2.5). One can assume that most authors carefully examine the merits of the documents they cite. Thus, in the case of frequently co-cited documents, and especially in the case of documents with a high CPA score, authors are assumed to have read and recognized the validity and contributions of the documents they cited together. Therefore, we regard it as unlikely that documents contain plagiarism originating from documents with which they are frequently co-cited. Furthermore, in the case that plagiarism is present, it is very unlikely that it has not yet been identified and reported in frequently co-cited documents. This consideration may help reduce false positives, although we have not yet collected empirical evidence for this hypothesis.

7.3.2.4 *Evaluating Intrinsic Citation-based PD*

Whether intrinsic[66] citation-based approaches are suitable in identifying plagiarism remains a question to be addressed by future research. Unexpected deviations in the type or style of citations may possibly point to plagiarism. For example, if a certain document section cites only non-open access publications, while the rest of the document cites only open access publications, this can potentially indicate copied sections of another author's literature review or copied paper structure and ideas. Similarly, if an author abbreviates other authors' first names, except in a few instances where the authors' first names are written out fully, this may be an indicator of unoriginal work. Additionally, if an author follows the convention of citing the first and last pages from works cited, yet in other sections only provides the beginning page number for a citation, the citation information may have been copied.

7.3.2.5 *Machine Learning of Similarity Characteristics*

If a larger suitable test collection that features a reliable ground truth should ever become available, one could consider the use of machine learning methods to optimize detection algorithms. Machine learning could improve CbPD by more accurately determining the typical combinations of citation-based and character-based similarity characteristics that cause a document to be suspicious.

7.3.3 Additional Applications

7.3.3.1 *Identification of Plagiarism Form*

As discussed in Section 4.5, the detection algorithms providing the best results differ depending on the plagiarism form present. This characteristic of the

---

[66] See *Stylometry for Intrinsic Plagiarism Detection* on page 31 for an explanation of intrinsic measures.

algorithms allows for the automatic identification of the form of plagiarism. For example, if a citation pattern is identical, yet textual similarity is relatively low, the plagiarism is likely a paraphrase. If citation similarity is high, but the text is in another language, it is possibly a translated plagiarism. Depending on the form of plagiarism, one could also adjust similarity thresholds.

7.3.3.2   *Visualization of Author Inspiration Trail*

When analyzing citation patterns, it is noticeable that review articles on identical or related topics tend to share a great deal of citation patterns. However, despite citing much of the same literature, later review articles rarely cite earlier review articles. Space limitations and readability concerns can justify why authors do not cite every document involved in the creation process of a paper. Thus, this should not necessarily be considered *plagiarism* as long as the similarities are not excessive. Nevertheless, identifying such similarities can be interesting to other authors.

As an example, assume Alice wrote a paper that Bob finds interesting. If Bob is especially interested in learning more about the topic in general, he may like to know which other publications Alice consulted while writing her article. Bob could look at the bibliography in Alice's article. However, the works cited in the bibliography are often only the most influential texts, or those addressing specific facts instead of giving a general introduction or literature review on the topic. The hypothesis is that identifying additional, often more general, publications aside from those cited becomes possible by running similar algorithms as for Citation-based Plagiarism Detection but using a lower similarity threshold.

Figure 55 illustrates the concept of an author inspiration trail. If Bob wrote *Doc B*, he may have also read *Doc A*, because both *Doc B* and *Doc A* cite documents [1], [2] and [3] in identical order. However, Bob does not cite Alice, who published earlier.

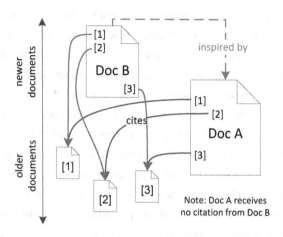

Figure 55: Potential to Identify Non-cited Documents

Identifying and displaying these currently invisible *inspiration trails*[67] is another possible application of CbPD. The goal would be to develop methods capable of identifying earlier papers that significantly affected the creation of later papers, even if the later papers did not cite the earlier ones.

7.3.3.3 *Sequential Pattern Analysis*

This thesis proposed and evaluated Citation-based Plagiarism Detection as a specialization of the broader approach we termed *Sequential Pattern Analysis*. CbPD applies Sequential Pattern Analysis for a particular use case – plagiarism detection – using a specific type of language-independent markers: academic citations.

Sequential Pattern Analysis using additional language-dependent and language-independent markers aside from citations could further increase the detection rates for global[68] plagiarism. Current PDS commonly employ a heuristic initial retrieval step using some form of vector space models or term

---

[67] The author first proposed the idea of inspiration trails at the ECDL doctoral consortium in 2010 [125].

[68] See Section 2.2.2, page 19, for an explanation of local vs. global plagiarism.

indices, see Section 2.2.1. These approaches consider the overlap and partially the distinctiveness of patterns, which equal indexed terms in this case, as the main criteria for identifying similar documents. Depending on the terms used, the order within patterns is also considered, e.g., when several characters, multiple words, or whole sentences represent a term. We hypothesize that additionally analyzing the proximity and order of shared patterns, i.e. matching character sequences, words, or longer text fragments, could improve retrieval accuracy. For instance, if two documents share technical terms, e.g., stating a certain bacterial culture, specifying a form of DNA sequencing, listing laboratory equipment and naming chemicals, the overlap in terms may too small and too common as to retrieve these documents as potentially suspicious. However, if these terms appear in similar order and proximity within both documents, they may indicate a similar research approach and/or experimental setup that are less common, thus interesting to an examiner.

Examples for additional language-independent characteristics used by Sequential Pattern Analysis include:

- Formulas (e.g., chemical formulas such as H_2O)

- Names (e.g., of author names, cities, countries)

- URIs (e.g., URLs)

- Dates (e.g., June 23, 1912)

- Patent numbers (e.g., 4,715,820, 3,685,001)

Aside from plagiarism detection, considering these and other characteristics could make Sequential Pattern Analysis applicable to further use cases.
For instance, considering the order and proximity of keywords, for example, descriptions of medical symptoms, could improve the retrieval accuracy for searches for medical diagnosis or treatment. A simple keyword search for symptoms may generate too many unrelated results, especially for common symptoms such as "headache". However, a search for symptoms in a specific

order, for example, the chronological order in which symptoms of a disease tend to occur, or when symptoms are discussed in close proximity within a specialized medical text may result in more relevant search results. Additionally, considering the distinctiveness of described symptoms could help to rank descriptions or case studies of rare diseases more prominently.

Considering the order, proximity and distinctiveness of names and/or dates could for instance improve the retrieval of historical text covering a particular event or period. Similarly, employing Sequential Pattern Analysis for patent retrieval could improve the search for specific prior art.

7.3.4 Further Evaluations

To date, the largest document collection examined using the citation-based approach for plagiarism detection was the PMC OAS. This corpus contained "only" ~234,000 publications. The CbPD approach, however, can easily be applied to much larger collections; refer to the *Comparison of Computational Efficiency* on page 176. We lack the licenses to access the 22 million articles in PubMed, of which only 2.8 million are freely available as full-text in PubMed Central [338].

The reason for choosing PMC OAS for an initial evaluation, and why we plan to re-examine PubMed's other collection more extensively in the future, is that academic fraud, including plagiarism and the fabrication or falsification of data can have serious negative effects to society, particularly in medicine. Fraudulent medical studies on the efficacy and safety of pharmaceuticals or health interventions can lead to serious maltreatment of patients[69]. An increasing

---

[69] Even without fabricating data, authors can endanger patients by recycling previously recorded data as part of several publications. In systematic reviews, results published more than once can receive an inappropriate weight. Systematic reviews of primary research are one of the most important instruments in evidence-based medicine to demonstrate the effects of pharmaceuticals, health and public health interventions, and social interventions [189]. In the worst case, plagiarized studies can distort systematic reviews and the conclusions drawn from these meta-analyses [349]. Several studies highlighted that although fraudulent studies make up a small share of all medical

number of scandals related to fraudulent research have been uncovered in the last decade. Prominent examples include a fabricated link between the measles, mumps and rubella vaccine and autism [87], falsified data in stem cell research [16], or a fabricated positive effect of painkillers on oral cancer [243].

Identifying fabricated or falsified data is difficult, especially by means of automatic detection. We found no study on scientific fraud, which analyzes how many studies containing fabricated or falsified data also contain plagiarism. However, the evaluation of CbPD using the PMC OAS revealed some examples of studies that both plagiarized and fabricated data. It seems plausible to assume that if authors intend to fabricate a study, they would not do so from scratch, but may try to resemble the structure of a previous study. In doing so, fabricated studies may resort to copying literature reviews or sections describing experimental setup from prior studies. CbPD can help in identifying such fraudulent studies. Further evaluations of the citation-based approach on corpora containing medical publications are thus a priority for mitigating the potentially damaging effects of plagiarism in medicine.

Further large-scale evaluations of the CbPD approach using scientific, multi-language corpora will be necessary. The evaluation using the PMC OAS corpus, while large-scale, was not applicable to translated plagiarism. The PMC OAS contains only medical texts in English. Figure 56 shows a retracted translated plagiarism [65] published in *Neuroscience Letters*. The English translation only contains sources that were also cited in the Chinese original. This citation-based similarity represents the *only* automatically recognizable similarity characteristic remaining in the texts.

---

research papers, they affect and potentially put at risk tens of thousands of patients [107, 315, 349].

Figure 56: Retracted Translated Plagiarism from Chinese to English

References

1. Ablamunits V (2005) The importance of APC. Journal of Autoimmune Disease 2:3, doi: 10.1186/1740-2557-2-3, PMC1087870

2. ACNP Software (2011) Plagiarism Detection Software. Online Source, retrieved Oct. 28, 2011 from: http://www.anticutandpaste.com

3. Ahlgren P, Colliander C (2009) Document–document Similarity Approaches and Science Mapping: Experimental Comparison of Five Approaches. Journal of Informetrics 3(1):49–63, doi: 10.1016/j.joi.2008.11.003

4. Ahlgren P, Jarneving B (2008) Bibliographic Coupling, Common Abstract Stems and Clustering: A Comparison of Two Document-document Similarity Approaches in the Context of Science Mapping. Scientometrics 76:273–290, 10.1007/s11192-007-1935-1

5. Ahtiainen A, Surakka S, Rahikainen M (2006) Plaggie: Gnu-licensed Source Code Plagiarism Detection Engine for Java Exercises. In: Proceedings of the 6th Baltic Sea Conference on Computing Education Research, pp 141–142, doi: 10.1145/1315803.1315831

6. Ali R, Beg SMM (2011) An overview of Web search evaluation methods. Computers and Electrical Engineering 37(6):835–848, doi: 10.1016/j.compeleceng.2011.10.005

7. Alkureishi LW, Burak Z, Alvarez JA, Ballinger J, Bilde A, Britten AJ, Calabrese L, Chiesa C, Chiti A, de Bree R, Gray HW, Hunter K, Kovacs AF, Lassmann M, Leemans CR, Mamelle G, McGurk M, Mortensen J, Poli T, Shoaib T, Sloan P, Sorensen JA, Stoeckli SJ, Thomsen JB, Trifiro G, Werner J, Ross GL (2009) Joint Practice Guidelines for Radionuclide Lymphoscintigraphy for Sentinel Node Localization in Oral/Oropharyngeal Squamous Cell Carcinoma. Ann Surg Oncol 16:3190–3210, PMID19795174, PMC2766455

8. Alkureishi LW, Burak Z, Alvarez JA, Ballinger J, Bilde A, Britten AJ, Calabrese L, Chiesa C, Chiti A, de Bree R, Gray HW, Hunter K, Kovacs AF, Lassmann M, Leemans CR, Mamelle G, McGurk M, Mortensen J,

Poli T, Shoaib T, Sloan P, Sorensen JA, Stoeckli SJ, Thomsen JB, Trifiro G, Werner J, Ross GL (2009) Joint Practice Guidelines for Radionuclide Lymphoscintigraphy for Sentinel Node Localization in Oral/Oropharyngeal Squamous Cell Carcinoma. Eur J Nucl Med Mol Imaging 36:1915–1936, PMID19784646, PMC2764079

9. Aller MA, Arias JL, Arias J (2007) The Mast Cell Integrates the Splanchnic and Systemic Inflammatory Response in Portal Hypertension. Journal of Translational Medicine 5:44, PMID17892556, PMC2034541

10. Aller MA, Arias JL, Cruz A, Arias J (2007) Inflammation: a Way to Understanding the Evolution of Portal Hypertension. Theoretical Biology and Medical Modelling 4:44, PMID17999758, PMC2206015

11. American Diabetes Association (2009) Diagnosis and classification of diabetes mellitus. Diabetes Care 32(Suppl. 1):62–67, doi: 10.2337/dc09-S062

12. American Diabetes Association (2010) Diagnosis and classification of diabetes mellitus. Diabetes Care 33(Suppl. 1):9–62, doi: 10.2337/dc10-S062

13. Amsler RA (1972) Applications of Citation-based Automatic Classification. Tech. rep., Linguistics Research Center, University of Texas at Austin, Austin, TX

14. Apache Software Foundation (2010) Apache OpenNLP. Online Source, retrieved May 29, 2012 from: http://incubator.apache.org/opennlp/

15. arXivorg (2007) 65 Admin Withdrawals. Online Source, retrieved Oct. 28, 2011 from: http://arxiv.org/new/withdrawals.aug.07.html

16. Associated Press (2006) Disgraced Korean Cloning Scientist Indicted. The New York Times, retrieved Oct. 31, 2012 from: http://www.nytimes.com/2006/05/12/world/asia/12korea.html

17. Autodesk Research (2012) Citeology: Visualizing Paper Genealogy. Online Source, retrieved Oct. 26, 2012 from: http://www.autodeskresearch.com/projects/citeology

18. Badge J, Scott J (2009) Dealing with Plagiarism in the Digital Age. Report for the Higher Education Academy EvidenceNet, retrieved Jul. 19,

2011 from http://evidencenet.pbworks.com/Dealing-with-plagiarism-in-the-digital-age

19. Baker BS (1992) A Program for Identifying Duplicated Code. In: Proceedings of the 24th Symposium on the Interface, College Station, TX, USA, pp 49–57

20. Baker BS (1993) On Finding Duplication in Strings and Software. Online Source, retrieved Jun. 16, 2010 from: http://cm.bell-labs.com/cm/cs/doc/-93/2-bsb-1.ps.gz

21. Ballard B (1989) Mutual Misconceptions: the Intellectual Problems of Overseas Students in Australia. Directions, Journal of Educational Studies 11(1):48–60

22. Bao J, Lyon C, Lane PCR, Wei J, Malcolm JA (2007) Comparing Different Text Similarity Methods. Tech. rep., Technical Report 461, Science and Technology Research Institute, University of Hertfordshire

23. Barrett R, Malcolm J (2006) Embedding Plagiarism Education in the Assessment Process. International Journal for Educational Integrity 2(1):38–45

24. Basile C, Benedetto D, Caglioti E, Cristadoro G, Esposti MD (2009) A Plagiarism Detection Procedure in Three Steps: Selection, Matches and "Squares". In: Proceedings of the 3rd PAN Workshop. Uncovering Plagiarism, Authorship and Social Software Misuse

25. Beel J, Gipp B (2009) Google Scholar's Ranking Algorithm: An Introductory Overview. In: Larsen B, Leta J (eds) Proceedings of the 12th International Conference on Scientometrics and Informetrics (ISSI'09), International Society for Scientometrics and Informetrics, Rio de Janeiro (Brazil), vol 1, pp 230–241

26. Beel J, Gipp B (2009) Google Scholar's Ranking Algorithm: The Impact of Citation Counts (An Empirical Study). In: Flory A, Collard M (eds) Proceedings of the 3rd IEEE International Conference on Research Challenges in Information Science (RCIS'09), IEEE, Fez, Morocco, pp 439–446, doi: 10.1109/RCIS.2009.5089308

27. Beel J, Gipp B (2010) Academic Search Engine Spam and Google Scholar's Resilience Against it. Journal of Electronic Publishing 13(3), doi: 10.3998/3336451.0013.305

28. Beel J, Gipp B (2010) Detection of a similarity of documents by Citation Proximity Analysis. Patent Application, wO/2010/078857

29. Beel J, Gipp B, Shaker A, Friedrich N (2010) SciPlore Xtract: Extracting Titles from Scientific PDF Documents by Analyzing Style Information (Font Size). In: Lalmas M, Jose J, Rauber A, Sebastiani F, Frommholz I (eds) Research and Advanced Technology for Digital Libraries, Proceedings of the 14th European Conference on Digital Libraries (ECDL'10), Springer, Glasgow (UK), Lecture Notes of Computer Science (LNCS), vol 6273, pp 413–416

30. Beel J, Gipp B, Wilde E (2010) Academic Search Engine Optimization (ASEO): Optimizing Scholarly Literature for Google Scholar and Co. Journal of Scholarly Publishing 41(2):176–190, doi: 10.3138/jsp.41.2.176, university of Toronto Press

31. Beel J, Gipp B, Langer S, Genzmehr M, Wilde E, Nürnberger A, Pitman J (2011) Introducing Mr. DLib, a Machine-readable Digital Library. In: Proceedings of the 11th ACM/IEEE Joint Conference on Digital Libraries (JCDL'11)

32. Beel J, Gipp B, Stiller JO (2011) Method for determining a similarity of objects. Patent Application, wO/2011/044865

33. Bernstein Y, Zobel J (2004) A Scalable System for Identifying Co-derivative Documents. In: String Processing and Information Retrieval, Lecture Notes in Computer Science, vol 3246, Springer, pp 1–11, doi: 10.1007/978-3-540-30213-1_6

34. Blackboard Inc (2011) Safe Assign. Online Source, retrieved Oct. 28, 2011 from: http://www.safeassign.com/

35. Bloomfield LA (2009) Software to detect plagiarism: WCopyfind. Online Source, retrieved Oct. 1, 2010 from: http://plagiarism.phys.virginia.edu/-Wsoftware.html

36. Stegemann Boehl S (1994) Fehlverhalten von Forschern. Thieme

37. Boekel MAv, Vossenaar ER, van den Hoogen FH, van Venrooij WJ (2002) Autoantibody Systems in Rheumatoid Arthritis: Specificity, Sensitivity and Diagnostic Value. Arthritis Res 4:87–93, PMID11879544, PMC128920

38. Boyack KW, Newman D, Duhon RJ, Klavans R, Patek M, Biberstine JR, Schijvenaars B, Skupin A, Ma N, Börner K (2011) Clustering More than Two Million Biomedical Publications: Comparing the Accuracies of Nine Text-Based Similarity Approaches. PLoS ONE 6(3):e18,029, doi: 10.1371/journal.pone.0018029

39. Braam RR, Moed HF, van Raan AFJ (1991) Mapping of Science by Combined Co-Citation and Word Analysis. I. Structural Aspects. Journal of the American Society for Information Science 42(4):233–251

40. Bretag T, Mahmud S (2009) Self-Plagiarism or Appropriate Textual Re-use? Journal of Academic Ethics 7:193–205, doi: 10.1007/s10805-009-9092-1

41. Brin S, Davis J, Garcia Molina H (1995) Copy Detection Mechanisms for Digital Documents. In: Proceedings of the 1995 ACM SIGMOD International Conference on Management of Data, ACM, pp 398–409, doi: 10.1145/223784.223855

42. Broder AZ, Glassman SC, Manasse MS, Zweig G (1997) Syntactic Clustering of the Web. Computer Networks and ISDN Systems 29(8-13):1157–1166, doi: 10.1016/S0169-7552(97)00031-7

43. Brooks T (1986) Evidence of complex citer motivations. Journal of the American Society for Information Science 37(1):34–36

44. Brown BS (2001) Explaining Variations in the Level of Academic Dishonesty in Studies of College Students: Some New Evidence. College Student Journal 35(4):529–538

45. Brown BS, Abramson J (1999) The Academic Ethics of Undergraduate Marketing Majors. Academy of Marketing Studies Journal 3(1):62–71

46. Brown BS, Weible R (2006) Changes in Academic Dishonesty among MIS Majors between 1999 and 2004. Journal of Computing in Higher Education 18:116–134

47. Brown KA, Aakre ME, Gorska AE, Price JO, Eltom SE, Pietenpol JA, Moses HL (2004) Induction by Transforming Growth Factor-beta1 of Epithelial to Mesenchymal Transition is a Rare Event in Vitro. Breast Cancer Res 6:215–231, PMID11250748, PMC13902

48. Bruhn A, Hernandez G, Bugedo G, Castillo L (2004) Effects of positive end-expiratory pressure on gastric mucosal perfusion in acute respiratory distress syndrome. Critical Care 8(5):306–311, doi: 10.1186/cc2905, PMID15469573, PMC1065018

49. Buckley C, Dimmick D, Soboroff I, Voorhees E (2007) Bias and the Limits of Pooling for Large Collections. Inf Retr 10(6):491–508, doi: 10.1007/s10791-007-9032-x

50. Bull J, Colins C, Coughlin E, Sharp D (2000) Technical Review of Plagiarism Detection Software Report. Tech. rep., Joint Information System Committee

51. Butakov S, Scherbinin V (2009) The Toolbox for Local and Global Plagiarism Detection. Computers & Education 52(4):781–788, doi: 10.1016/j.compedu.2008.12.001

52. Buyko E, Wermter J, Poprat M, Hahn U (2006) Automatically Adapting an NLP Core Engine to the Biology Domain. In: Proceedings of the Joint BioLINK-Bio-Ontologies Meeting. A Joint Meeting of the ISMB Special Interest Group on Bio-Ontologies and the BioLINK Special Interest Group on Text Data Mining in Association with ISMB, pp 65–68

53. Calado P, Cristo M, Moura E, Ziviani N, Ribeiro Neto B, Gonçalves MA (2003) Combining Link-based and Content-based Methods for Web Document Classification. In: Proceedings of the 12th international conference on Information and knowledge management, ACM, pp 394–401, doi: 10.1145/956863.956938

54. Calado P, Cristo M, Gonçalves MA, de Moura ES, Ribeiro Neto B, Ziviani N (2006) Link-based Similarity Measures for the Classification of Web Documents. Journal of the American Society for Information Science and Technology 57:208–221, doi: 10.1002/asi.v57:2

55. Callahan A, Hockema S, Eysenbach G (2010) Contextual Cocitation: Augmenting Cocitation Analysis and its Applications. Journal of the American Society for Information Science and Technology 61:1130–1143, doi: 0.1002/asi.21313

56. Campbell DM, Chen WR, Smith RD (2000) Copy Detection Systems for Digital Documents. In: Tester T, Hubertus Tv (eds) Proceedings of the Conference on Advances in Digital Libraries, IEEE, Los Alamitos, CA, USA, LNS, vol 64654, pp 78–88, doi: 10.1109/ADL.2000.848372

57. Barrón Cedeño A, Rosso P (2009) On Automatic Plagiarism Detection Based on n-Grams Comparison. In: Advances in Information Retrieval, Lecture Notes in Computer Science, vol 5478, Springer, pp 696–700, doi: 10.1007/978-3-642-00958-7_69

58. Barrón Cedeño A, Rosso P, Pinto D, Juan A (2008) On Cross-lingual Plagiarism Analysis using a Statistical Model. In: Proceedings of the ECAI08 Workshop on Uncovering Plagiarism, Authorship and Social Software Misuse, CEUR-WS.org, CEUR Workshop Proceedings, vol 377

59. Ceska Z (2008) Plagiarism Detection Based on Singular Value Decomposition. In: Advances in Natural Language Processing, Lecture Notes in Computer Science, vol 5221, Springer, pp 108–119, doi: 10.1007/978-3-540-85287-2_11

60. CFL Software Ltd (2011) CopyCatch. Online Source, retrieved Oct. 1, 2011 from: http://cflsoftware.com/

61. Chan B, Koren G (2003) Pharmacological Treatment for Pregnant Women who Smoke Cigarettes. Tobacco Induced Diseases 1:165–174, PMID19570257, PMC2671545

62. Chan B, Koren G (2003) Pharmacological Treatment for Pregnant Women who Smoke Cigarettes. Tobacco Induced Diseases 1:165–174, PMID19570257, PMC2669555

63. Chang WI, Lawler EL (1994) Sublinear Approximate String Matching and Biological Applications. Algorithmica 12:327–344, doi: 10.1007/BF01185431

64. Chatzimarkakis   G   (2000)   Informationeller   Globalismus:
     Kooperationsmodell   globaler   Ordnungspolitik   am   Beispiel   des
     elektronischen Geschäftsverkehrs. Dissertation, Faculty of Philosophy,
     University of Bonn, retracted as plagiarism by the University of Bonn on
     Jul. 13, 2011.

65. Chen Y, Liu C, Xu X, Zhang X, Shen W (2012) Simple Mental
     Arithmetic is not so Simple: An ERP Study of the Split and Odd-even
     Effects in Mental Arithmetic. Neuroscience Letters 510, Issue 1:62–66,
     retraction   notice: http://www.sciencedirect.com/science/article/pii/-
     S0304394012000201

66. Chennagiri RJ, Critchley P, Giele H (2004) Duplicate publication in the
     Journal of Hand Surgery. British Journal of Hand Surgery 29:625–628,
     doi: 10.1016/j.jhsb.2004.04.005, PMID15542228

67. Chong M, Specia L, Mitkov R (2010) Using Natural Language
     Processing for Automatic Detection of Plagiarism. In: Proceedings of the
     4th International Plagiarism Conference 2010, Newcastle upon Tyne, UK

68. Chowdhury A, Frieder O, Grossman D, McCabe M (2002) Collection
     Statistics for Fast Duplicate Document Detection. ACM Transactions on
     Information   Systems   (TOIS)   20(2):171–191,   doi:
     10.1145/506309.506311

69. Clarke R (2006) Plagiarism by Academics: More Complex Than It
     Seems. Journal of the Association for Information Systems 7(2):91–121

70. Clarke SJ, Willett P (1997) Estimating the recall performance of Web
     search engines. Aslib Proceedings 49(7):184–189, doi: 10.1108/eb051463

71. Clough P (2000) Plagiarism in Natural and Programming Languages an
     Overview of Current Tools and Technologies. Tech. rep., Department of
     Computer Science, University of Sheffield

72. Clough P, Stevenson M (2011) Developing a Corpus of Plagiarised Short
     Answers. Language Resources and Evaluation 45:5–24, 10.1007/s10579-
     009-9112-1

73. Cohen MB (2006) The Best in CytoJournal: 2005. Cytojournal
     2006(3:21), doi: 10.1186/1742-6413-3-21, PMC1570476

74. Cole CA (2002) Academic Dishonesty among College Students: Themes of the Professional Literature, 1950-1997. Phd. thesis, The University of Texas at Austin

75. Cole SL, Vassar R (2007) The Alzheimer's Disease Beta-secretase Enzyme, BACE1. Mol Neurodegener 2:22, PMID18005427, PMC2211305

76. Cole SL, Vassar R (2007) The Basic Biology of BACE1: a Key Therapeutic Target for Alzheimer's Disease. Current Genomics 8:509–530, PMID19415126, PMC2647160

77. Collberg C, Kobourov S (2005) Self-plagiarism in Computer Science. Commununications of the ACM 48(4):88–94, doi: 10.1145/1053291.1053293

78. Cooper WS (1968) Expected search length: a single measure of retrieval effectiveness based on the weak ordering action of retrieval systems. Journal of the American Society for Information Science and Technology 19(1):30–41, doi: 10.1002/asi.5090190108

79. Couto T, Cristo M, Gonçalves MA, Calado P, Ziviani N, Moura E, Ribeiro Neto B (2006) A Comparative Study of Citations and Links in Document Classification. In: Proceedings of the 6th ACM/IEEE-CS Joint Conference on Digital Libraries, ACM, pp 75–84, doi: 10.1145/1141753.1141766

80. Cristo M, Calado P, de Moura E, Ziviani N, Ribeiro Neto B (2003) Link Information as a Similarity Measure in Web Classification. In: String Processing and Information Retrieval, Lecture Notes in Computer Science, vol 2857, Springer, pp 43–55

81. Crochemore M, Rytter W (2002) Jewels of Stringology. World Scientific Publishing

82. Crown DF, Spiller MS (1998) Learning from the Literature on Collegiate Cheating: A Review of Empirical Research. Journal of Business Ethics 17:683–700, doi: 10.1023/A:1017903001888

83. Culwin F (2006) An Active Introduction to Academic Misconduct and the
     Measured Demographics of Misconduct. Assessment & Evaluation in
     Higher Education 31(2):167–182, doi: 10.1080/02602930500262478

84. Culwin F (2009) The Efficacy of Turnitin and Google. In: Proceedings of
     the 10th Annual Conference of the Subject Centre for Information and
     Computer Sciences, HE Academy, Subject Centre for ICS

85. Culwin F, Warwick J, Child M (2008) An Empirical Investigation of
     Student Behaviour when Non-originality Detection is Made Available
     before Submission. In: Proceedings of the 3rd International Plagiarism
     Conference, Newcastle upon Tyne, UK

86. Dean J, Henzinger MR (1999) Finding Related Pages in the World Wide
     Web. Computer Networks 31:1467–1479, doi: 10.1016/S1389-
     1286(99)00022-5

87. Deer B (2004) Revealed: MMR Research Scandal. The Sunday Times,
     retrieved Oct. 31, 2012 from: http://briandeer.com/mmr/lancet-deer-1.htm

88. Devi SL, Rao PRK, Ram VS, Akilandeswari A (2010) External
     Plagiarism Detection - Lab Report for PAN at CLEF 2010. In: Notebook
     Papers of CLEF 2010 LABs and Workshops

89. Devlin M (2002) Plagiarism Detection Software: How Effective is it? In:
     Assessing Learning in Australian Universities, Centre for the Study of
     Higher Education, University of Melbourne and the Australian
     Universities Teaching Committee

90. Dickinson HO, Hrisos S, Eccles MP, Francis J, Johnston M (2010)
     Statistical Considerations in a Systematic Review of Proxy Measures of
     Clinical Behaviour. Implementation Science 5:20, PMID20187923,
     PMC2846869

91. Divita G, Browne A, Loane R (2006) dTagger: a POS Tagger. In:
     Proceedings of the Annual AMIA Symposium, pp 200–203

92. Déjà Vu (2011) A Study of Scientific Publication Ethics. Online Source,
     retrieved May 29, 2012 from: http://dejavu.vbi.vt.edu/dejavu/

93. Docoloc UG & Co KG (2011) Docoloc. Online Source, retrieved Aug. 8,
     2011 from: http://www.docoloc.com

94. Dreher H (2007) Automatic Conceptual Analysis for Plagiarism Detection. Information and Beyond: The Journal of Issues in Informing Science and Information Technology 4:601–614

95. Durani P (2006) Duplicate publications: redundancy in plastic surgery literature. Journal of Plastic, Reconstructive & Aesthetic Surgery 59:975–7, doi: 10.1016/j.bjps.2005.11.039, PMID16920591

96. Egghe L, Rousseau R (1990) Introduction to Informetrics : Quantitative Methods in Library, Documentation and Information Science. Elsevier Science Publishers, http://hdl.handle.net/10760/6011

97. Meyer zu Eissen S, Stein B (2006) Intrinsic Plagiarism Detection. In: Proceedings of the 28th European Conference on IR Research, Springer, London, UK, Lecture Notes in Computer Science, vol 3936, pp 565–569, doi: 10.1007/11735106_66

98. Meyer zu Eissen S, Stein B, Kulig M (2007) Plagiarism Detection without Reference Collections. In: Proceedings of the 30th Annual Conference of the Gesellschaft für Klassifikation e.V., Springer, Berlin, Germany, pp 359–366, doi: 10.1007/978-3-540-70981-7_40

99. Aaron Elkiss, Siwei Shen, Anthony Fader, Günes, Erkan, David States, Dragomir Radev (2008) Blind Men and Elephants: What Do Citation Summaries Tell Us About a Research Article? Journal of the American Society for Information Science and Technology 59(1):51–62, doi: 10.1002/asi.20707

100. Ephorus BV (2011) Ephorus. Online Source, retrieved Aug. 8, 2011 from: https://www.ephorus.com/en/home

101. Epstein SK (2004) Extubation failure: an outcome to be avoided. Critical Care 8(5):310–312, doi: 10.1186/cc2927, PMID15469587, PMC1065026

102. Ercegovac Z, Richardson Jr JV (2004) Academic Dishonesty, Plagiarism Included, in the Digital Age: a Literature Review. College and Research Libraries 65(4):301–318

103. Ernst H (1959) Design and Evaluation of a Literature Retrieval Scheme. Master's thesis, Massachusetts Institute of Technology, cited according to: E. Garfield. Science Citation Index - A New Dimension in Indexing.

Science, 144 (3619): 649–654, May 1964. doi: 10.1126/science.144.3619.649.

104. Errami M, Hicks JM, Fisher W, Trusty D, Wren JD, Long TC, Garner HR (2008) Déjà Vu — a Study of Duplicate Citations in Medline. Bioinformatics 24(2):243–249, doi: 10.1093/bioinformatics/btm574, http://bioinformatics.oxfordjournals.org/content/24/2/243.full.pdf+html

105. Errami M, Sun Z, Long TC, George AC, Garner HR (2009) Déjà Vu: a Database of Highly Similar Citations in the Scientific Literature. Nucleic Acids Research 37(Suppl. 1):D921–D924, doi: 10.1093/nar/gkn546, http://nar.oxfordjournals.org/content/37/suppl_1/D921.full.pdf+html

106. Eto M (2012) Evaluations of Context-based Co-Citation Searching. Scientometrics 94(2):651–673, doi: 10.1007/s11192-012-0756-z

107. Fang FC, Steen RG, Casadevall A (2012) Misconduct Accounts for the Majority of Retracted Scientific Publications. Proceedings of the National Academy of Sciences 109(42):17,028–17,033, doi: 10.1073/pnas.1212247109

108. Fano RM (1956) Documentation in Action, Reinhold Publ. Co., New York, chap Information Theory and the Retrieval of Recorded Information, pp 238–244

109. Fellbaum C (1998) WordNet: an Electronic Lexical Database (Language, Speech, and Communication). The MIT Press

110. Ferrini F, Salio C, Lossi L, Merighi A (2009) Ghrelin in central neurons. Current Neuropharmacology 7(1):37–49, doi: 10.2174/157015909787602779, PMID19721816, PMC2724662

111. Finkel RA, Zaslavsky AB, Monostori K, Schmidt HW (2002) Signature Extraction for Overlap Detection in Documents. In: Proceedings of the 25th Australasian Computer Science Conference, Australian Computer Society Inc., Melbourne, Australia, Conferences in Research and Practice in Information Technology, vol 4, pp 59–64

112. Fiori R, Chiappa R, Gaspari E, Simonetti G (2010) A Rare Case of Popliteal Venous Aneurysm. Case Reports in Medicine 2010(Artuicle ID 579256), doi: 10.1155/2010/579256, PMID20224754, PMC2836132

113. Fishman T (2009) "We know it when we see it" is not good enough: toward a standard definition of plagiarism that transcends theft, fraud, and copyright. In: Proceedings of the 4th Asia Pacific Conference on Educational Integrity, http://www.bmartin.cc/pubs/09-4apcei/4apcei-Fishman.pdf

114. Couzin Frankel J, Grom J (2009) Plagiarism Sleuths. Science 324(5930):1004–1007, doi: 10.1126/science.324_1004, http://www.sciencemag.org/content/324/5930/1004.full.pdf

115. Fraser GE, Franke AA, Jaceldo-Siegl K, Bennett H (2010) Reliability of Serum and Urinary Isoflavone Estimates. Biomarkers 15:135–139

116. Fröhlich G (2006) Plagiate und unethische Autorenschaften. Information - Wissenschaft & Praxis 57(2):81—89

117. Garfield E (1964) Science Citation Index - a New Dimension in Indexing. Science 144(3619):649–654, doi: 10.1126/science.144.3619.649

118. Garfield E, Sher I (1963) New factors in the evaluation of scientific literature through citation indexing. American Documentation 14(3):195–201

119. Garfield E, Sher IH, Torpie RJ (1964) The Use of Citation Data in Writing the History of Science. Institute for Scientific Information

120. Garner BA (2011) Garner's Dictionary of Legal Usage, 3rd edn. Oxford University Press

121. Ghafouri M, Amini S, Khalili K, Sawaya BE (2006) HIV-1 Associated Dementia: Symptoms and Causes. Retrovirology 3:28, PMID16712719, PMC1513597

122. Gipp B (2006) (Co-)Citation Proximity Analysis - A Measure to Identify Related Work. Doctoral Proposal, otto-von-Guericke University, Germany, Supervisor: Prof. Claus Rautenstrauch

123. Gipp B (2009) Very Large Business Applications (VLBA): Systemlandschaften der Zukunft, Shaker Verlag, Magdeburg, chap Entwicklung neuer Verfahren zur Bestimmung von Dokumentenähnlichkeiten mittels Referenz- und Zitationsanalyse, pp

163–173. 3. Workshop des Centers for Very Large Business Applications (CVLBA)

124.   Gipp B (2010) Measuring Document Relatedness by Citation Proximity Analysis and Citation Order Analysis. In: Lalmas M, Jose J, Rauber A, Sebastiani F, Frommholz I (eds) Proceedings of the 14th European Conference on Digital Libraries (ECDL'10): Research and Advanced Technology for Digital Libraries, Springer, Lecture Notes of Computer Science (LNCS), vol 6273

125.   Gipp B (2011) Identifying Related Work and Plagiarism by Citation Analysis. Bulletin of IEEE Technical Committee on Digital Libraries (TCDL) 7(1)

126.   Gipp B, Beel J (2009) Citation Proximity Analysis (CPA) - A new approach for identifying related work based on Co-Citation Analysis. In: Larsen B, Leta J (eds) Proceedings of the 12th International Conference on Scientometrics and Informetrics (ISSI'09), International Society for Scientometrics and Informetrics, Rio de Janeiro (Brazil), vol 2, pp 571–575, iSSN 2175-1935

127.   Gipp B, Beel J (2010) Citation Based Plagiarism Detection - a New Approach to Identify Plagiarized Work Language Independently. In: Proceedings of the 21st ACM Conference on Hypertext and Hypermedia, ACM, pp 273–274, doi: 10.1145/1810617.1810671

128.   Gipp B, Beel J (2011) Method and System for Detecting a Similarity of Documents. Patent Application, http://www.patentlens.net/patentlens/-patent/US_2011_0264672_A1/en/, uS 2011/0264672 A1

129.   Gipp B, Meuschke N (2011) Citation Pattern Matching Algorithms for Citation-based Plagiarism Detection: Greedy Citation Tiling, Citation Chunking and Longest Common Citation Sequence. In: Proceedings of the 11th ACM Symposium on Document Engineering, ACM, Mountain View, CA, USA, pp 249–258, doi: 10.1145/2034691.2034741

130.   Gipp B, Beel J, Hentschel C (2009) Scienstein: A Research Paper Recommender System. In: Proceedings of the International Conference on Emerging Trends in Computing (ICETiC'09), Kamaraj College of

Engineering and Technology India, IEEE, Virudhunagar (India), pp 309–315

131. Gipp B, Taylor A, Beel J (2010) Link Proximity Analysis - Clustering Websites by Examining Link Proximity. In: Lalmas M, Jose J, Rauber A, Sebastiani F, Frommholz I (eds) Proceedings of the 14th European Conference on Digital Libraries (ECDL'10): Research and Advanced Technology for Digital Libraries, Springer, Lecture Notes of Computer Science (LNCS), vol 6273, pp 449–452

132. Gipp B, Meuschke N, Beel J (2011) Comparative Evaluation of Text- and Citation-based Plagiarism Detection Approaches using GuttenPlag. In: Proceedings of 11th ACM/IEEE-CS Joint Conference on Digital Libraries (JCDL'11), ACM, Ottawa, Canada, pp 255–258, doi: 10.1145/1998076.1998124

133. Gipp B, Meuschke N, Breitinger C, Lipinski M, Nürnberger A (2013) Demonstration of the First Citation-based Plagiarism Detection Prototype. In: Proceedings of the 36th International ACM SIGIR conference on research and development in Information Retrieval, ACM, Dublin, Ireland, pp 1119–1120, doi: 10.1145/2484028.2484214

134. Gipp B, Meuschke N, Lipinski M, Nürnberger A (2013) CITREC: An Evaluation Framework for Citation-Based Similarity Measures Based on TREC Genomics and PMC, to be published

135. Gipp B, Meuschke N, Breitinger C (2014) Citation-based Plagiarism Detection: Practicability on a Large-scale Scientific Corpus. Journal of the American Society for Information Science and Technology

136. Glänzel W (2003) Bibliometrics as a Research Field - a Course on Theory and Application of Bibliometric Indicators. Course Handout, retrieved Jul. 13, 2010 from: http://nsdl.niscair.res.in/bitstream/123456789/968/1/

137. Goan T, Fujioka E, Kaneshiro R, Gasch L (2006) Identifying Information Provenance in Support of Intelligence Analysis, Sharing, and Protection. In: Intelligence and Security Informatics, Lecture Notes in Computer Science, vol 3975, Springer, pp 692–693, doi: 10.1007/11760146_93

138. Goldbach-Mansky R, Lee J, McCoy A, Hoxworth J, Yarboro C, Smolen JS, Steiner G, Rosen A, Zhang C, Ménard HA, Zhou Zhi Jie, Palosuo T, Van Venrooij aWR Walther J, Klippel SRH John H, Gabalawy Sani H E (2000) Rheumatoid Arthritis Associated Autoantibodies in Patients with Synovitis of Recent Onset. Arthritis Research 2:236–243, PMID11056669, PMC17811

139. Griffith BC, Small HG, Stonehill JA, Dey S (1974) The Structure of Scientific Literatures II: toward a Macro- and Microstructure for Science. Science Studies 4(4):339–365

140. Grman J, Ravas R (2011) Improved Implementation for Finding Text Similarities in Large Collections of Data. In: Notebook Papers of CLEF 2011 LABs and Workshops, Amsterdam, Netherlands

141. Grose R (2004) Common Ground in the Transcriptional Profiles of Wounds and Tumors. Genome Biology 5:228, PMID15186486, PMC463068

142. Grozea C, Popescu M (2010) Encoplot - Performance in the Second International Plagiarism Detection Challenge. In: Notebook Papers of CLEF 2010 LABs and Workshops, Padua, Italy

143. Grozea C, Gehl C, Popescu M (2009) ENCOPLOT: Pairwise Sequence Matching in Linear Time Applied to Plagiarism Detection. In: Proceedings of the 3rd PAN Workshop. Uncovering Plagiarism, Authorship and Social Software Misuse

144. Gruner S, Naven S (2005) Tool Support for Plagiarism Detection in Text Documents. In: Proceedings of the 2005 ACM Symposium on Applied Computing, ACM, pp 776–781, doi: 10.1145/1066677.1066854

145. Gutbrod MA (2007) Nachhaltiges E-Learning durch Sekundäre Dienste. Dissertation, Institute of Operating Systems and Computer Networks, Technische Universität Braunschweig

146. Guttenberg KTz (2009) Verfassung und Verfassungsvertrag: Konstitutionelle Entwicklungsstufen in den USA und der EU. Dissertation, Faculty of Law, Business Administration and Economics,

University of Bayreuth, retracted as plagiarism by the University of Bayreuth on May 5, 2011.

147. GuttenPlag Wiki (2011) Eine kritische Auseinandersetzung mit der Dissertation von Karl-Theodor Freiherr zu Guttenberg: Verfassung und Verfassungsvertrag. Konstitutionelle Entwicklungsstufen in den USA und der EU. Online Source, retrieved Apr. 25, 2012 from: http://-de.guttenplag.wikia.com/wiki/GuttenPlag_Wiki

148. Gyan S, Sushma S, Maneesh S, Rajesh S, Misra M (2010) Successful microsurgical penile replantation following self amputation in a schizophrenic patient. Indian Journal of Urology 26(3):434–437, doi: 10.4103/0970-1591.70589

149. Haller S (2003) Das Sanierungsgebiet Hemshof in Ludwigshafen am Rhein: Eine Bilanz von 30 Jahren baulicher Erneuerung und sozialer Veränderung. Dissertation, Faculty of Philosophy III: Educational Science, University of Halle, http://sundoc.bibliothek.uni-halle.de/diss-online/03/06H158/prom.pdf, retracted as plagiarism by the Martin-Luther-University Halle-Wittenberg on Apr. 18, 2012.

150. Hariharan S, Kamal S, Faisal AVM, Azharudheen SM, Raman B (2010) Detecting Plagiarism in Text Documents. In: Proceedings of the International Conference on Recent Trends in Business Administration and Information Processing, Springer, Trivandrum, Kerala, India, Communications in Computer and Information Science, vol 70, pp 497–500, doi: 10.1007/978-3-642-12214-9_86

151. Heather J (2010) Turnitoff: Identifying and Fixing a Hole in Current Plagiarism Detection Software. Assessment & Evaluation in Higher Education 35(6):647–660, doi: 10.1080/02602938.2010.486471

152. Heinrich-Heine University of Düsseldorf (2013) Der Fakultätsrat der Philosophischen Fakultät. Online, retrieved Apr. 3, 2013 from: http://-www.phil-fak.uni-duesseldorf.de/organisation/fakultaetsrat/

153. Heinrich-Heine University of Düsseldorf (2013) Promotionsprüfungsverfahren Prof. Dr. Schavan - Aktuelle Sitzung des Fakultätsrats der Philosophischen Fakultät und Presseerklärung vom

05.02.2013. Press Release, retrieved Feb. 25, 2013 from: http://www.uni-duesseldorf.de/home/startseite/news-detailansicht/article/aktuelle-sitzung-des-fakultaetsrats-der-philosophischen-fakultaet-und-presseerklaerung-vom-0502.html

154. Heintze N (1996) Scalable Document Fingerprinting. In: 1996 USENIX Workshop on Electronic Commerce

155. Hetzner E (2008) A Simple Method for Citation Metadata Extraction using Hidden Markov Models. In: Proceedings of the 8th ACM/IEEE-CS Joint Conference on Digital Libraries, ACM, pp 280–284, doi: 10.1145/1378889.1378937

156. Heun M (2007) Finanzmarktsimulation mit Multiagentensystemen: Entwicklung eines methodischen Frameworks. Deutscher Universitäts-Verlag

157. Hill JD, Page EF (2009) An Empirical Research Study of the Efficacy of Two Plagiarism-Detection Applications. Journal of Web Librarianship 3(3):169–181, doi: 10.1080/19322900903051011

158. Hoad TC, Zobel J (2003) Methods for Identifying Versioned and Plagiarised Documents. Journal of the American Society for Information Science and Technology 54(3):203–215, doi: 10.1002/asi.10170

159. Hohenester S, Oude Elferink RPJ, Beuers U (2009) Primary Biliary Cirrhosis. Seminars in Immunopathology 31:283–307, PMID19603170, PMC2758170

160. Holmes DI (1998) The Evolution of Stylometry in Humanities Scholarship. Literary and Linguistic Computing 13(3):111–117, doi: 10.1093/llc/13.3.111, http://llc.oxfordjournals.org/content/13/3/111.full.pdf+html

161. Howard RM (2007) Understanding "Internet plagiarism". Computers and Composition 24(1):3–15, doi: 10.1016/j.compcom.2006.12.005

162. Hrisos S, Eccles MP, Francis JJ, Dickinson HO, Kaner EF, Beyer F, Johnston M (2009) Are There Valid Proxy Measures of Clinical Behaviour? A Systematic Review. Implementation Science 4:37, PMID19575790, PMC2713194

163. Integru (2012) Review 6: Aurelia Cristina Nechifor, Ecaterina Andronescu (minister of research), 2003 – plagiarism and falsification of data. Online Source, retrieved Feb. 28, 2013 from: http://integru.org/-reviews/andronescu-2003

164. iParadigms LLC (2013) Turnitin Webpage - Content. Online Source, retrieved Feb. 28, 2013 from: http://turnitin.com/en_us/products/-originalitycheck/content

165. Jalel A, Soumaya GS, Hamdaoui MH (2009) Dermatology Life Quality Index Scores in Vitiligo: Reliability and Validity of the Tunesian Version. Indian Journal of Dermatology 54(4):3–330, doi: 10.4103/0019-5154.57607, PMID20101332, PMC2807707

166. Janssens F, Tran Quoc V, Glänzel W, De Moor B (2006) Integration of Textual Content and Link Information for Accurate Clustering of Science Fields. In: Proceedings of the I International Conference on Multidisciplinary Information Sciences & Technologies, pp 615–619

167. Janssens F, Zhang L, De Moor B, Glänzel W (2009) Hybrid Clustering for Validation and Improvement of Subject-classification Schemes. Information Processing and Management 45:683–702, doi: 10.1016/j.ipm.2009.06.003

168. Jarneving B (2005) A Comparison of Two Bibliometric Methods for Mapping of the Research Front. Scientometrics 65(2):245–263

169. Juola P (2008) Authorship Attribution. Foundations and Trends Information Retrieval 1:233–334, doi: 10.1561/1500000005

170. Kakkonen T, Mozgovoy M (2010) Hermetic and Web Plagiarism Detection Systems for Student Essays — an Evaluation of the State-of-the-Art. Journal of Educational Computing Research 42(2):135–159, doi: 10.2190/EC.42.2.a

171. Kang N, Gelbukh A, Han S (2006) PPChecker: Plagiarism Pattern Checker in Document Copy Detection. In: Text, Speech and Dialogue, Lecture Notes in Computer Science, vol 4188, Springer, pp 661–667, doi: 10.1007/11846406_83

172. Kasprzak J, Brandejs M (2010) Improving the Reliability of the Plagiarism Detection System - Lab Report for PAN at CLEF 2010. In: Notebook Papers of CLEF 2010 LABs and Workshops, Padua, Italy

173. Kasprzak J, Brandejs M, Kripac M (2009) Finding Plagiarism by Evaluating Document Similarities. In: Proceedings of the 3rd PAN Workshop. Uncovering Plagiarism, Authorship and Social Software Misuse

174. Kessler MM (1963) An Experimental Study of Bibliographic Coupling Between Technical Papers. IEEE Transactions on Information Theory 9:49–51

175. Khmelev DV, Teahan WJ (2003) A Repetition Based Measure for Verification of Text Collections and for Text Categorization. In: Proceedings of the 26th Annual International ACM SIGIR Conference on Research and Development in Information Retrieval, ACM, pp 104–110, doi: 10.1145/860435.860456

176. Kidwell LA, Wozniak K, Laurel JP (2003) Student Reports and Faculty Perceptions of Academic Dishonesty. Teaching Business Ethics 7:205–214, doi: 10.1023/A:1025008818338

177. Ko P, Aluru S (2003) Space Efficient Linear Time Construction of Suffix Arrays. Journal of Discrete Algorithms 2676:200–210, doi: 10.1007/3-540-44888-8_15

178. Koppel M, Schler J, Argamon S (2011) Authorship Attribution in the Wild. Language Resources and Evaluation 45(1):83–94, doi: 10.1007/s10579-009-9111-2

179. Kreider R, Almada A, Antonio J, Broeder C, Earnest C, Greenwood M, Incledon T, Kalman D, Kleiner S, Leutholtz B, Lowery L, Mendel R, Stout J, Willoughby D, Ziegenfuss T (2004) ISSN Exercise & Sport Nutrition Review: Research & Recommendations. Journal of the International Society of Sports Nutrition 1(1):1–44, doi: 10.1186/1550-2783-1-1-1, PMC2129137

180. Kreider RB, Wilborn CD, Taylor L, Campbell B, Almada AL, Collins R, Cooke M, Earnest CP, Greenwood M, Kalman DS, Kerksick CM, Kleiner

SM, Leutholtz B, Lopez H, Lowery LM, Mendel R, Smith A, Spano M, Wildman R, Willoughby DS, Ziegenfuss TN, Antonio J (2010) ISSN Exercise & Sport Nutrition Review: Research & Recommendations. Journal of the International Society of Sports Nutrition 7:7, PMID20181066, PMC2853497

181. Kulkarni AP, Agarwal V (2008) Extubation failure in intensive care unit: Predictors and management. Indian Journal of Critical Care Medicine 12(1):1–9, doi: 10.4103/0972-5229.40942, PMID19826583, PMC2760915

182. Kumagi T, Heathcote EJ (2008) Primary Biliary Cirrhosis. Orphanet Journal of Rare Diseases 3:1

183. Kurtz S (1999) Reducing the Space Requirement of Suffix Trees. Software-Practice and Experience 29(13):1149–1171, doi: 10.1002/(SICI)1097-024X(199911)29:13<1149::AID-SPE274>3.0.CO;2-O

184. Lachlan P (2012) The Sherlock Plagiarism Detector. Online Source, retrieved Jul. 11, 2012 from: http://sydney.edu.au/engineering/it/~scilect/-sherlock/

185. Lancaster T (2003) Effective and Efficient Plagiarism Detection. Phd thesis, School of Computing, Information Systems and Mathematics, South Bank University, retrieved on Jul. 9, 2013 from http://-academia.edu/168972/Effective_and_Efficient_Plagiarism_Detection

186. Lane P (2011) Ferret Copy Detection Software. Online Source, retrieved Oct. 1, 2011 from: http://homepages.feis.herts.ac.uk/~comqpcl/ferret.html

187. Larsen B (2004) References and citations in automatic indexing and retrieval systems - experiments with the boomerang effect. PhD thesis, Department of Information Studies, Royal School of Library and Information Science, Copenhagen

188. LeBaron B (2005) Agent-based Computational Finance. In: Handbook of Computational Economics, International Business School, Brandeis University, retrieved May 28, 2013 from: people.brandeis.edu/~blebaron/-wps/hbook.pdf

189. Leucht S, Kissling W, Davis JM (2009) How to Read and Understand and Use Systematic Reviews and Meta-analyses. Acta Psychiatrica Scandinavica 119(6):443–450, doi: 10.1111/j.1600-0447.2009.01388.x

190. Leung CH, Chan YY (2007) A Natural Language Processing Approach to Automatic Plagiarism Detection. In: Proceedings of the 8th ACM SIGITE Conference on Information Technology Education, ACM, pp 213–218, doi: 10.1145/1324302.1324348

191. Lewis J, Ossowski S, Hicks J, Errami M, Garner HR (2006) Text Similarity: an Alternative Way to Search Medline. Bioinformatics 22(18):2298–2304, doi: 10.1093/bioinformatics/btl388

192. Liberati A, Altman DG, Tetzlaff J, Mulrow C, Gøtzsche PC, Ioannidis JP, Clarke M, Devereaux PJ, Kleijnen J, Moher D (2009) The Prisma Statement for Reporting Systematic Reviews and Meta-analyses of Studies that Evaluate Healthcare Interventions: Explanation and Elaboration. BMJ 339:1–27, PMID19189221, PMC2764094

193. Liberati A, Altman DG, Tetzlaff J, Mulrow C, Gøtzsche PC, Ioannidis JP, Clarke M, Devereaux PJ, Kleijnen J, Moher D (2009) The Prisma Statement for Reporting Systematic Reviews and Meta-analyses of Studies that Evaluate Health Care Interventions: Explanation and Elaboration. PLoS Medicine 6:1–28, doi: e1000100. doi:10.1371/journal.pmed.1000100, PMID19192942, PMC2634792

194. Lim VKG, See SKB (2001) Attitudes toward, and Intentions to Report, Academic Cheating among Students in Singapore. Ethics & Behavior 11(3):261–274, doi: 10.1207/S15327019EB1103_5

195. Lipinski M, Yao K, Breitinger C, Beel J, Gipp B (2013) Evaluation of Header Metadata Extraction Approaches and Tools for Scientific PDF Documents. In: Proceedings of the 13th ACM/IEEE-CS Joint Conference on Digital Libraries (JCDL), ACM, New York, NY, USA, pp 385–386, doi: 10.1145/2467696.2467753, http://doi.acm.org/10.1145/-2467696.2467753

196. Little J, Higgins JP, Ioannidis JP, Moher D, Gagnon F, von Elm E, Khoury MJ, Cohen B, Davey Smith G, Grimshaw J, Scheet P, Gwinn M,

Williamson RE, Zou GY, Hutchings K, Johnson CY, Tait V, Wiens M, Golding J, van Duijn C, McLaughlin J, Paterson A, Wells G, Fortier I, Freedman M, Zecevic M, King R, Infante Rivard C, Stewart A, Birkett N (2009) Strengthening the Reporting of Genetic Association Studies (STREGA): an Extension of the STROBE Statement. PLoS Med 6:1–13, doi: 10.1371/journal.pmed.1000022, PMID19192942, PMC2634792

197. Little J, Higgins JP, Ioannidis JP, Moher D, Gagnon F, von Elm E, Khoury MJ, Cohen B, Davey Smith G, Grimshaw J, Scheet P, Gwinn M, Williamson RE, Zou GY, Hutchings K, Johnson CY, Tait V, Wiens M, Golding J, van Duijn C, McLaughlin J, Paterson A, Wells G, Fortier I, Freedman M, Zecevic M, King R, Infante Rivard C, Stewart A, Birkett N (2009) Strengthening the Reporting of Genetic Association Studies (STREGA): an Extension of the STROBE Statement. Eur J Epidemiol 24:37–55, PMID19189221, PMC2764094

198. Liu S, Chen C (2011) The Effects of Co-citation Proximity on Co-citation Analysis. In: Proceedings of the Conference of the International Society for Scientometrics and Informetrics

199. Liu S, Chen C (2012) The Proximity of Co-Citation. Scientometrics 91(2):495–511, doi: 10.1007/s11192-011-0575-7

200. Liu X, Yu S, Moreau Y, De Moor B, Glänzel W, Janssens FAL (2009) Hybrid Clustering of Text Mining and Bibliometrics Applied to Journal Sets. In: Proceedings of the SIAM International Conference on Data Mining, Sparks, NV, USA, pp 49–60

201. Liu X, Yu S, Janssens FAL, Glänzel W, Moreau Y, De Moor B (2010) Weighted Hybrid Clustering by Combining Text Mining and Bibliometrics on a Large-Scale Journal Database. Journal of the American Society for Information Science and Technology 61(6):1105–1119, doi: 10.1002/asi.21312

202. Long TC, Errami M, George AC, Sun Z, Garner HR (2009) Responding to Possible Plagiarism. Science 323(5919):1293–1294, doi: 10.1126/science.1167408, http://www.sciencemag.org/content/323/5919/1293.full.pdf

203. Lyon C, Malcolm J, Dickerson B (2001) Detecting Short Passages of Similar Text in Large Document Collections. In: Proceedings of the Conference on Empirical Methods in Natural Language Processing, pp 118–125

204. Lyon C, Barrett R, Malcolm J (2003) Experiments in Electronic Plagiarism Detection Computer Science Department. Tech. Rep. TR 388, School of Computer Science, University of Hertfordshire

205. MacPherson H, Altman DG, Hammerschlag R, Li Y, Wu T, White A, Moher D, Altman DG, Moher D, MacPherson H, Hammerschlag R, Li Y, Wu T, Birch S, Boutron I, Bovey M, Fei Y, Gagnier J, Hopewell S, Hopwood V, Jena S, Linde K, Liu J, Trinh K, Veitch E, White A, Yamashita H (2010) Revised Standards for Reporting Interventions in Clinical Trials of Acupuncture (STRICTA): Extending the CONSORT Statement. Acupunct Med 28:83–93, PMID20615861, PMC3002761

206. MacPherson H, Altman DG, Hammerschlag R, Youping L, Taixiang W, White A, Moher D, Burton A, Hopton A, Jenna S, Prady S, Stuardi T, Altman D, Moher D, MacPherson H, Hammerschlag R, Youping L, Taixiang W, Bovey M, Hopwood V, White A, Anastasi J, Birch S, Bosco J, Citkovitz C, Coeytaux R, Cohen M, Colbert A, Elden H, Filho RdeC, Forbes A, Foster N, Gagnier J, Goldby M, Gronlund M, Harris R, Irnich D, Langevin H, Lixing L, Lee A, Hyangsook L, Myeongsoo L, Sanghoon L, Lewith G, Linde K, Liu J, Milley R, Mist S, Melchart D, Molsberger A, Napadow V, Niemtzow R, Jongbae P, Saghaei M, Saputra K, Schnyer R, Shang C, Sherman K, Byung Cheul S, Smith C, Stener Victorin E, Trinh K, Vas J, Vickers A, White P, Witt C, Yamashita H, Zaslawski C, Birch S, Boutron I, Bovey M, Yutong F, Gagnier J, Hopewell S, Hopwood V, Jena S, Linde K, Jianping L, Trinh K, Veitch E, White A, Yamashita H (2010) Revised Standards for Reporting Interventions in Clinical Trials of Acupuncture (STRICTA): Extending the CONSORT Statement. PLoS Medicine 7:1–11, doi: 10.1371/journal.pmed.1000261, PMID20543992, PMC2882429

207. Malthan D (2011) PlagAware. Online Source, retrieved Oct. 1, 2011 from: http://www.plagaware.com

208. Manber U (1994) Finding Similar Files in a Large File System. In: Proceedings of the USENIX Winter Technical Conference, USENIX Association, Berkeley, CA, USA, pp 2–11

209. Manning CD, Raghavan P, Schütze H (2009) An Introduction to Information Retrieval, online edition edn. Cambridge University Press, Cambridge, England

210. Markram H, Rinaldi T, Markram K (2007) The Intense World Syndrome - an Alternative Hypothesis for Autism. Frontiers in Neuroscience 1:77–96

211. Markram K, Markram H (2010) The Intense World Theory - a Unifying Theory of the Neurobiology of Autism. Frontiers in Human Neuroscience 4:224, PMID21191475, PMC3010743

212. Marsden H, Carroll M, Neill JT (2005) Who Cheats At University? a Self-report Study of Dishonest Academic Behaviours in a Sample of Australian University Students. Australian Journal of Psychology 57(1):1–10, doi: 10.1080/00049530412331283426

213. Marshakova-Shaikevich I (1973) System of Document Connections Based on References. Scientific and Technical Information Serial of VINITI 6(2):3–8

214. Martin B (2007) Obstacles to Academic Integrity. In: Proceedings of the 3rd Asia-Pacific Conference on Educational Integrity, University of South Australia, Adelaide, pp 21–26

215. Martinson BC, Anderson MS (2005) Scientists Behaving Badly. Nature 435(7043):737–738, doi: 10.1038/435737a

216. Martyn J (1964) Bibliographic coupling. Journal of Documentation 20(4):236, doi: 10.1108/eb026352

217. Mathers C, Murray C (2003) Introduction of article-processing charges for Population Health Metrics. Population Health Metrics 1(1:8), doi: 10.1186/1478-7954-1-8, PMID14613521, PMC272941

218. Maurer H, Zaka B (2007) Plagiarism - a Problem and How to Fight It. In: Proceedings of World Conference on Educational Multimedia, Hypermedia and Telecommunications, AACE, Vancouver, Canada, pp 4451–4458

219. Maurer H, Kappe F, Zaka B (2006) Plagiarism - a Survey. Journal of Universal Computer Science 12(8):1050–1084, doi: 10.3217/jucs-012-08-1050

220. McCabe DL (2005) Cheating among College and University Students: A North American Perspective. International Journal for Academic Integrity 1(1):1–11

221. McCabe DL, Trevino LK (1993) Academic Dishonesty: Honor Codes and Other Contextual Influences. The Journal of Higher Education 64(5):522–538

222. McCabe DL, Trevino LK (1996) What We Know about Cheating in College: Longitudinal Trends and Recent Developments. Change 28(1):28–33

223. McCabe DL, Butterfield KD, Trevino LK (2006) Academic Dishonesty in Graduate Business Programs: Prevalence, Causes, and Proposed Action. Academy of Management Learning and Education 5(3):294

224. Mcnamee P, Mayfield J (2004) Character N-Gram Tokenization for European Language Text Retrieval. Information Retrieval 7:73–97, doi: 10.1023/B:INRT.0000009441.78971.be

225. Meho L, Yang K (2007) Impact of data sources on citation counts and rankings of LIS faculty: Web of Science vs. Scopus and Google Scholar. Journal of the American Society for Information Science and Technology 58(13):2105–25

226. Koch Mehrin S (2001) Historische Währungsunion zwischen Wirtschaft und Politik : die Lateinische Münzunion 1865 - 1927. Dissertation, Faculty of Philosophy, University of Heidelberg, retracted as plagiarism by the University of Heidelberg on Jun. 15, 2011.

227. Merton RK (1968) The Matthew Effect in Science. Science 159(3810):56–63, doi: 10.1126/science.159.3810.56

228. Meuschke N, Gipp B (2013) State of the Art in Detecting Academic Plagiarism. International Journal for Educational Integrity 9(1):50–71

229. Meuschke N, Gipp B, Breitinger C (2012) CitePlag: A Citation-based Plagiarism Detection System Prototype. In: Proceedings of the 5th International Plagiarism Conference, Newcastle upon Tyne, UK

230. Micol D, Ferrández Ó, Llopis F, Muñoz R (2010) A Textual-Based Similarity Approach for Efficient and Scalable External Plagiarism Analysis - Lab Report for PAN at CLEF 2010. In: CLEF (Notebook Papers/LABs/Workshops)

231. Miller G, Charles W (1991) Contextual correlates of semantic similarity. Language and cognitive processes 6(1):1–28

232. Monostori K, Zaslavsky A, Schmidt H (2000) Document Overlap Detection System for Distributed Digital Libraries. In: Proceedings of the 5th ACM Conference on Digital Libraries, ACM, pp 226–227, doi: 10.1145/336597.336667

233. Monostori K, Zaslavsky A, Bia A (2001) Using the MatchDetectReveal System for Comparative Analysis of Texts. In: Proceedings of the 6th Australasian Document Computing Symposium, Coffs Harbour, Australia, pp 51–58

234. Monostori K, Zaslavsky A, Schmidt H (2001) Efficiency of Data Structures for Detecting Overlaps in Digital Documents. Australian Computer Science Communications 23:140–147

235. Monostori K, Finkel R, Zaslavsky A, Hodász G, Pataki M (2002) Comparison of Overlap Detection Techniques. In: Proceedings of the International Conference on Computational Science, Springer, Amsterdam, Netherlands, Lecture Notes in Computer Science, vol 2329, pp 51–60

236. Monostori K, Zaslavsky A, Schmidt H (2002) Suffix Vector: Space- and Time-efficient Alternative to Suffix Trees. Australian Computer Science Communications 24(1):157–165, doi: 10.1145/563857.563820

237. Garnacho Montero J, Amaya Villar R (2006) A validated clinical approach for the management of aspergillosis in critically ill patients:

ready, steady, go! Critical Care 10(2):132–133, doi: 10.1186/cc4860, PMID16584528, PMC1550917

238. Muhr M, Zechner R Mario Kern, Granitzer M (2009) External and Intrinsic Plagiarism Detection Using Vector Space Models. In: Proceedings of the 3rd PAN Workshop. Uncovering Plagiarism, Authorship and Social Software Misuse, pp 47–55

239. Muhr M, Kern R, Zechner M, Granitzer M (2010) External and Intrinsic Plagiarism Detection Using a Cross-Lingual Retrieval and Segmentation System - Lab Report for PAN at CLEF 2010. In: Notebook Papers of CLEF 2010 LABs and Workshops, Padua, Italy

240. Neville LM, O'Hara B, Milat AJ (2009) Computer-tailored Dietary Behaviour Change Interventions: A Systematic Review. Health Education Research 24:699–720, PMID19286893, PMC2706490

241. Neville LM, O'Hara B, Milat AJ (2009) Computer-tailored Physical Activity Behavior Change Interventions Targeting Adults: a Systematic Review. The International Journal of Behavioral Nutrition and Physical Activity 6:30, PMID19490649, PMC2700068

242. Nikolaou C, Althammer S, Beato M, Guigo R (2010) Structural Constraints Revealed in Consistent Nucleosome Positions in the Genome of S. Cerevisiae. Epigenetics Chromatin 3:20, PMID21073701, PMC2994855

243. Norwegian Board of Health Supervision (2007) Case involving scientific fraud 2005-2006. Press Release, retrieved Oct. 31, 2012 from: http://-www.helsetilsynet.no/no/Norwegian-Board-of-Health-Supervision/-Decisions-in-individual-cases/Case-involving-scientific-fraud-2005-2006/

244. Noyons E, van Raan A (1994) Bibliometric Cartography of Scientific and Technological Developments of an R & D Field. Scientometrics 30:157–173, doi: 10.1007/BF02017220

245. Oberreuter G, L'Huillier G, Ríos SA, Velásquez JD (2010) FastDocode: Finding Approximated Segments of N-Grams for Document Copy Detection. In: Notebook Papers of CLEF 2010 LABs and Workshops, Padua, Italy

246. Oberreuter G, L'Huillier G, Ríos SA, Velásquez JD (2011) Approaches for Intrinsic and External Plagiarism Detection. In: Notebook Papers of CLEF 2011 LABs and Workshops, Amsterdam, Netherlands

247. O'Shea J, Bandar Z, Crockett K, McLean D (2008) A Comparative Study of Two Short Text Semantic Similarity Measures. In: Proceedings of the 2nd KES International Conference on Agent and Multi-agent Systems, Springer, pp 172–181

248. Palkovskii Y (2009) "Counter Plagiarism Detection Software" and "Counter Counter Plagiarism Detection" Methods. In: Proceedings of the 3rd Workshop on Uncovering Plagiarism, Authorship and Social Software Misuse and 1st International Competition on Plagiarism Detection

249. Papadakis MA, Wofsy D (2010) Plagiarism on Personal Statements: a Disturbing Symptom of a Broader Trend. Annals of Internal Medicine 153(2):128–129

250. Park C (2003) In Other Peoples Words: Plagiarism by University Students – Literature and Lessons. Assessment Evaluation in Higher Education 28(5):471–488, doi: 10.1080/02602930301677

251. Pawelzik B (2005) Algorithmen zur Plagiaterkennung. Student research project, Technische Universität Braunschweig Institut für Betriebssysteme und Rechnerverbund

252. Pera MS, Ng YK (2011) SimPaD: a Word-Similarity Sentence-Based Plagiarism Detection Tool on Web Documents. Web Intelligence and Agent Systems 9(1):24–41, doi: 10.3233/WIA-2011-0203

253. Pereira ARJ, Ziviani N (2004) Retrieving Similar Documents from the Web. Journal of Web Engineering 2(4):247–261

254. Pertsemlidis A, Garner H (2004) Engineering in Genomics: Text Comparison Based on Dynamic Programming. IEEE Engineering in Medicine and Biology Magazine 23(6):66–71, doi: 10.1109/MEMB.2004.1378640

255. Phelan T (1999) A Compendium of Issues for Citation Analysis. Scientometrics 45:117–136, doi: 10.1007/BF02458472

256. Piao S, Tsuruoka Y (2008) A Highly Accurate Sentence and Paragraph Breaker. Online Source, retrieved Jan. 28, 2011 from: http://-text0.mib.man.ac.uk:8080/scottpiao/sent_detector

257. Pinto D, Civera J, Barrón Cedeño A, Juan A, Rosso P (2009) A Statistical Approach to Crosslingual Natural Language Tasks. Journal of Algorithms 64(1):51–60, doi: 10.1016/j.jalgor.2009.02.005

258. Potsdamer Neuste Nachrichten Online (2012) Plagiatsstreit an der BTU um Vattenfall-Chef. Online Source, retrieved Aug. 2, 2012 from http://-www.pnn.de/brandenburg-berlin/663296/

259. Potthast M, Stein B, Anderka M (2008) A Wikipedia-based Multilingual Retrieval Model. In: Proceedings of the 30th European Conference on Advances in Information Retrieval, Springer, pp 522–530

260. Potthast M, Stein B, Eiselt A, Barrón Cedeño A, Rosso P (2009) Overview of the 1st International Competition on Plagiarism Detection. In: Proceedings of the 3rd Workshop on Uncovering Plagiarism, Authorship and Social Software Misuse and 1st International Competition on Plagiarism Detection, vol 502, pp 1–9

261. Potthast M, Barrón Cedeño A, Eiselt A, Stein B, Rosso P (2010) Overview of the 2nd International Competition on Plagiarism Detection. In: Notebook Papers of CLEF 2010 LABs and Workshops, Padua, Italy

262. Potthast M, Stein B, Barrón Cedeño A, Rosso P (2010) An Evaluation Framework for Plagiarism Detection. In: Proceedings of the 23rd International Conference on Computational Linguistics, Association for Computational Linguistics, Beijing, China, pp 997–1005

263. Potthast M, Barrón Cedeño A, Stein B, Rosso P (2011) Cross-language Plagiarism Detection. Language Resources and Evaluation 45(1):45–62, doi: 10.1007/s10579-009-9114-z

264. Potthast M, Eiselt A, Barrón-Cedeño A, Stein B, Rosso P (2011) Overview of the 3rd International Competition on Plagiarism Detection. In: Notebook Papers of CLEF 2011 LABs and Workshops, Amsterdam, Netherlands

265. Potthast M, Gollub T, Hagen M, Kiesel J, Michel M, Oberländer A, Tippmann M, Barrón Cedeño A, Gupta P, Rosso P, Stein B (2012) Overview of the 4th International Competition on Plagiarism Detection. In: CLEF 2012 Evaluation Labs and Workshop - Working Notes Papers, http://www.uni-weimar.de/medien/webis/research/events/pan-12/pan12-web/index.html

266. Pouliquen B, Steinberger R, Ignat C (2003) Automatic Identification of Document Translations in Large Multilingual Document Collections. In: Proceedings of the International Conference Recent Advances in Natural Language Processing, pp 401–408

267. Prechelt L, Philippsen M, Malpohl G (2000) JPlag: Finding Plagiarisms among a Set of Programs. Technical Report 2000-1, Universität Karlsruhe, Fakultät für Informatik, Germany

268. Oxford University Press (2009) A Dictionary of Psychology [electronic resource]. Oxford Reference Online, Oxford University Press, http://www.oxfordreference.com/

269. Price AR (2006) Cases of Plagiarism Handled by the United States Office of Research Integrity 1992-2005. Plagiary: Cross-Disciplinary Studies in Plagiarism, Fabrication, and Falsification 1:46–56

270. Solla Price DJd (1965) Networks of Scientific Papers. Science 149(3683):510–515, doi: 10.1126/science.149.3683.510

271. PrioInfo AB (2011) URKUND. Online Source, retrieved Oct. 1, 2011 from: http://www.urkund.com

272. Project SAX (2004) Simple API for XML (SAX). Online Source, retrieved May 29, 2012 from: http://www.saxproject.org/

273. Rakovski CC, Levy ES (2007) Academic Dishonesty: Perceptions of Business Students. College Student Journal 41(2):466

274. Ran EY, Mordechai N (2007) Optimal Single-Class Classification Strategies. In: Proceedings of the 20th Annual Conference on Neural Information Processing Systems, MIT Press, Vancouver, Canada, pp 377–384

275. Razera D, Verhagen H, Cerratto Pargman T, Ramberg R (2010) Plagiarism Awareness, Perception, and Attitudes among Students and Teachers in Swedish Higher Education – A Case Study. In: Proceedings of the 4th International Plagiarism Conference, Newcastle upon Tyne, UK

276. Resnik P (1999) Semantic Similarity in a Taxonomy: An Information-Based Measure and its Application to Problems of Ambiguity in Natural Language. Journal of Artificial Intelligence Research 11:95–130

277. Roberts P, Anderson J, Yanish P (1997) Academic Misconduct: Where Do We Start? Paper presented at the Annual Conference of the Northern Rocky Mountain Educational Research Association, retrieved Oct. 25, 2010 from: http://www.eric.ed.gov/ERICWebPortal/search/-permalinkPopup.jsp?accno=ED415781

278. Rossaint R, Bouillon B, Cerny V, Coats TJ, Duranteau J, Fernandez Mondejar E, Hunt BJ, Komadina R, Nardi G, Neugebauer E, Ozier Y, Riddez L, Schultz A, Stahel PF, Vincent JL, Spahn DR (2010) Management of bleeding following major trauma: an updated European guideline. Critical Care 14:R52, PMID20370902, PMC2887168

279. Rudman J (1997) The State of Authorship Attribution Studies: Some Problems and Solutions. Computers and the Humanities 31:351–365, doi: 10.1023/A:1001018624850

280. Saß V (2009) Regulierung im Mobilfunk. Dissertation, Department of Law, University of Konstanz, http://d-nb.info/99505147X, retracted as plagiarism by the University of Konstanz on May 11, 2011.

281. Sarkar S, Bhattacharya P, Kumar I, Mandal K (2009) Changes of splanchnic perfusion after applying positive end expiratory pressure in patients with acute respiratory distress syndrome. Indian Journal of Critical Care Medicine 13(1):12–16, doi: 10.4103/0972-5229.53109, PMID19881173, PMC2772258

282. Scaife B (2007) IT Consultancy Plagiarism Detection Software Report for JISC Plagiarism Advisory Service. Tech. rep., Joint Information System Committee

283. Scanlon PM, Neumann DR (2002) Internet Plagiarism among College Students. Journal of College Student Development 43(3):374–385

284. Scheers NJ, Dayton CM (1987) Improved Estimation of Academic Cheating Behavior Using the Randomized Response Technique. Research in Higher Education 26:61–69, doi: 10.1007/BF00991933

285. Scherbinin V, Butakov S (2009) Using Microsoft SQL Server Platform for Plagiarism Detection. In: Proceedings of the 3rd PAN Workshop. Uncovering Plagiarism, Authorship and Social Software Misuse

286. Schleimer S, Wilkerson DS, Aiken A (2003) Winnowing: Local Algorithms for Document Fingerprinting. In: Proceedings of the ACM SIGMOD International Conference on Management of Data, ACM, pp 76–85, doi: 10.1145/872757.872770

287. Scott D, Palmer R (2003) The Influence of Tobacco Smoking on Adhesion Molecule Profiles. Tobacco Induced Diseases 1:7–25, PMID19570245, PMC2669563

288. Scott D, Palmer R (2003) The Influence of Tobacco Smoking on Adhesion Molecule Profiles. Tobacco Induced Diseases 1:7–25, PMID19570245, PMC2671531

289. Scott JE (2004) The Pulmonary Surfactant: Impact of Tobacco Smoke and Related Compounds on Surfactant and Lung Development. Tobacco Induced Diseases 2:3–25, PMID19570267, PMC2669453

290. Scott JE (2004) The Pulmonary Surfactant: Impact of Tobacco Smoke and Related Compounds on Surfactant and Lung Development. Tobacco Induced Diseases 2(1):3–25, PMID19570267, PMC2671518

291. Seglen PO (1997) Why the Impact Factor of Journals Should Not Be Used for Evaluating Research. BMJ 314(7079):497

292. Semmelweis University of Budapest (2012) University Senate Revokes Pál Schmitt's Doctoral (Dr. Univ.) Title. Press Release, retrieved Mar. 30, 2012 from: http://www.semmelweis-univ.hu/news/2556/university-senate-revokes-pal-schmitt%E2%80%99s-doctoral-dr-univ-title/

293. Shen Y, Li SC, Tian CG, Cheng M (2009) Research on Anti-Plagiarism System and the Law of Plagiarism. In: Proceedings of the 1st

International Workshop on Education Technology and Computer Science, pp 296–300, doi: 10.1109/ETCS.2009.327

294. Sher IH, Garfield E (1966) New Tools for Improving and Evaluating the Effectiveness of Science. In: Proceedings of the Conference on Research Program Effectiveness, Gordon and Breach, Washington, D.C., USA, pp 135–146

295. Shibata N, Kajikawa Y, Takeda Y, Matsushima K (2009) Comparative Study on Methods of Detecting Research Fronts Using Different Types of Citation. Journal of the American Society for Information Science and Technology 60:571–580, doi: 10.1002/asi.v60:3

296. Shidham VB, Pitman MB, Demay RM, Atkinson BF (2008) CytoJournal's move to the new platform: More on financial model to the support open-access charter in cytopathology, publication quality indicators, and other issues. Cytojournal 5(15), doi: 10.4103/1742-6413.44572, PMID19495401, PMC2669682

297. Shivakumar N, Garcia Molina H (1995) SCAM a Copy Detection Mechanism for Digital Documents. In: Proceedings of the 2nd Annual Conference on the Theory and Practice of Digital Libraries, Austin, TX, USA

298. Shivakumar N, Garcia Molina H (1996) Building a Scalable and Accurate Copy Detection Mechanism. In: Proceedings of the 1st ACM International Conference on Digital Libraries, ACM, pp 160–168, doi: 10.1145/226931.226961

299. Si A, Leong V Hong, Lau RWH (1997) CHECK: a Document Plagiarism Detection System. In: Proceedings of the ACM Symposium on Applied Computing, ACM, pp 70–77, doi: 10.1145/331697.335176

300. SkyLine Inc (2011) Plagiarism Detector. Online Source, retrieved Oct. 1, 2011 from: http://www.plagiarism-detector.com

301. Small H (1973) Co-citation in the Scientific Literature: A New Measure of the Relationship Between Two Documents. Journal of the American Society for Information Science 24:265–269

302. Small H, Griffith BC (1974) The Structure of Scientific Literatures I: Identifying and Graphing Specialties. Science Studies 4(1):17–40

303. Smith H, Ridgway J (2008) Why Students Cheat (In Their Own Words as Well as those of Others). In: Proceedings of the 3rd International Plagiarism Conference, Newcastle upon Tyne, UK

304. Smith LC (1981) Citation Analysis. Library Trends 30(1):83–106

305. Smyth B (2003) Computing Patterns in Strings. Pearson Addison-Wesley, Harlow, England; New York

306. Snapper JW (1999) On the Web, Plagiarism Matters More Than Copyright Piracy. Ethics and Information Technology 1:127–135, doi: 10.1023/A:1010083703905

307. Sorokina D, Gehrke J, Warner S, Ginsparg P (2006) Plagiarism Detection in arXiv. Technical report computer science, Cornell University, TR2006-2046

308. Spahn DR, Cerny V, Coats TJ, Duranteau J, Fernandez Mondejar E, Gordini G, Stahel PF, Hunt BJ, Komadina R, Neugebauer E, Ozier Y, Riddez L, Schultz A, Vincent JL, Rossaint R (2007) Management of Bleeding Following Major Trauma: a European Guideline. Critical Care 11:R17, PMID17298665, PMC2151863

309. Spiegel Online (2013) Titelentzug vor Gericht: Schavan hat Klage eingereicht. Online Source, retrieved Feb. 21, 2013 from: http://-www.spiegel.de/unispiegel/studium/schavan-reichte-klage-gegen-entzug-des-doktortitels-ein-a-884435.html

310. Stamatatos E (2009) A Survey of Modern Authorship Attribution Methods. Journal of the American Society for Information Science and Technology 60(3):538–556, doi: 10.1002/asi.21001

311. Stamatatos E (2009) Intrinsic Plagiarism Detection Using Character n-gram Profiles. In: Proceedings of the 3rd PAN Workshop. Uncovering Plagiarism, Authorship and Social Software Misuse

312. Stamatatos E (2011) Plagiarism Detection Using Stopword N-grams. Journal of the American Society for Information Science and Technology 62(12):2512–2527, doi: 10.1002/asi.21630

313. Standler RB (2001) Plagiarism in Colleges in USA. Online Source, retrieved Oct. 27, 2011 from: http://www.rbs2.com/plag.htm

314. Stanford Natural Language Processing Group (2010) Stanford CoreNLP - a Suite of Core NLP Tools. Online Source, retrieved May 29, 2011 from: http://nlp.stanford.edu/software/corenlp.shtml

315. Steen RG (2011) Retractions in the Medical Literature: How Many Patients are Put at Risk by Flawed Research? Journal of Medical Ethics 37:688–692, doi: 10.1136/jme.2011.043133

316. Stein B, Meyer zu Eissen S (2006) Near Similarity Search and Plagiarism Analysis. In: Proceedings of the 29th Annual Conference of the Gesellschaft für Klassifikation e.V., Springer, Magdeburg, pp 430–437, doi: 10.1007/3-540-31314-1_52

317. Stein B, Meyer zu Eissen S, Potthast M (2007) Strategies for Retrieving Plagiarized Documents. In: Proceedings of the 30th Annual International ACM SIGIR Conference, ACM, pp 825–826, doi: 10.1145/1277741.1277928

318. Stein B, Koppel M, Stamatatos E (eds) (2007) Plagiarism Analysis Authorship Identification, and Near Duplicate Detection, CEUR Workshop Proceedings, vol 276, CEUR-WS.org, in Proceedings of the SIGIR 2007 International Workshop, held in conjunction with the 30th Annual International ACM SIGIR Conference, Amsterdam, Netherlands

319. Stein B, Lipka N, Prettenhofer P (2011) Intrinsic Plagiarism Analysis. Language Resources and Evaluation 45(1):63–82, doi: 10.1007/s10579-010-9115-y

320. Steinberger R, Pouliquen B, Hagman J (2002) Document Similarity Calculation Using the Multilingual Thesaurus EUROVOC. In: Proceedings of the 3rd International Conference on Computational Linguistics and Intelligent Text Processing, Springer, London, UK, pp 415–424

321. Sun Z, Errami M, Long T, Renard C, Choradia N, Garner H (2010) Systematic Characterizations of Text Similarity in Full Text Biomedical

Publications. PLoS ONE 5(9):e12,704, doi: 10.1371/journal.pone.0012704

322. Suárez P, González JC, Villena Román J (2010) A Plagiarism Detector for Intrinsic Plagiarism. In: Notebook Papers of CLEF 2010 LABs and Workshops, Padua, Italy

323. Sutherland-Smith W (2005) Pandora's Box: Academic Perceptions of Student Plagiarism in Writing. Journal of English for Academic Purposes 4(1):83–95, doi: 10.1016/j.jeap.2004.07.007

324. Swazey JP, Anderson MS, Louis KS (1993) Ethical Problems in Academic Research a Survey of Doctoral Candidates and Faculty Raises Important Questions About the Ethical Environment of Graduate Education and Research. American Scientist 81:542–553

325. Symvoulakis EK, Klinis S, Peteinarakis I, Kounalakis D, Antonakis N, Tsafantakis E, Lionis C (2008) Diagnosing a popliteal venous aneurysm in a primary care setting: A case report. Journal of Medical Case Reports 2, doi: 10.1186/1752-1947-2-307, PMID18808663, PMC2556343

326. Tan Z (2009) Erratum: Neural Protection by Naturopathic Compounds-an Example of Tetramethylpyrazine From Retina to Brain. Journal of Ocular Biology, Diseases, and Informatics 2:137–144, PMID20046848, PMC2798986

327. Tan Z (2009) Neural Protection by Naturopathic Compounds-an Example of Tetramethylpyrazine From Retina to Brain. Journal of Ocular Biology, Diseases, and Informatics 2:57–64, PMID19672463, PMC2723671

328. Tashiro T, Ueda T, Hori T, Hirate Y, Yamana H (2007) EPCI: Extracting Potentially Copyright Infringement Texts from the Web. In: Proceedings of the 16th International Conference on World Wide Web, ACM, pp 1151–1152, doi: 10.1145/1242572.1242740

329. Thornton DE (2010) Detect, Deter, and Disappear: the Plagiarism Prevention Project at Bilkent University, Turkey. In: Proceedings of the 4th International Plagiarism Conference, Newcastle upon Tyne, UK

330. Tran N, Alves P, Ma S, Krauthammer Michael (2009) Enriching PubMed Related Article Search with Sentence Level Co-citations. In: Proceedings

of the Annyual AMIA Symposium, pp 650–654, http://-www.ncbi.nlm.nih.gov/pmc/articles/PMC2815371/

331. Trof RJ, Beishuizen A, Debets Ossenkopp YJ, Girbes ARJ, Groeneveld ABJ (2007) Management of invasive pulmonary aspergillosis in non-neutropenic critically ill patients. Intensive Care Medicine 33(10):1694–1703, doi: 10.1007/s00134-007-0791-z, PMID17646966, PMC2039828

332. Trost K (2009) Psst, Have You Ever Cheated? A Study of Academic Dishonesty in Sweden. Assessment & Evaluation in Higher Education 34(4):367–376, doi: 10.1080/02602930801956067

333. Tsatsaronis G, Varlamis I, Giannakoulopoulos A, Kanellopoulos N (2010) Identifying Free Text Plagiarism Based on Semantic Similarity. In: Proceedings of the 4th International Plagiarism Conference, Newcastle upon Tyne, UK

334. Tsatsaronis G, Varlamis I, Vazirgiannis M (2010) Text Relatedness Based on a Word Thesaurus. Journal of Artificial Intelligence Research 37(1):1–40

335. U S National Library of Medicine (2011) Medline® Bibliographic Database. Online Source, retrieved Sep. 29, 2011 from: http://-www.nlm.nih.gov/pubs/factsheets/medline.html

336. Ukkonen E (1992) Constructing Suffix Trees On-Line in Linear Time. In: Proceedings of the IFIP 12th World Computer Congress on Algorithms, Software, Architecture - Information Processing, North-Holland Publishing Co., Amsterdam, Netherlands, vol 1, pp 484–492

337. Unser M (1999) Behavioral Finance am Aktienmarkt. Uhlenbruch

338. US National Center for Biotechnology Information (2011) PubMed Central. Online Source, retrieved Sep. 27, 2011 from: http://-www.ncbi.nlm.nih.gov/pmc/

339. Uzuner Ö, Katz B, Nahnsen T (2005) Using Syntactic Information to Identify Plagiarism. In: Proceedings of the 2nd Workshop on Building Educational Applications Using Natural Language Processing, Ann Arbor, MI, USA

340. Veldhuis JD, Bowers CY (2010) Integrating GHS into the Ghrelin System. International Journal of Peptides 2010(Article ID 879503), doi: 10.1155/2010/879503, PMID20798846, PMC2925380

341. Ventura LM (2009) Erratum: Psychoneuroimmunology: Application to Ocular Diseases. Journal of Ocular Biology, Diseases, and Informatics 2:109–118, PMID20046843, PMC2798981

342. Ventura LM (2009) Psychoneuroimmunology: Application to Ocular Diseases. Journal of Ocular Biology, Diseases, and Informatics 2:84–93, PMID19672468, PMC2723676

343. Verma AS, Singh UP, Dwivedi PD, Singh A (2010) Contribution of CNS Cells in Neuroaids. Journal of Pharmacy And Bioallied Sciences 2:300–306, PMID21180461, PMC2996080

344. Vile JR (1991) American Views of the Constitutional Amending Process: An Intellectual History of Article V. The American Journal of Legal History 35(1):44–69, http://www.jstor.org/stable/845582

345. Virk MS, Lieberman JR (2007) Tumor Metastasis to Bone. Arthritis Research and Therapy 9 Suppl. 1:S5, PMID17634144, PMC1924520

346. Vladutz J G & Cook (1984) Bibliographic coupling and subject relatedness. Proceedings of the American Society for Information Science 21:204–207

347. Vohra A, Vohra D (2006) Pro XML Development with Java Technology. Apress, Berkeley, CA, USA

348. Volk D (2003) Die Begrenzung kriegerischer Konflikte durch das moderne Völkerrecht. Dissertation, Faculty of Law, University of Würzburg

349. von Elm E, Poglia G, Walder B, Tramèr MR (2004) Different Patterns of Duplicate Publication: an Analysis of Articles Used in Systematic Reviews. JAMA: The Journal of the American Medical Association 291(8):974–980, doi: 10.1001/jama.291.8.974

350. VroniPlag Wiki (2012) VroniPlag - Collaborative Documentation of Plagiarism. Online Source, retrieved May 9, 2012 from: http://-de.vroniplag.wikia.com

351. Kevin W Boyack, Henry Small, Richard Klavans (2012) Improving the Accuracy of Co-citation Clustering Using Full Text. In: Proceedings of 17th International Conference on Science and Technology Indicators

352. Wang Y, Kitsuregawa M (2002) Evaluating Contents-link Coupled Web Page Clustering for Web Search Results. In: Proceedings of the 11th International Conference on Information and Knowledge Management, ACM, pp 499–506, doi: 10.1145/584792.584875

353. Weber-Wulff D (2004) Portal Plagiat - Softwaretest 2004. Online Source, retrieved May 29, 2012 from: http://plagiat.htw-berlin.de/ff-alt/05hilfen/-programme.html

354. Weber-Wulff D (2008) On the Utility of Plagiarism Detection Software. In: Proceedings of the 3rd International Plagiarism Conference, Newcastle upon Tyne, UK

355. Weber-Wulff D (2008) Portal Plagiat - Softwaretest 2008. Online Source, retrieved May 29, 2012 from: http://plagiat.htw-berlin.de/software/2008/

356. Weber-Wulff D (2010) Portal Plagiat - Softwaretest 2010. Online Source, retrieved May 29, 2012 from: http://plagiat.htw-berlin.de/software/2010-2/

357. Weber-Wulff D (2010) Test Cases for Plagiarism Detection Software. In: Proceedings of the 4th International Plagiarism Conference, Newcastle upon Tyne, UK

358. Weber-Wulff D (2011) Copy, Shake, and Paste - a Blog about Plagiarism written by a Professor for Media and Computing at the HTW. Online Source, retrieved Oct. 28, 2011 from: http://copy-shake-paste.blogspot.com

359. Weber-Wulff D (2012) Cottbus Refuses to Rescind Doctorate. Online Source, retrieved Jul. 27, 2012 from http://copy-shake-paste.blogspot.com/2012/06/cottbus-refuses-to-rescind-doctorate.html

360. Weber-Wulff D (2012) Portal Plagiat - Softwaretest Report 2012. Online Source, retrieved Nov. 27, 2012 from: http://plagiat.htw-berlin.de/-collusion-test-2012/

361. Weber-Wulff D, Köhler K (2011) Kopienjäger - Cloud-Software vs. menschliche Crowd in der Plagiaterkennung. iX Magazin für Professionelle Informationstechnik 6:78

362. Weber-Wulff D, Wohnsdorf G (2006) Strategien der Plagiatsbekämpfung. Information: Wissenschaft & Praxis 57:90–98, doi: ISSN 1434-4653, https://www.uni-hohenheim.de/fileadmin/einrichtungen/agrar/Studium/-Plagiate/strategien_plagiate.pdf

363. Weinberg BH (1974) Bibliographic Coupling: a Review. Information Storage and Retrieval 10:189–196

364. Whitley BE (1998) Factors Associated with Cheating among College Students: A Review. Research in Higher Education 39:235–274, doi: 10.1023/A:1018724900565

365. Wikipedia (2011) Suffix Tree. Online Source, retrieved Aug. 30, 2011 from: http://en.wikipedia.org/wiki/Suffix_tree

366. Williams D (2010) Academic Integrity: Pots and Kettles? In: Proceedings of the 4th International Plagiarism Conference, Newcastle upon Tyne, UK

367. Wise MJ (1993) String Similarity via Greedy String Tiling and Running Karp-Rabin Matching. Online Preprint, retrieved May 29, 2012 from: http://vernix.org/marcel/share/RKR_GST.ps.

368. Yoon SH, Kim SW, Park S (2010) A Link-based Similarity Measure for Scientific Literature. In: Proceedings of the 19th International Conference on World Wide Web, ACM, pp 1213–1214, doi: 10.1145/1772690.1772880

369. Yoon SH, Kim SW, Park S (2011) C-Rank: a Link-based Similarity Measure for Scientific Literature Databases. arXivorg Computing Research Repository abs/1109.1059:1–11

370. Zhan S, Byung Ryul A, Ki Yol E, Min Koo K, Jin Pyung K, Moon Kyun K (2008) Plagiarism Detection Using the Levenshtein Distance and Smith-Waterman Algorithm. In: Proceedings of the 3rd International Conference on Innovative Computing Information and Control, pp 569–569, doi: 10.1109/ICICIC.2008.422

371. Zou D, Long WJ, Ling Z (2010) A Cluster-Based Plagiarism Detection Method. In: Notebook Papers of CLEF 2010 LABs and Workshops, 22-23 September, Padua, Italy

372. Zujewski J, Vaughn Cooke A, Flanders KC, Eckhaus MA, Lubet RA, Wakefield LM (2001) Transforming Growth Factors-beta Are Not Good Biomarkers of Chemopreventive Efficacy in a Preclinical Breast Cancer Model System. Breast Cancer Research 3:66–75, PMID11250748, PMC13902

Appendix

The Appendix includes a list of related publications, the preliminary corpus analysis, the CPA/CbPD patent application, material related to the prototype, and other resources.

A   Preliminary PMC OAS Corpus Analysis

This chapter[70] describes the preliminary analysis of the PMC OAS collection. This analysis served to provide an insight into the characteristics and capabilities for each of the detection algorithms before applying them to detect suspicious document similarities.

A.1   Bibliographic Coupling

We analyzed Bibliographic Coupling (BC), both the number (absolute Bibliographic Coupling strength, s_{BC}) or fraction (relative Bibliographic Coupling strength, r_{BC}) of references that two documents have in common for two reasons. First, we expected s_{BC} and r_{BC} to be valuable criteria for constraining the scope of the CbPD analysis to document pairs more likely to share a significant citation-based similarity. Additionally, such a reduction of collection size increases computing speed. Second, we wished to test the extent to which BC strength can point to suspicious document similarities. To investigate these two questions, we analyzed the distribution of bibliographically coupled document pairs in the PMC OAS.

Figure 57 plots the cumulated number of document pairs (vertical axis) with an absolute Bibliographic Coupling strength that is greater or equal to the value on the horizontal axis. The average absolute BC strength was $\mu(s_{BC}) = 1.21$ with a standard deviation of $\sigma(s_{BC}) = 0.95$. The distribution was strongly skewed toward lower values. A clear majority, 84 %, of the bibliographically coupled document pairs had a $s_{BC} = 1$.

---

[70]   This chapter was written in collaboration with Norman Meuschke.

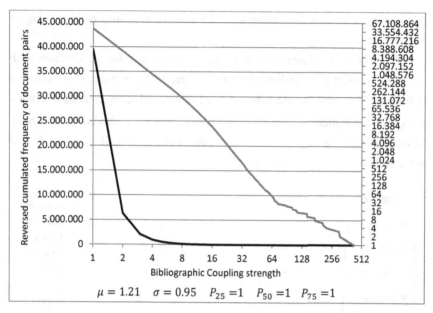

Figure 57: Bibliographic Coupling Strength among Documents in PMC OAS

The goal of the subsequent CbPD evaluation was to identify highly uncommon citation-based document similarities. To test the extent to which high BC strengths reflect highly uncommon citation-based document similarities, we chose to preliminarily analyze the approximately 3 % of document pairs with the highest s_{BC}. We performed the selection of the respective document pairs by stetting $s_{BC} \geq 4$ as a minimum threshold for inclusion. This threshold retained 972,919 distinct document pairs (2.5 % of the bibliographically coupled document pairs) for analysis.

Setting a required minimum s_{BC} potentially excluded documents containing few references. This is problematic, because even documents with few total references may have a substantial relative BC strength (r_{BC}). Having a large fraction of references in common represents a significant citation-based document similarity although $s_{BC} = 4$ may be undercut. Therefore, we also chose to include documents with $s_{BC} < 4$ if r_{BC} is high. To determine the threshold above which r_{BC} should be uncommonly high, we analyzed the distribution of r_{BC} over all bibliographically coupled document pairs (see Figure 58).

On average, the fraction of references a document has in common with another document (r_{BC}) makes up a minor share, ~3 %, of a document's overall references. We chose to select the ~5 % of bibliographically coupled document pairs with the highest r_{BC}. To do so, we set $r_{BC} = 9$ % as a minimum threshold. In other words, we included document pairs with $s_{BC} < 4$, if they had 9 % or more of their references in common.

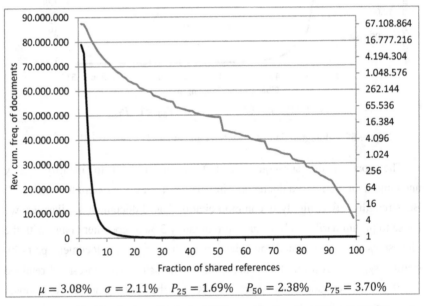

Figure 58: Distribution of Relative Bibliographic Coupling Strength (rBC)

In addition to using Bibliographic Coupling to limit the scope of the analysis, we also wanted to evaluate its usefulness in detecting suspiciously similar, potentially plagiarized documents. Since we compare all documents against all others in a *n:n* comparison, the number of detected similarities requires finding a reasonable confinement of documents for manual inspection. To achieve this, we considered the following two criteria.

First, we selected the top 10,000 document pairs with the highest s_{BC}. To rely not only on absolute counts, we consolidated these documents with the 10,000 document pairs that had the highest r_{BC}. In total, 13,911 document pairs fulfilled one or both criteria. We plotted the selected document pairs according to their absolute and relative BC strength as shown in the scatter plot in Figure 59. Selecting the top 10,000 documents for both criteria causes the clear breakup in the data points in both dimensions of the plot.

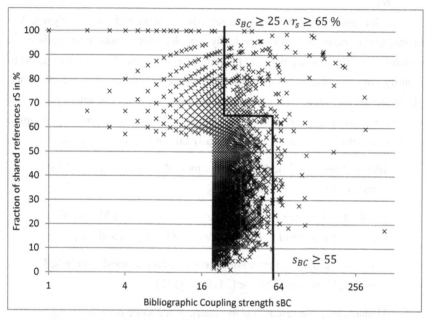

Figure 59: Document Pairs with High Absolute and Relative BC Strength

Examining the left upper plot area, we can conclude that in an *n:n* detection scenario, an isolated examination of r_{BC} is not a valuable similarity indicator for $s_{BC} \lesssim 20$. For almost any $s_{BC} \lesssim 20$ a substantial number of documents exist that share between 60 % and 80 % of their references with other documents. For $s_{BC} \leq 8$, even 100 % shared references are common. Samples indicated that documents with $s_{BC} \leq 8$, but a large r_{BC} are typically very short. These short documents have most of their references in common with much longer documents. The scatter plot suggests that in the given $n{:}n$ detection scenario, high thresholds must be set for s_{BC} and r_{BC} to limit the document space to a number that allows manual inspection. We defined three heuristic criteria to select and examine the most similar documents, i.e. the documents lying to the upper right of the thresholds, indicated by straight lines in Figure 59. We chose document pairs with $s_{BC} \geq 55$ and consolidated them with documents with lower absolute BC strengths ($s_{BC} \geq 25$), but higher relative BC strengths $r_{BC} \geq 65$.

322 document pairs matched the selection criteria and were analyzed. We differentiated between bibliographically coupled documents with authors in common (277 document pairs) and no authors in common (45 document pairs) to identify potential plagiarism as opposed to duplicate publications. We examined 10 document pairs that had no authors in common and 30 document pairs with authors in common. The examined samples showed that strongly coupled documents with authors in common typically fall into these categories:

- Identical text published in different journals, e.g., [192] and [193], [196] and [197], or [7] and [8]

- Duplicates, i.e. the same journal article appeared in PMC multiple times, e.g., [289] and [290], [287] and [288], or [61] and [62]

- Errata including a complete new version of a previously published text, e.g., [326] and [327], or [341] and [342]

- Updates on prior research using many of the same references, e.g., [180] and [179], [278] and [308], or [211] and [210]

Errata and multiple copies, which are likely erroneous submissions of the same text to PMC®, are clearly unsuspicious. The appropriateness of simultaneous publication of the same article in different journals is case-dependent. Duplicate publication can be justified if the goal is reaching a broader audience or increasing the dissemination of key findings. If the publication mainly serves interests of the author without contributing to the scientific community and without acknowledging prior publications in other venues, duplicate publication represents undue behavior. As far as we can judge, the listed examples of updates seem to provide new information, and hence are legitimate examples of highly similar texts.

Most examined documents that shared no common authors were review articles on related or identical topics that shared a significant number of references. We found no blatant copy & paste plagiarism. Bibliographic Coupling does not provide clues as to which of these documents might contain suspiciously similar content. Overall, Bibliographic Coupling provides a rough measure of document similarity in the given $n{:}n$ detection setting, in which we regard all documents as potentially suspicious and compare them against all others. Bibliographic Coupling can identify identical and highly related documents that contain a large number of common references.

We assume that s_{BC} and r_{BC} can be more valuable for indicating suspicious document similarities in a $1{:}n$ detection scenario, in which one potentially suspicious document is compared against a genuine reference collection. To substantiate this assumption, we analyzed the distribution of documents with $r_{BC} \geq 9\,\%$, which we set as a threshold for suspicion, depending on the number of documents the respective fraction of references is shared with (see Figure 60).

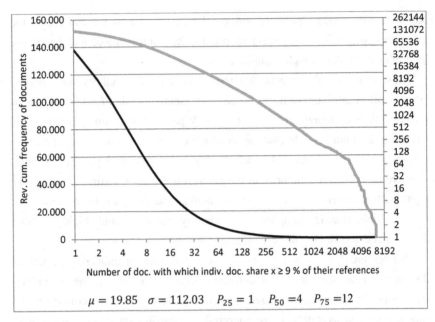

$$\mu = 19.85 \quad \sigma = 112.03 \quad P_{25} = 1 \quad P_{50} = 4 \quad P_{75} = 12$$

Figure 60: Distribution of Documents Sharing $r \geq 9\,\%$ of References

The median of the distribution is four; the upper quartile is 12. This means that 50 % of all ~168,000 bibliographically coupled documents share 9 % or more of their references with a maximum of four other documents and 75 % do so with a maximum of 12 documents. We find it realistic to assume that examiners would be willing and able to manually check four to 12 documents when told that the amount of reference overlap is uncommon and may point to suspicious similarity. Thus, we assume that in a majority of cases in a *1:n* detection setting, r_{BC} is a valuable criterion to identify potentially similar documents in preparation for a manual inspection.

Similarly, the number of documents for which an "unusually" high s_{BC} exists is a more restrictive and thus a more valuable selector in a *1:n* detection setting. As previously mentioned, we derived $s_{BC} = 4$ as the threshold for potential suspicion. Figure 61 shows the distribution of documents that are bibliographically coupled to other documents with $s_{BC} \geq 4$. The median is 3, the upper quartile 10. In other words, 75 % of bibliographically coupled documents are "strongly" coupled to a maximum of 10 other documents. Again, in a *1:n* detection setting, this generally appears to be a reasonable number for manual inspection.

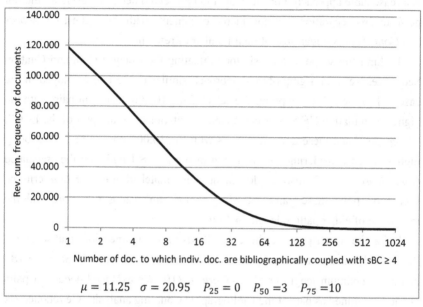

$$\mu = 11.25 \quad \sigma = 20.95 \quad P_{25} = 0 \quad P_{50} = 3 \quad P_{75} = 10$$

Figure 61: Distribution of Documents with BC Strength ≥ 4

A.2 Longest Common Citation Sequence

The Longest Common Citation Sequence (LCCS), as described in Section 4.4.2, is a detection algorithm, which allows slight transpositions in matching citations or skipping over gaps of non-matching citations. The LCCS measures global document similarity in the form of a single value. To test the detection capabilities of the LCCS approach and to understand the influence of continuity and rarity of matching citations in terms of the *CF-Score* and *Cont.-Score*, we used both scores as the dimensions of a scatter plot.

CF-Score and *Cont.-Score* both depend on the pattern length, i.e. the number of matching citations, which makes them additive scores. Documents that differ from the majority of documents with comparable numbers of matching citations represent notable outliers in one or both dimensions. To prevent scores of documents with many references from masking outliers obtained from shorter documents, separately analyzing documents with similar numbers of references is a reasonable approach. For the evaluation presented here, however, we did not perform this separation, but considered documents with the highest *CF-Scores* and *Cont.-Scores*, regardless of their number of references.

To limit the scope of analysis for evaluating the Longest Common Citation Sequence, we used a graph-based approach similar to the one employed in the case of Bibliographic Coupling. We selected the 10,000 document pairs with the highest cumulative *CF-Scores* calculated for citations that are part of the LCCS. We consolidated these document pairs with the 10,000 document pairs scoring highest when considering the maximum of the LCCS length and the associated *Cont.-Score*. 15,392 distinct document pairs matched the selection criteria. Figure 62 plots these pairs according to the dimensions *CF-Score* and the maximum of either pattern length or *Cont.-Score*.

Using the scatter plot, we chose thresholds for both dimensions that separated the most dominant outliers. We selected document pairs with *CF-Score* $\geq$ 480 and/or a maximum length or *Cont.-Score* $\geq$ 310. We excluded document pairs already examined as part of the Bibliographic Coupling analysis. We retained six document pairs with authors in common and 49 document pairs with no authors in common.

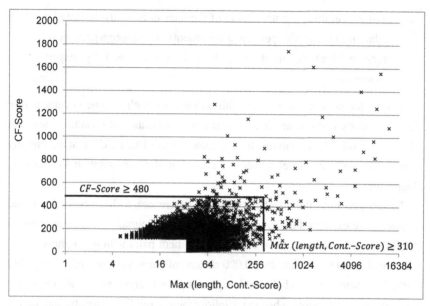

Figure 62: Document Pairs with High Similarity Scores in the LCCS Assessment

Examining a sample of 15 document pairs from the group with authors in common yielded:

- Six duplicate submissions of the respective journal to PMC.

- Six updates on prior research. The updates featured Longest Common Citation Sequence scores of 286, 283, 198, 135, 91 and 88 citations. However, as far as we were able to judge the articles, they presented new findings.

- Three document pairs appeared to be slightly reworded reports on identical literature reviews submitted to different journals. The three documents pairs [76] and [75], [241] and [240], [90] and [162] respectively featured longest common citation sequences of 218, 178 and 129, a majority of sequences in direct succession (without gaps of non-matching citations). Two pairs were submitted to the respective journals within one month, and another pair within three months. None of the later documents indicated a relation to the earlier published documents. The appropriateness of such publications must be judged in context and by expert examiners.

Among the six document pairs with no common authors, one document pair was an annually updated medical standard, which mentioned no authors and had a LCCS of 364. The remaining five document pairs had LCCS lengths ranging from 26 to 48. The articles were related, but did not show indications of plagiarism.

To analyze how the number of shared references influences LCCS-based similarity, we examined the relation of absolute Bibliographic Coupling strength to LCCS length. We selected the 10,000 document pairs with the highest LCCS and consolidated them with the 10,000 document pairs with the highest s_{BC}. We omitted documents we had checked as part of prior analysis and created a scatter plot with the dimensions absolute Bibliographic Coupling strength and LCCS length (see Figure 63). By visually examining the most prominent outliers, we defined heuristic thresholds for including document pairs in a manual check. We selected document pairs if their LCCS had a length of $l > 64$. We also included document pairs with shorter LCCS ($l > 39$) if their absolute Bibliographic Coupling strength was comparably low ($s_{BC} < 16$). 96 documents matched the selection criteria, of which 18 had no authors in common, while 68 had authors in common.

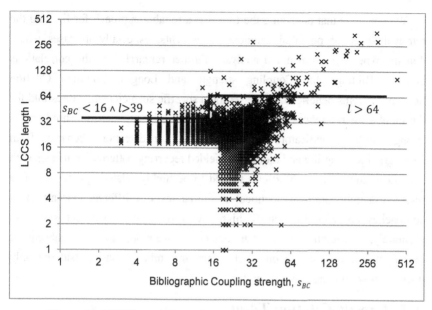

Figure 63: LCCS Length Dependent on Bibliographic Coupling Strength

The results from checking documents with authors in common were in line with earlier findings. LCCS lengths ranged from 40 to 108. Among the highest-scoring document pairs, we identified one duplicate submission to PMC, which was probably erroneous. Furthermore, we found one identical text published in two journals [206] and [205]. The duplicate publication appeared to be sanctioned because it presented a standardized reporting scheme. We also found similar, yet non-identical, reviews published in different journals, e.g., [10] and [9]. The two articles had a LCCS of length $l = 91$ in this class of articles.

Of the 18 article pairs with no authors in common, eight were review articles (see for example [159] and [182]). The pattern of highly related periodic review articles was dominant. The remaining article pairs were highly related research papers in very specific areas of research. One example of such a document pair is [242] and [115], which both discuss nucleotide distributions in the DNA of specific cell cultures and have a LCCS of 50. We did not find indications for plagiarism in these articles.

We conclude that analyzing the LCCS is a reliable approach for limiting the retrieval space of potential candidate documents, especially in cases where domain experts perform a *1:n* analysis. Further research into the correlations between Bibliographic Coupling strength and Longest Common Citation Sequences seems beneficial before setting a specific suspiciousness threshold for the number of references in common. Once established, such thresholds are a strong similarity indicator, especially in a *1:n* detection scenario. Both Bibliographic Coupling and the LCCS yielded recurring patterns for articles with authors in common. Such articles tended to be highly related updates on prior research or publications of identical or similar texts in different journals. Both approaches are able to identify high levels of global document similarity accurately, especially in a *1:n* detection scenario. In our subsequent investigations, we focused on local document similarity and considered only documents sharing no common authors.

A.3   Greedy Citation Tiling

Greedy Citation Tiling (GCT) , as described in Section 4.4.3, identifies all longest substrings of matching citations, so-called citation tiles, within the citation sequences of two documents. Citation tiles are composed solely of matching citations in identical order. To gain an understanding of the document similarities that lead to high scores in a GCT analysis, we reduced the number of documents to the ones most similar. To achieve this reduction, we analyzed the distribution of citation tile lengths in order to set a suitable threshold. Given the distribution (see Figure 64), we disregarded all documents that did not contain at least one citation tile of length three.

We also wished to estimate the selective power of the chosen similarity threshold in a *1:n* detection setting. For this purpose, we analyzed the distribution of documents sharing citation tiles of length three or more with other documents depending on the number of documents the tiles were shared with (see Figure 65). The upper quartile of the distribution is two. In other words, 75 % of documents that share a citation tile of length three or more do so with a maximum of two other documents. Therefore, we assume that citation tiles of

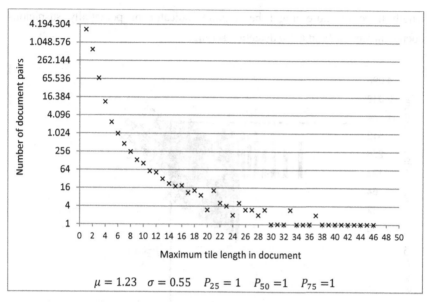

$$\mu = 1.23 \quad \sigma = 0.55 \quad P_{25} = 1 \quad P_{50} = 1 \quad P_{75} = 1$$

Figure 64: Distribution of Maximum Citation Tile Lengths

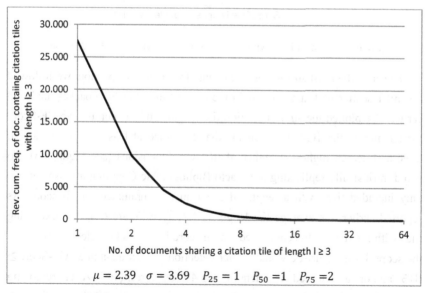

$$\mu = 2.39 \quad \sigma = 3.69 \quad P_{25} = 1 \quad P_{50} = 1 \quad P_{75} = 2$$

Figure 65: Distribution of Documents with Citation Tiles of Length $l \geq 3$

length three or more might be a good indicator of potentially suspicious document similarity in a *1:n* detection setting.

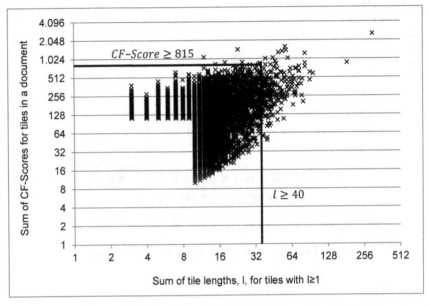

Figure 66: Document Pairs with Highest Similarity Scores in GCT Assessment

To select the most suspicious documents for manual inspection, we followed a similar scatter plot approach as in the case of the other approaches analyzed earlier. We plotted the sum of citation tile lengths and the cumulative CF-Score for all tiles in the 10,000 documents that contained at least one tile of length three and scored highest in either of the two dimensions (see Figure 66). To avoid intrinsically replicating a de-facto Bibliographic Coupling assessment, we only included tiles with a length of $l > 1$ in the cumulated length score. As reported earlier, the average tile length is 1.23 (see Figure 64), thus excluding tiles with $l \leq 1$ from the cumulated length score increases the selective power of the score. Using heuristic visual outlier detection, we set a summed CF-Score $\geq$ 815 and/or a summed tile length $l \geq 40$ as thresholds. After removing previously analyzed documents, 153 distinct documents remained, of which eight document pairs had no authors in common.

Six of these article pairs were reviews, one article pair was a periodically republished medical standard and another was a related research paper. All articles listed consecutive prior studies. The following table shows a typical example of a text excerpt with long citation tiles taken from two review articles written by different authors. The publishing dates of both articles are apart by ~4 years. The references 111 to 119 in [121] and 64 to 72 in [343] refer to the same sources in identical order. We were able to identify similar examples using the LCCS and to a lesser extent using Bibliographic Coupling.

Table 25: In-text Citation Tile (Example 1)

Text excerpt from [121]	Text excerpt from [343]
"Following entry to the brain, monocytes, lymphocytes, activated macrophage, microglia and astrocytes release cytokines, reactive oxygen species, and other neurotoxins that disrupt normal cellular functioning, modify neurotransmitter action, and may lead to leukoencephalopathy and ultimately neuronal apoptosis [111,112]. Some of these neurotoxins include TNF-α, arachidonic acid, platelet activating factors (PAF), nitric oxide (NO), and quinolinic acid (QUIN). NO is synthesized by endothelial cells, macrophages and neurons and might be associated with the NMDA type glutamate associated neurotoxicity. A high level of inducible NO synthase has been found in the brain of HAD patients [113]. In HIV-1 patients who also are/were drug addicted (e.g. cocaine, heroine), a 40-fold increase in expression of NO synthase in neurons of temporal lobes was reported [114]. TNF-α is released by HIV-1 infected macrophage microglia and particularly affects oligodendrocytes [115]. It has been shown that TNF-α mRNA level in the subcortical regions of HAD patients' CNS are higher than in AIDS patients without neurological symptoms [116]. In addition, TNF-α can damage the BBB,	"This may cause alterations in neurotransmitter action and causes leukoencephalopathy resulting in neuronal apoptosis.[64,65] TNF-α, platelet activating factor (PAF), nitric oxide (NO), and quinolinic acid (QUIN) also behave like neurotoxicant and cause neurotoxicity. NO is produced by microvascular endothelial cells, macrophages, and neurons which may result in N-methyl-D-aspartate (NMDA) type glutamate-associated neurotoxicity. Elevated levels of NO synthase has been reported in the brain of HAD patients, while a 40-fold increase in expression of NO synthase in neurons of drug addict HIV patients.[66,67] TNF-α is produced by macrophages and microglia and it mainly affects oligodendrocytes.[68] An elevated level of TNF-α mRNA has been reported in HIV patients with neurological complications.[69] TNF-α causes damage to BBB and facilitates entry of peripheral blood cells.[70] Pro-inflammatory cytokines like TNF-α, IL-1, and IFN-α are found to be present in elevated level in AIDS patients.[71,72]"

as shown in an in-vivo model, which could facilitate entry into the brain of HIV-1 protein(s) and cytokines secreted in the periphery [117]. Not only the level of pro-inflammatory cytokines, such as TNF-α, IL-1 and IFN-γ, anti-inflammatory cytokines including TGF-β and IL-6, and soluble cytokine receptors is elevated in AIDS patients, but the cytokine production is correlated with the gravity of the neuropathology [118,119]."

We also found empirical examples that citation tiles of length three or more have a high predictive value for local document similarity. We randomly selected the following two text excerpts from article pairs that shared exactly one citation tile of length three (and potentially additional citations, but for the given selection, no other matching pattern was allowed to be longer than two).

Table 26: In-text Citation Tile (Example 2)

Text excerpt from ([138], p.1)	Text excerpt from ([37], p. 90)
"In RA, RF is detected in 70-80 % of patients with established disease, and is an integral part of the definition of this disorder. AKA, APF, AFA, and anti-Sa have all been shown to be associated with RA, and appear to be more specific than RF for this disease [1,2,3,4,5,6,7,8,9]."	"Vincent et al. [48] could detect AFA in 41 % of RA sera with 99 % specificity. When combining the AFA immunoblot assay with AKA testing, a much higher sensitivity (64 %), without loss of specificity, could be achieved [48]. However, the sensitivity of the assay appears to be dependent on the method for purification of the filaggrin. Slack et al. calculated sensitivities of 12 and 16 for two different filaggrin preparations, while only one of five positive sera reacted with both preparations [49]. The AFA-ELISA is somewhat more sensitive (47–54 %) than the immunoblot assay [50,51] ..."

In [138] and [37] the citations 3–5 and 48–50 represent references to identical sources in matching order. Aside from this tile of length three, the articles share 20 other single citations. Both paragraphs and the articles as a whole discuss auto-antibodies related to rheumatic diseases. The articles are clearly not a plagiarism, but are semantically highly related. The article [37] shares a citation tile of length three only with the article [138]. The article [138] shares citation tiles of length three with two other documents.

Table 27: In-text Citation Tile (Example 3)

Text excerpt from ([372], p. 216)	Text excerpt from ([47], p. 73)
"In RA, RF is detected in 70–80 % of patients with established disease, and is an integral part of the definition of this disorder. AKA, APF, AFA, and anti-Sa have all been shown to be associated with RA, and appear to be more specific than RF for this disease [1,2,3,4,5,6,7,8,9]." "In contrast to the growth inhibitory effects of TGF β1 in the early stages of carcinogenesis, TGF β1 can also act as a promoter of tumor cell invasion and metastasis in the later stages of tumorigenesis [5,6]. Increased production of TGF β1 is observed in epidermal [35], gastric [36], renal [37], breast [38 41], and prostate carcinomas [42] when compared with normal tissues."	"There is considerable evidence to suggest that, at late stages in tumorigenesis, TGF βs can actually promote the tumorigenic process, particularly if the epithelial cells have lost responsiveness to the growth regulatory effects of TGF β by this time [9,39,40,41]. Thus, advanced human tumors show increased levels of TGF β expression [42,43,44], and TGF βs are known to suppress the immunosurveillance system, to enhance angiogenesis, invasion and metastasis, and to increase drug resistance [45,46,47,48]."

In [372] and [47] the citations 39 to 41 and 42 to 44 represent references to identical sources in matching order. Aside from the tile of length three, the documents share two other single citations. None of the documents shares a tile of length three or more with any other articles. The paragraphs of both articles describe the effect of a tumor growth factor in early and later stages of cancer. Both articles are not a plagiarism, but the relatedness of the paragraph is evident.

These examples show that citation tiles of length three or more are highly predictive indicators for legitimate or potentially illegitimate local content similarity. Identifying legitimate, yet highly similar text segments can, for example, be used to improve academic literature recommender systems. Thus, the GCT approach can be valuable to improve general information retrieval and particular plagiarism detection systems. As the empirical examples show, GCT can identify highly related text segments that differ significantly in wording. However, due to its exact matching approach, GCT fails when shared citations are scaled or their order is transposed.

A.4 Citation Chunking

For a first test of Citation Chunking (Cit-Chunk), we evaluated the variation of Citation Chunking that splits up both documents into chunks and includes citations in chunks dependent on the previous shared citations (see Section 4.4.4 for details). The algorithm adds a shared citation to a chunk if n non-matching citations, where $n \leq 1$ or $1 > n \leq s$, separate it from the last preceding matching citation. The variable s equals the number of citations in the chunk under construction. Once the algorithm has chunked both documents, it compares each chunk of one document to each chunk of the other document regardless of the order of citations.

As in the case of the other similarity measures in our experiments, we had to limit the large number of documents with matching citation chunks to allow for a more detailed analysis. To define a suitable exclusion threshold for documents, we analyzed the distribution of maximum chunk lengths (see Figure 67).

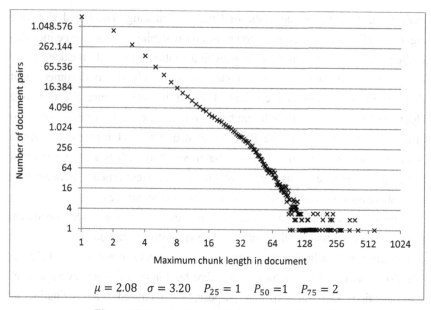

$$\mu = 2.08 \quad \sigma = 3.20 \quad P_{25} = 1 \quad P_{50} = 1 \quad P_{75} = 2$$

Figure 67: Distribution of Maximum Chunk Lengths

The distribution shows that Citation Chunking, on average, yielded longer maximum patterns than Greedy Citation Tiling (see the distribution of maximum citation tile lengths in Figure 64, page 279, for a comparison). In addition, the number of document pairs that shared a maximum pattern of specified length decreased more slowly in the case of Citation Chunking than in the case of GCT. Furthermore, the overall number of identified citation chunks, ~3.5 million, was lower than the number of identified citation tiles, ~12.4 million. These characteristics indicate that Citation Chunking includes more matching citations into patterns than the GCT approach, which represents the expected behavior. The results also support the assumption that the number of text segments containing matching citations in close proximity, yet not necessarily in the same order, is significantly higher than that of text segments with perfectly matching citation tiles.

Figure 67 shows that the number of documents with long citation chunks was significantly higher than the number of documents with long citation tiles, which indicates a negative characteristic of Citation Chunking. The tested chunking algorithm allows an increasing number of non-matching citations to be included in the pattern if a higher number of matching citations is already included in the chunk under construction. This characteristic negatively affects documents that share many references and citations, because in such a case the chunking algorithm tends to form a small number of very long chunks. Approximately 10 million document pairs in the PMC OAS shared $r \geq 64$ references, refer to *Bibliographic Coupling* in A.1. Thus, the effect likely afflicts a large portion of the corpus. The effect was especially strong for review articles, because they often share up to several hundred references with other articles.

Given the distribution of documents in Figure 67, we excluded document pairs from the assessment that did not share at least one citation chunk of length four or greater. This limited the number of documents to approximately 143,000. We also examined the usefulness of this threshold in regard to an "average case" $1{:}n$ detection scenario. For this purpose, we analyzed the distribution of documents sharing citation chunks of length $l \geq 4$ depending on the number of documents that shared the respective patterns. Figure 68 shows the corresponding plot, which indicates that a citation chunk of length four is not as selective as a citation tile of length three (compare this to the distribution of citation tiles in Figure 65, page 279).

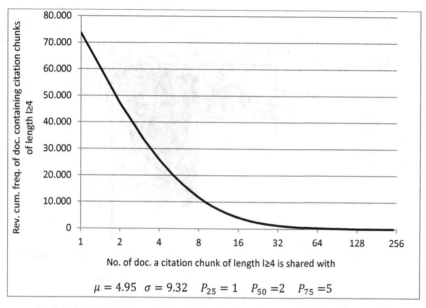

Figure 68: Distribution of Documents sharing a Cit. Chunk Length of $l >= 4$

Nonetheless, setting the minimum chunk length to four caused the upper quartile of the distribution in Figure 68 to equal five. Thus, 75 % of documents in the corpus that shared citation chunks of length four or more did so with a maximum of five other documents. To further confine the sub-collection to be analyzed, we employed a similar graph-based approach as for the other similarity measures. We used the sum of *CF-Scores* and the maximum of the *Cont.-Score* or chunk length as the dimensions of a scatter plot. To avoid replicating a de-facto Bibliographic Coupling analysis (the majority of citation chunks have a length of one) we only considered the *Cont.-Score* or the length of chunks with length $l > 1$ for inclusion in the graph. We selected the 10,000 documents that met the selection criteria and featured the highest scores in either of the two dimensions. Figure 69 shows the resulting scatter plot.

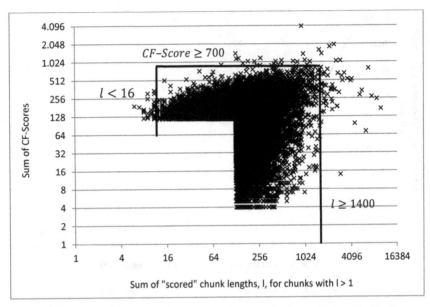

Figure 69: Document Pairs Yielding High Similarity Scores Using Cit-Chunk

Consistent with the evaluations of the similarity functions presented earlier, we visually selected outliers as indicated in Figure 69. The analysis of maximum chunk length had already indicated that Citation Chunking is prone to degenerate into a de-facto global similarity measure for documents sharing many references. Manually inspecting the highest scoring documents verified this expected result. A total of 128 document pairs matched the selection criteria, of which 47 had no authors in common. The large majority of these documents were review articles, which we already covered in the description of prior similarity functions. While Citation Chunking is able to identify such highly related documents, the measure did not provide a significant benefit over the LCCS approach.

For documents with many shared references, citation chunks tend to become so large that a majority of a document's citations are included in a chunk. For instance, the highest scoring document in the assessment yielded a citation chunk length of 139. We assume that such high similarities would also be detected using the Bibliographic Coupling or LCCS approach.

The strength of Citation Chunking lies in its ability to pinpoint specific local similarities. To illustrate this capacity, we analyzed the portion of selected documents with the shortest lengths (l < 16 as indicated in Figure 69), but a high CF-Score. Consider the following example from the group of documents with shorter citation chunks, but a high CF-Score. The two documents [141] and [345] share a single citation chunk of length four, consisting of four citations of two distinct references that are repeated to outline various facts. Because the matching citations are transposed, we state alphanumeric keys formed of first author name and publication year in bold type in addition to the original numeric citations given in the texts. The two texts were not cases of plagiarism, but clearly related. As mentioned previously, the average specificity of citation chunks is not as high as that of citation tiles. For instance, the article [141] shared citation chunks of length four or more with eight additional documents, while the article [345] shared citations with the indicated document only.

Table 28: In-text Citation Chunk Example

Text excerpt from ([141], p. 228)	Text excerpt from ([345], p. 1)
"[...] recent findings that challenge the dogma that metastases arise from a relatively small population of cells within a tumor that have a particularly high metastatic potential. Rather, microarray studies comparing metastatic and non-metastatic adenocarcinomas identified a molecular signature correlating with metastasis, and suggested that the bulk of cells within the tumor share this signature, and thus the metastatic potential is encoded within the bulk of the primary tumor [13 |**Ramaswarmy03**|]. This signature, defined as 17 differentially regulated genes, correlated with metastatic potential in solid tumors from a variety of organs, supporting the concept of a common pathway towards metastasis, and suggesting the existence of common therapeutic targets in different cancers. Gene-expression profiling has also been reported to be useful for predicting the clinical outcome of breast cancer [14 |**van'tVeer02**|]".	"According to the traditional model of metastasis, the potential to metastasize resides in a small subset of tumor cells that have acquired this property through a set of mutations that occur during the later stages of tumor progression [11]. An emerging concept has recently challenged this existing model of metastasis by demonstrating that the potential to metastasize is encoded in the bulk of the tumor and is present early in tumor pathogenesis [11, 12 |**van'tVeer02**| 13 |**Ramaswarmy03**|, 14]."

In summary, we found that a chunk length of three to four is sufficient in most cases to predict local text similarity with high accuracy. Citation Chunking is most valuable for texts that share smaller or average numbers of citations. The approach is also capable of highlighting highly related texts with numerous citations in very close proximity, which is common in review articles. However, if documents share many references overall, the algorithm begins to lose its most valuable feature of highlighting the specific areas of highest similarity. The algorithm treats citation chunks like a bucket. Once this bucket gets too large, and potentially contains many non-matching citations, a manual analysis becomes cumbersome.

A.5 Character-based PDS Sherlock

To compare the CbPD detection performance to a character-based PDS, we also analyzed parts of the PMC OAS with the plagiarism detector *Sherlock* developed at the University of Sydney [184]. We chose Sherlock as a baseline approach for the following reasons:

- Sherlock offers a fingerprinting detection approach, which is representative for most currently available PDS. Sherlock employs word-based text chunking and a probabilistic selection strategy for computing each document's fingerprint.

- Sherlock allows customizing the length of chunks and the probability of retaining chunks during the selection step. By default, Sherlock partitions the input texts into chunks of three words, selects on average one out of 16 chunks formed and discards the rest. For our experiment, we increased the probability of retaining chunks to one out of eight on average to perform a finer-grained comparison. Sherlock reports the document similarities identified as a percentage calculated as: $sim = \frac{100 l_s}{l_{D1} + l_{D2} - l_s}$ where l_s is the length of passages identified as similar in both documents and l_{D1} and l_{D2} denote the overall length of the two documents.

- Sherlock is a lightweight open source C program, which we could easily adapt to the requirements of the evaluation. While most other available PDS are closed source or limit the number of analyzable documents, Sherlock does not enforce a limit on analyzable documents.

The required computational effort prohibited the use of Sherlock to analyze the entire test collection derived from the PMC OAS (185,170 documents) in an *n:n* analysis (17,143,871,865 comparisons). Refer to *Comparison of Computational Efficiency*, page 176, for more details.

A.6 Character-based PDS Encoplot

To compare the detection performance of CbPD to more than one character-based PDS, we additionally analyzed documents from the PMC OAS with Encoplot, a PDS developed by Grozea et al. [143]. We chose Encoplot as a baseline approach for the following reasons:

-   The system is a state-of-the-art research prototype. Encoplot won the PAN comparison of PDS in 2009 and constantly ranged among the best-performing PDS in subsequent PAN comparisons [260, 261, 264].

-   Encoplot employs elaborate n-gram string matching for an n:n comparison of documents, i.e. the system compares each document to every other document in the collection. During each comparison of a document pair, the system matches all unique character n-gram pairs in the two documents. This approach guarantees high detection accuracy for literal text matches. The system extracts all character n-grams of length 16 from two documents under comparison into two separate lists, sorts the lists of n-grams, and uses a modified merge sort algorithm to identify matching n-grams. A limitation of Encoplot's detection algorithm is that it matches the first occurrence of an n-gram in one document to the first occurrence of that n-gram in the second document, the second occurrence to the second and so on. If the number of n-gram occurrences in the documents is different, Encoplot does not identify all possible matches. For example, if Document 1 contains the n-gram "abc" twice and Document 2 contains "abc" four times, Encoplot only matches the first two occurrences of "abc" in Document 2 to the two occurrences of "abc" in Document 1.

- Encoplot is optimized for speed and offers a worst case performance of $O(n)$.

Despite Encoplot's efficiency, an $n{:}n$ comparison of the 185,170 documents in the PMC OAS test collection would still require 17,143,871,865 comparisons, as in the case of Sherlock. The processing time required by Encoplot to perform these comparisons is just as infeasible as an $n{:}n$ comparison using Sherlock. Refer to *Comparison of Computational Efficiency*, page 176, for details.

B Technical Details of the CitePlag Prototype

Section B.1 describes the implementation of the sentence-word-tagger and Section B.2 describes the data parser, two subcomponents of the CitePlag prototype. Section B.3 presents the procedure for the consolidation of reference identifiers in the PMC OAS.

B.1 Sentence-Word-Tagger (SW-Tagger)

The SW-Tagger identifies individual sentences and words in NXML texts and marks them with delimiters that do not impair the validity of the original XML markup. Identifying parts of speech (POS) is a common task in the field of Natural Language Processing (NLP). The ambiguity of natural language makes accurately identifying POS challenging. One example of a highly ambiguous grapheme in natural language is the period. Aside from indicating the conclusion of a sentence, a period can also be a decimal point, or a delimiter within an email address.

The peculiarities of life science texts pose additional challenges to POS identification and force researchers to adjust POS taggers specifically for this field to achieve good POS detection performance. Articles in the life sciences frequently refer to chemical substances, abbreviations, or other domain-specific entities that are difficult to match to ordinary sentence structures. Due to the challenges of identifying POS in life science texts, we incorporated an existing POS tagger into the CitePlag document parser to detect sentence boundaries. Existing and potentially suitable POS taggers for the life sciences include OpenNLP, dTagger, SPToolkit and Stanford Core NLP [52, 91, 256, 314]. We evaluated OpenNLP [14] in combination with the extensions for POS tagging in life sciences proposed by Buyko et al. [52], Stanford CoreNLP [314], and SPToolkit [256] on their suitability for integration into the CitePlag document parser. For each of the three tools, we manually inspected five annotated documents. Although the test was too small to be statistically significant, the results of all tools were in line with results reported in earlier studies [52, 256].

All three tools achieved precision and recall values of ~99 % for word and sentence boundary detection.

In terms of processing time per document, SPToolkit, which required ~30*ms*, was superior to OpenNLP and Stanford CoreNLP, which both required ~1.5*s*. We attribute this difference in runtime to the complexity of the different detection approaches the systems employ. SPToolkit relies on comparably less complicated heuristic rule sets, while OpenNLP and Stanford CoreNLP use sophisticated machine-learning procedures.

Another advantage of SPToolkit over OpenNLP and Stanford CoreNLP is that the output format of SPToolkit's sentence detector is easier to integrate with the other sub-components of the document parser than that of OpenNLP or Stanford CoreNLP. SPToolkit provides its output as a plain Java string object that is universally usable. OpenNLP or Stanford CoreNLP discard the original XML markup and create individually formatted output files. This tagging behavior would require changes to the tools' source codes to produce an output that includes sentence and word markup in addition to the original XML tags.

Given the test results, we incorporated SPToolkit into the CitePlag document parser. All three of the tools tested showed nearly identical precision and recall in sentence detection, yet SPToolkit offered both better runtime performance and a favorable output format. By default, SPToolkit is not able to process XML texts. Therefore, the SW-Tagger substitutes all XML tags in the original documents with unique placeholder strings of the form Z*§*running no.*/§ and stores the tag content in an index for later reinsertion. After the substitution, the SW-Tagger runs the sentence detection procedures of SPToolkit.

SPToolkit does not feature word boundary detection. To avoid using a runtime-intensive POS tagger based on machine learning, we adapted and incorporated word markup heuristics commonly found in similar POS tools into the SW-Tagger. The SW-Tagger marks up word boundaries with plain text annotations similar to the ones employed for tagging sentences. These annotations do not interfere with the original XML markup. The SW-Tagger restores the original markup after the detection of sentences and words by resubstituting the inserted placeholder strings with the original tag content from the stored index.

The algorithm uses regular expressions in Java™ and was designed for use after a separate tagger, in our case SentParDetector [256], has identified sentence boundaries. The output of the sentence tagger has to list each sentence in a separate line and mark the beginning of a sentence with a specific character sequence. In the given case, the SW-Tagger replaces the XML style markups produced by SentParDetector and all original XML markups with the following character sequences prior to the word boundary detection:

*§S/§ denotes the beginning of a sentence.

_z*§000/§ denotes an individual XML tag, which the SW-Tagger replaced with this placeholder string. The numbering 000 corresponds to an individual unique ascending number for each tag in the document. This way, the SW-Tagger can reinsert the original tags after the sentence and word markup process to retain the original document structure information.

The SW-Tagger uses the following regular expression, which includes alternative tests for two main patterns. We list the entire expression in multiple sub-expressions to comment on the sub-patterns these sub-expressions match. The first main pattern, which the regular expression searches for, represents words separated by one or multiple whitespaces.

To identify such patterns, the SW-Tagger uses the following sub-expression to search for the last alphanumeric character in a character sequence that is not part of a markup substitution mentioned above:

"(?:(?:[a-zA-Z0-9](?!\\w|/§|([\\.,]?[0-9]+?)))"+

Note that the SW-Tagger treats numeric expressions or abbreviations as words. While we consider this behavior reasonable for CbPD, it might not be desirable for other applications.

The following sub-expression allows any non-alphanumeric character, except for white spaces or characters that are part of a markup substitution, to follow the first sub-pattern of pattern 1.

```
"(?:[^\\w\\s]|(?:[S0-9]+(?=/§)))*"+
```

This sub-expression causes the SW-Tagger to ignore, e.g., punctuation marks or brackets between words. The next sub-expression tests for a white-space character, which is mandatory in order to match pattern 1.

```
"(?:\\s)"+
```

Any non-alphanumeric character, except for whitespaces and characters that are part of a markup substitution, can follow the whitespace. This sub-expression allows additional punctuation marks, brackets and similar characters before the next word starts.

```
"(?:[^\\w]|(?:S/§)|(?:[0-9]+(?=/§)))*"+
```

The last sub-expression belonging to the test for pattern 1 searches for an alphanumeric character that is not part of a markup substitution. If the SW-Tagger finds such a character, it assumes the beginning of a new word.

```
"(?:[a-zA-Z0-9](?!/§)))"+
```

If the SW-Tagger fails to match the first main pattern, it checks for a second one, which represents words that are separated by an XML tag, but no whitespaces.

```
"|"+
```

The SW-Tagger attempts to match the second pattern by looking for the last alphanumeric character in a sequence (word or numeric expression) that is not part of a markup substitution, but directly followed by a markup substitution.

```
"(?:(?:[a-zA-Z0-9](?!(?:\\w)|(?:/§)|(?:[\\.,]?
[0-9]+?))[,\\.;\\?!\""'\\=/:&+\\-\\$%°]*(?=\\*§[0-9]+/§
))"+
```

Non-alphanumeric characters, markup substitutions or a sentence markup can follow the first sub-pattern of pattern 2.

```
"(?:[^\\w]|(?:S/§)|(?:[0-9]+(?=/§)))*"+
```

This sub-expression causes the SW-Tagger to ignore punctuation marks, brackets or sentence boundaries between words. The end of the second main pattern must be an alphanumeric character that is not part of a markup substitution.

`"(?:[a-zA-Z0-9](?!(?:/$))))"`

To check the quality of the SW-Tagger's markup procedure, we randomly sampled four documents from four journals and inspected the markup for three paragraphs in each document. For words, we found 2,092 correctly identified instances, six incorrect separations and no misses. Five of the six errors originated from one document that states the names of places and tribes in native African languages. These words contained unusual combinations of diacritics and hyphens that caused the word split-up heuristics to fail. The SW-Tagger's word markup procedure achieved a precision of 99 % and a recall of 100 %. The detection for sentences was error-free in the sample. Overall, we are confident that the SW-Tagger's markup procedure is highly accurate.

B.2   Data Parser

The data parser extracts all information necessary for a CbPD analysis from NXML texts. This task requires evaluating the original XML markup and the plain text markup for sentences and words that the SW-Tagger introduced to the documents during the pre-processing step. We implemented the data parser according to the Simple API for XML (SAX) [272]. SAX allows easy extraction of citation positions compared to other APIs for XML parsing and offers high processing speed ([347], p. 36).

SAX follows a push approach for accessing data in XML documents. This means a parser implementing the SAX API reads and triggers (i.e. "pushes") a notification when it detects one of five predefined events. Encountering the start or end tag of the whole document or arbitrary elements represents one event each, thus totaling four events. The fifth event is the encountering of literal character data. Only the application that invokes the SAX parser defines reactions for events that the SAX parser reports. For this purpose, the invoking application must provide callback handlers to the SAX parser. These handlers contain and execute programming logic dependent on the event they receive from the SAX parser.

The content handler is the callback handler of the data parser that extracts document metadata, citations, and references. For most data elements, such as document IDs, author names, and references, this extraction is straightforward. Likewise, citations are easy to parse when the respective NXML text contains individual tags for every citation.

However, some texts state several citations in an abbreviated fashion, for example, "[3 – 8]" without offering XML markup for all citations in the range. To recognize these notations, we implemented an additional check to see if citations occur within a range of 13 or less characters. We chose thirteen characters by assuming that a notation similar to this: "[110] – [115]" is the likely maximum length of an abbreviated citation range. If citations occur within the 13-character-interval, the content handler uses regular expressions to check whether the literal character data between the citation tags actually represents a citation range.

To keep track of sentence and word counts, we adapted the method of the callback handler that reacts to event notifications for literal character data. We use regular expressions to recognize the sentence and word markup introduced in the pre-processing step. After gathering all data for an element, for example a citation, the content handler submits the element to the database.

In order to analyze research papers, while ignoring additional content in PMC, including editorial letters, book reviews, etc., we selected only those documents in the PMC OAS of the following types: "research-article", "review-article", "case-report", "brief-report", "report" and "other". We also excluded documents containing more than one text body or no text body. Samples indicated that documents without a text body are mostly scanned versions of older articles that express only metadata in NXML. Documents with multiple text body parts were usually conference reviews that list summaries of proceeding articles. Both of these document types are not relevant for a plagiarism analysis. The exclusions affected ∼13,000 documents. In total, we imported 221,220 documents to the CitePlag database.

B.3   Consolidation of Reference Identifiers

We consolidated available document identifiers after importing the data into the CitePlag database. When possible, we assigned all identifiers available for a document to all references that likely point to that document and corrected reference records in the database that had incorrect identifiers assigned to them. To achieve this, we identified all likely valid relationships between identifiers and documents by applying the following procedure:

First, we selected all PMIDs, MEDIDs, DOIs, RefTitKeys, and RefAuthKeys and took each of these identifiers as a seed to build all combinations with other identifiers. For example, taking PMIDs as the seed, we selected all pairwise combinations of PMID-DOI, PMID-MEDID, PMID-RefAuthKey, and PMID-RefTitKey. To improve accuracy, we only considered identifier combinations that were identical in at least two documents. During this process, we recognized that RefAuthKey is too error-prone for use as a seed, because we do not disambiguate author names. If we encountered non-unique combinations of identifiers, we chose the combination used by the majority of authors and ignored the other combinations. Assuming that the most frequently used combination of, for example, a given PMID and DOI, is likely the correct mapping, we consolidated all ambiguous pairwise mappings of document identifiers.

Second, we joined the consolidated pairwise-unique mappings of document identifiers using the respective seed identifier in the mappings as the join criterion. This step yielded the following four combined mappings for the respective seed identifiers:

1. PMID-DOI-MEDID-RefAuthKey-RefTitKey

2. DOI-PMID-MEDID-RefAuthKey-RefTitKey

3. MEDID-PMID-DOI-RefAuthKey-RefTitKey

4. RefTitKey-PMID-DOI MEDID-RefAuthKey

Third, we joined the mappings 1 through 4 consecutively to the table of all references using the respective seed identifier of the mappings as the join criterion. If reference records matched one of the mappings in at least one additional identifier aside from the seed identifier, we updated all data fields of the reference record to equal the mapping. Mapping 4, which uses the artificially computed RefTitKey as the seed identifier, is more error-prone than the other mappings. Therefore, we used mapping 4 only to alter records that offered no other document identifier.

Table 29: Consolidation of Reference Identifiers

		Before Consolidation		After Consolidation	
		No. of Ref.	No. of dist. IDs	No. of Ref.	No. of dist. IDs
Total		6,921,249			
Document Identifier	PMID	5,470,266	2,367,554	5,572,531	2,364,433
	no PMID, DOI	195,359	158,652	192,705	141,357
	no PMID, no DOI, MEDID	84	81	82	79
	No identifiers, authors, title	831,899	655,841	733,183	597,220
	No title and/or authors	423,641	-	422,748	-

Table 29 displays the availability of document identifiers for references before and after the consolidation. The table states the number of references for which the respective type of document identifier is available. Authors most often stated PMIDs when citing sources. DOIs and MEDIDs were the second and third most frequent choice. The table shows the quantities of available document identifiers according to the most commonly used document identifier for an individual reference. For example, if the string for a reference included a PMID and a DOI, we counted it for the PMID category only. The table also lists the totals for distinct document identifiers before and after consolidation.

During the consolidation, we assigned PMIDs to ~100,000 references that had no assigned PMIDs before consolidation. We were able to reduce the number of references without numeric identifiers by ~58,000. Additionally, we reduced the number of distinct PMIDs by ~3,000 and the number of distinct DOIs by ~17,000. This reduction in distinct identifiers suggests that we significantly reduced the numbers of non-unique identifiers.

B.4 Database Documentation

This section presents more details on the database structure of the CitePlag prototype briefly introduced in Section 5.2. A database dump (530 GB) is available upon request from the author.

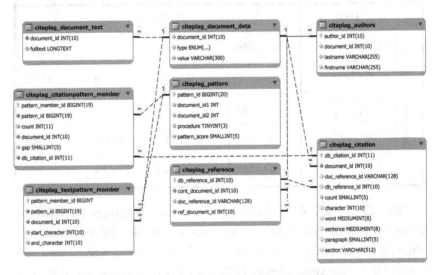

Figure 70: ER Data Model for the CitePlag Database

The following list explains the attributes of all tables in the CitePlag database.

citeplag_document_data

- *document_id* → the database-internal ID assigned to documents for which the full text is available in the database and to "placeholder" documents representing documents referenced within full texts.

- *type* → a flag that identifies the type of additional data stored for documents, e.g., title or external document identifiers (PubMed IDs, PMCIDs, DOIs). The ENUM type provides the possibility to add further types, which are not yet considered, in the future.

- *value* → an attribute holding the actual data of a certain type, e.g., title.

citeplag_document_text

- *document_id* → the database-internal ID of the document for which the full text is stored.

- *fulltext* → the full text of the document.

citeplag_author

- *author_id* → the database-internal ID for all authors.

- *document_id* → the ID of the document in which the author appeared. Currently, authors are not disambiguated, i.e. if an author appears in multiple documents, there will be multiple records with the same name in citePlag_authors.

- *last_name, first_name* → the author name.

citeplag_citation

- *db_citation_id* → the database-internal ID for all citations.

- *document_id* → the database-internal ID of the document that contains the citation.

- *doc_reference_id* → the ID for references in NXML-documents. It is unique only within the NXML-document. In-text citations within a NXML-document specify the ID of their corresponding reference.

- *db_reference_id* → the unique database-internal ID for references.

- *count* → a sequential number of a citation within a document's full text.

- *character, word, sentence, paragraph, section* → the positional information of a citation within a document's full text.

citeplag_reference

- *db_reference_id* → the database-internal ID for references.

- *cont_document_id* → the document_id of the document that contains the reference.

- *doc_reference_id* → an ID for references used in NXML-documents; is unique only within the NXML-document.

- *ref_document_id* → the document_id of the document that is referenced. The referenced document is not necessarily part of the PMC OAS. Therefore, many "placeholder documents" for which no full text is available are contained in the database.

citeplag_pattern

- *pattern_id* → the database-internal ID for all patterns.

- *document_id1, document_id2* → the document_ids of the two documents for which the matching pattern has been identified.

- *procedure* → the ID that denominates the detection algorithm, which was used to identify the pattern, see Table 30 for a short description and an overview of IDs for the detection approaches.

- *pattern_score* → similarity score of the identified pattern. For citation patterns, the score equals the length of the pattern, for character-based patterns see table above.

Table 30: Overview of Detection Algorithms and their Database-internal IDs

Class	Detection Algorithm	ID
LCCS	LCCS	1
	LCCS distinct	11
GCT	shared citations only	2
	all citations	21
	all citations, matches all shared citations once a match has been found	22
Citation Chunking	one document chunked, only adjacent citations considered, no merge performed	30
	one document chunked, only adjacent citations considered, merge	31
	one document chunked dependent on predecessor, no merge	32
	one document chunked dependent on predecessor, merge	33
	one document chunked dependent on textual proximity, no merge	34
	one document chunked dependent on textual proximity, no merge	35
	both documents chunked, only adjacent citations considered, no merge	40
	both documents chunked, only adjacent citations considered, merge	41
	both documents chunked dependent on predecessor, no merge	42
	both documents chunked dependent on predecessor,	43

	merge	
	both documents chunked dependent on textual proximity, no merge	44
	both documents chunked dependent textual proximity, no merge	45
Encoplot Similarity	Encoplot (global score of document = percentage of similarity)	50
	Encoplot (scores of multiple patterns per document, details on patterns in textpattern_member table)	51
CPA	Basic CPA	60
Bibliographic Coupling	Bibliographic Coupling (score = coupling strength of both documents, no pattern_members)	70
	Bibliographic Coupling / Coupling units (score = total citations of a shared reference, pattern_members: citations that form the coupling)	71
Co-Citation	Co-Citation = number of documents that cite the two documents together	80
Lucene	Lucene MoreLikeThis measure computed on the full text	90

citeplag_citationpattern_member

- *pattern_member_id* → database-internal ID for all citation_pattern_members

- *pattern_id* → database-internal ID of the pattern formed by the citation_pattern_members

- *document_id* → document_ID of the document that contains the citations. Storing this ID here is redundant, because the citation identified by db_citation_id contains the same information. However, in practice the redundancy saves a join of citeplag_citationpattern_member to citeplag_citation, which significantly improves performance, because citeplag_citation-pattern_member is a very large table (approximately 1.4 billion records).

- *count* → sequential position of the pattern member within the pattern

- gap → number of non-matching citations between two matching citations in a citation pattern

- *db_citation_id* → ID of the citation that represents the pattern member

citeplag_textpattern_member

- *pattern_member_id* → database-internal ID for all text_pattern_members

- *pattern_id* → database-internal ID of the pattern formed by the text_pattern_members

- *document_id* → document_ID of the document that features the text similarity

- *start_character, end_character* → character count at the start- and ending position of the identified text overlap

C   Data and Source-code Downloads

Various files are publicly available for download on the thesis website:
http://citeplag.org/thesis/

- This doctoral thesis (PDF)

- Introductory video to CbPD

- Source code: CitePlag prototype (zip file)

- Related publications (PDF)

- The figures and tables used in the thesis (zip file)

- GuttenPlag Wiki evaluation, from Section 6.3 (Excel file)

- VroniPlag Wiki evaluation data, from Section 6.3 (Excel file)

- Heun plagiarism examination, from Section 6.3.3 (Excel file)

CbPD Evaluation Findings (password required)

To access the non-publically accessible password-protected data, including the user study suspiciousness-ratings for the scientific publications of the PMC OAS that have not yet been retracted, please contact the author[71].

The following non-public downloads are available:

- PMC OAS database dump with description (SQL file, 530 GB)

- PMC OAS findings of suspicious publications, as discussed in *Examples of CbPD-identified Cases* on page 188 (Excel file)

---

[71]   bela@gipp.com

Involved Organizations

- DKE – Data & Knowledge Engineering Group, Otto-von-Guericke University, Germany

- HTW – Hochschule für Technik und Wirtschaft, Germany

- UC Berkeley – University of California, Berkeley, CA, USA

- VLBA Lab – SAP / Very Large Business Applications Lab (VLBA), Germany

D   Related Publications

Content included in this dissertation has been published with co-authors at conferences and in journals. These publications and their respective locations in the doctoral thesis are listed here.

JCDL / TPDL Doctoral consortium [125]: See Chapter 7 and Section 7.3

> B. Gipp. Identifying Related Work and Plagiarism by Citation Analysis. *IEEE-TCDL Bulletin*, 7, 2011.

CbPD Algorithms [129]: See Chapter 4

> B. Gipp and N. Meuschke. Citation Pattern Matching Algorithms for Citation-based Plagiarism Detection: Greedy Citation Tiling, Citation Chunking and Longest Common Citation Sequence. In *Proceedings of the 11th ACM Symposium on Document Engineering*, pages 249–258, Mountain View, CA, USA, 2011. ACM. doi: 10.1145/2034691.2034741

CPA concept publication [126]: See Section 3.2.5

> B. Gipp and J. Beel. Citation Proximity Analysis (CPA) - A new approach for identifying related work based on Co-Citation Analysis. In B. Larsen and J. Leta, editors, *Proceedings of the 12th International Conference on Scientometrics and Informetrics (ISSI'09)*, volume 2, pages 571–575, Rio de Janeiro (Brazil), July 2009. International Society for Scientometrics and Informetrics. ISSN 2175-1935.

CbPD concept [127]: See Chapter 4

> B. Gipp and J. Beel. Citation Based Plagiarism Detection - a New Approach to Identify Plagiarized Work Language Independently. In *Proceedings of the 21st ACM Conference on Hypertext and Hypermedia*, pages 273–274. ACM, 2010. doi: 10.1145/1810617.1810671

CbPD Prototype [133, 229]: See Chapter 5

B. Gipp, N. Meuschke, C. Breitinger, M. Lipinski, and A. Nürnberger. Demonstration of the First Citation-based Plagiarism Detection Prototype. In *The 36th International ACM SIGIR conference on research and development in Information Retrieval*, 2013. doi: 10.1145/2484028.2484214

N. Meuschke, B. Gipp, and C. Breitinger. CitePlag: A Citation-based Plagiarism Detection System Prototype. In *Proceedings of the 5th International Plagiarism Conference*, Newcastle upon Tyne, UK, 2012.

CbPD Evaluation using GuttenPlag [132]: See Chapter 6

B. Gipp, N. Meuschke, and J. Beel. Comparative Evaluation of Text- and Citation-based Plagiarism Detection Approaches using GuttenPlag. In *Proceedings of 11th ACM/IEEE-CS Joint Conference on Digital Libraries (JCDL'11)*, pages 255–258, Ottawa, Canada, 2011. ACM. doi: 10.1145/1998076.1998124

State-of-the-Art in Detecting Academic Plagiarism [228]: See Chapter 2

N. Meuschke and B. Gipp. State of the Art in Detecting Academic Plagiarism. *International Journal for Educational Integrity*, 9 (1): 50–71, June 2013.

Measuring Document Relatedness by Citation Proximity Analysis and Citation Order Analysis [124]: See Chapter 4

B. Gipp. Measuring Document Relatedness by Citation Proximity Analysis and Citation Order Analysis. In M. Lalmas, J. Jose, A. Rauber, F. Sebastiani, and I. Frommholz, editors, *Proceedings of the 14th European Conference on Digital Libraries (ECDL'10): Research and Advanced Technology for Digital Libraries*, volume 6273 of *Lecture Notes of Computer Science (LNCS)*. Springer, September 2010.

Scienstein [130]: See Section 3.2.5

B. Gipp, J. Beel, and C. Hentschel. Scienstein: A Research Paper Recommender System. In *Proceedings of the International Conference on Emerging Trends in Computing (ICETiC'09)*, pages 309–315, Virudhunagar (India), 2009. Kamaraj College of Engineering and Technology India, IEEE.

CPA / CbPD Approach [123]: See Section 3.2.5 and Chapter 4

B. Gipp. *Very Large Business Applications (VLBA): Systemlandschaften der Zukunft*, chapter Entwicklung neuer Verfahren zur Bestimmung von Dokumentenaehnlichkeiten mittels Referenz- und Zitationsanalyse, pages 163–173. 3. Workshop des Centers for Very Large Business Applications (CVLBA). Shaker Verlag, Magdeburg, October 2009.

Link-Proximity Analysis [131]: See Chapter 7.3

B. Gipp, A. Taylor, and J. Beel. Link Proximity Analysis - Clustering Websites by Examining Link Proximity. In M. Lalmas, J. Jose, A. Rauber, F. Sebastiani, and I. Frommholz, editors, *Proceedings of the 14th European Conference on Digital Libraries (ECDL'10): Research and Advanced Technology for Digital Libraries*, volume 6273 of *Lecture Notes of Computer Science (LNCS)*. Springer, September 2010.

Patent applications:

B. Gipp and J. Beel. Method and system for detecting a similarity of documents. Patent Application, 10 2011. URL http://-www.patentlens.net/patentlens/patent/US_2011_0264672_A1/en/. US 2011/0264672 A1.

Indirectly Related Publications:

CitRec [134]: See Chapter 7.3

B. Gipp, N. Meuschke, M. Lipinski, and A. Nürnberger. CITREC: An Evaluation Framework for Citation-Based Similarity Measures based on TREC Genomics and PMC. To be published.

SciPlore Xtract: Extracting Titles from Scientific PDF Documents by Analyzing Style Information [29]: See Chapter 7.3

J. Beel, B. Gipp, A. Shaker, and N. Friedrich. SciPlore Xtract: Extracting Titles from Scientific PDF Documents by Analyzing Style Information (Font Size). In M. Lalmas, J. Jose, A. Rauber, F. Sebastiani, and I. Frommholz, editors, *Research and Advanced Technology for Digital Libraries, Proceedings of the 14th European Conference on Digital Libraries (ECDL'10)*, volume 6273 of *Lecture Notes of Computer Science (LNCS)*, pages 413–416, Glasgow (UK), Sept. 2010. Springer.

MrDLib [31]: See Chapter 7.3

J. Beel, B. Gipp, S. Langer, M. Genzmehr, E. Wilde, A. Nürnberger, and J. Pitman. Introducing Mr. DLib, a Machine-readable Digital Library. In *Proceedings of the 11th ACM/IEEE Joint Conference on Digital Libraries (JCDL'11)*, 2011.

Impact of Citations in Google Scholar [25, 27, 30]: See Chapter 7.3

J. Beel and B. Gipp. Google Scholar's Ranking Algorithm: An
Introductory Overview. In B. Larsen and J. Leta, editors, *Proceedings of
the 12th International Conference on Scientometrics and Informetrics
(ISSI'09)*, volume 1, pages 230–241, Rio de Janeiro (Brazil), July 2009.
International Society for Scientometrics and Informetrics.

J. Beel and B. Gipp. Academic search engine spam and Google
Scholar's resilience against it. *Journal of Electronic Publishing*, 13 (3),
Dec. 2010. doi: 10.3998/3336451.0013.305.

J. Beel, B. Gipp, and E. Wilde. Academic Search Engine Optimization
(ASEO): Optimizing Scholarly Literature for Google Scholar and Co.
Journal of Scholarly Publishing, 41 (2): 176–190, Jan. 2010. doi:
10.3138/jsp.41.2.176. University of Toronto Press.

Evaluation of Header Metadata Extraction Approaches and Tools for
Scientific PDF Documents [195]: See Section 5.1 and 7.3.1

M. Lipinski, K. Yao, C. Breitinger, J. Beel, and B. Gipp. Evaluation of
Header Metadata Extraction Approaches and Tools for Scientific PDF
Documents. In *Proceedings of the 13th ACM/IEEE-CS joint conference
on Digital Libraries (JCDL)*, JCDL '13, New York, NY, USA, 2013.
ACM. doi: 10.1145/2467696.2467753.

E   Patent Application

The author filed three patent applications in Europe and the USA related to the ideas and research presented in this thesis [28, 32, 128]. The following text is a copy of the US-Patent application for Co-citation Proximity Analysis [128]. For additional information please visit:

http://www.patentstorm.us/applications/20110264672/description.html

The following patent is included in this appendix:

METHOD AND SYSTEM FOR DETECTING A SIMILARITY OF DOCUMENTS

Cross Reference to Related Applications
The present application is a continuation of International Application Number PCT/DE2009/000017 filed on January 8, 2009, the entire contents of which are incorporated herein by reference.

Field of the Invention
The present invention relates to a method and a system for detecting a similarity of documents. The invention particularly relates to a method and a system for detecting a similarity of documents, wherein similar documents are detected and possibly provided based on a predetermined document.

US 20110264672A1

(19) **United States**

(12) **Patent Application Publication** (10) Pub. No.: **US 2011/0264672 A1**
Gipp et al. (43) **Pub. Date:** **Oct. 27, 2011**

(54) **METHOD AND SYSTEM FOR DETECTING A SIMILARITY OF DOCUMENTS**

(76) Inventors: **Bela Gipp**, Magdeburg (DE);
Joeran Beel, Springe (DE)

(21) Appl. No.: **13/174,882**

(22) Filed: **Jul. 1, 2011**

Related U.S. Application Data

(63) Continuation of application No. PCT/DE2009/000017, filed on Jan. 8, 2009.

Publication Classification

(51) Int. Cl.
G06F 17/30 (2006.01)

(52) U.S. Cl. **707/749**; 707/E17.008; 707/E17.108

(57) **ABSTRACT**

The invention relates to a method and a system for detecting a similarity of documents. The similarity of documents is detected with the help of an analysis of citations in one or more citation document(s), wherein the distance between the individual citations is used as criterion of the analysis. On the basis of the determined distance between two citations, respectively, a similarity value is determined, which is characteristic of the cited documents. A small distance between two citations leads to a high similarity of the cited documents. In case of several citations with regard to documents from several citation documents, the similarity values for the citation pairs from the individual citation documents are used for determining a final similarity value.

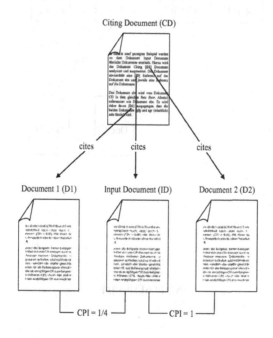

Patent Application Publication   Oct. 27, 2011 Sheet 1 of 3   US 2011/0264672 A1

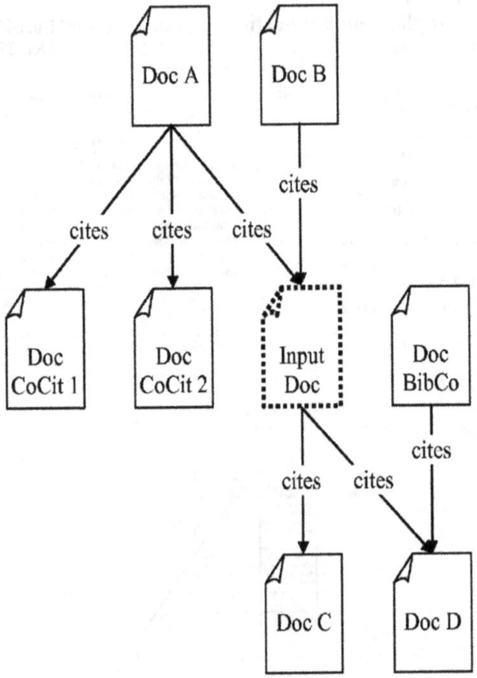

Fig. 1
State of the art

Patent Application Publication   Oct. 27, 2011 Sheet 2 of 3   US 2011/0264672 A1

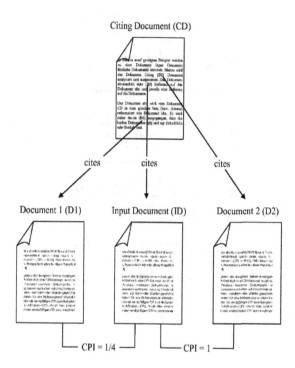

Fig. 2

322   Appendix

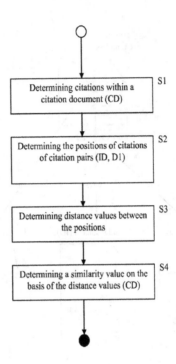

Fig. 3

US 2011/0264672 A1

Oct. 27, 2011

1

METHOD AND SYSTEM FOR DETECTING A SIMILARITY OF DOCUMENTS

CROSS REFERENCE TO RELATED APPLICATIONS

[0001] The present application is a continuation of International Application Number PCT/DE2009/000017 filed on Jan. 8, 2009, the entire contents of which are incorporated herein by reference.

FIELD OF THE INVENTION

[0002] The present invention relates to a method and a system for detecting a similarity of documents. The invention particularly relates to a method and a system for detecting a similarity of documents, wherein similar documents are detected and possibly provided based on a predetermined document.

STATE OF THE ART

[0003] Every year, millions of scientific publications are published as printed documents, electronic documents or as Internet pages. This makes it difficult to search for or find relevant publications concerning a certain subject area, since it is impossible to read all the publications.

[0004] Search engines are known, being specially adapted to the search for scientific publications. Search engines for scientific documents, such as Google Scholar by Google Inc., use two approaches in order to support the search for relevant publications, to be specific the word-based analysis of documents and the so-called citation analysis.

[0005] In case of the word-based analysis, the searching person enters one or more keyword(s), preferably of a subject area concerning the search to be performed. The underlying system detects one or more document(s) basing on the keywords. Preferentially, the system detects and proposes documents containing these keywords as often as possible. It is disadvantageous that the system also proposes documents, which are not thematically related to the searched subject area. In the worst case, irrelevant documents are wrongly classified as particularly relevant due to a preset sort sequence of the search engines, because the keywords are found particularly often in these documents. In addition to the automated search by means of the search engines, the searching person has to perform a manual filtering of the documents proposed by the search engine.

[0006] In case of the citation analysis, the searching person enters a document (input document), which is considered to be interesting or relevant for a certain subject area. On the basis of this input document, the search machine proposes documents which cite the input document (e.g. by means of references) or which are cited by the input document or the like. FIG. 1 illustrates the method of the citation analysis. In case the searching person considers the input document Input Doc to be relevant or interesting, the search engine could propose the following documents:

[0007] (1) documents which cite the input document Input Doc, i.e. the documents Doc A and Doc B;

[0008] (2) documents which are cited by the input document Input Doc, i.e. the documents Doc C and Doc D;

[0009] (3) documents which cite the same documents as the input document Input Doc, i.e. the document Doc BiboCo. This method is also known as bibliographic coupling;

[0010] (4) documents which are also cited by the documents detected according to (1) (Doc A and Doc B), i.e. the documents Doc CoCit 1 and Doc CoCit 2. This method is also known as co-citation analysis.

[0011] The citation analysis provides an initial indication that the cited documents or the citing documents might bear a certain reference with regard to the content, but it does not provide information on the degree of similarity of these documents to one another.

[0012] The present invention is based on the problem to provide a method and a device to be able to perform an enhanced search for similar documents.

SUBJECT MATTER AND DEFINITION OF THE INVENTION

[0013] This problem is solved by a method with the features according to claim 1, a method with the features according to claim 15 as well as a system with the features according to claim 19.

[0014] Preferred embodiments of the invention are quoted in the following description as well as in the further claims.

[0015] According to this, a first aspect of the invention is to provide a method for detecting a similarity of documents, wherein the documents are at least once cited by at least one citing document, and wherein the method comprises at least the following steps:

[0016] detecting the positions of the citations with regard to the cited documents within the at least one citation document;

[0017] detecting a distance value between the positions of the citations within the at least one citation document;

[0018] calculating a similarity value (the so-called citation proximity index, CPI) for the documents, wherein the similarity value depends on the distance value between the two citations citing the documents, and wherein the similarity value indicates the similarity of the two documents to one another.

[0019] The degree of similarity (as similarity value CPI) is advantageously indicated in addition to a reference with regard to the content of the documents to one another, thus enabling a more differentiated search for similar documents. It particularly enables an enhanced computer-based similarity search.

[0020] According to a preferred embodiment of the invention, a smaller similarity value is calculated for a higher distance value. That is, the greater the distance between two citations within a citation document, the smaller the similarity or the similarity value of the cited documents and vice versa.

[0021] A value between a first limit value, i.e. a first threshold value and a second limit value i.e. a second threshold value can be calculated as similarity value CPI. The first limit value (or a value close to the first limit value) can indicate a low similarity and the second limit value (or a value close to the second limit value) can indicate a high similarity of the two documents and vice versa. The values 0 or 1 can be, for example, provided as limit values. These values are only exemplary. Other values can be provided.

[0022] In an embodiment, the distance can also be indicated ordinally scaled, such as "a=citations in the same sentence" or "b=citations in the same paragraph" etc.

[0023] The distance or the distance value between the citations within the citation document can be detected in different ways. According to a preferred embodiment of the invention, the distance value can be detected as follows:

US 2011/0264672 A1   Oct. 27, 2011

2

[0024] with the help of the character distance (number of the characters between the citations);

[0025] with the help of the word distance (number of words between the citations);

[0026] with the help of the sentence distance (number of sentences between the citations);

[0027] with the help of the paragraphs (number of paragraphs between the citations or citations within the same paragraph);

[0028] with the help of the chapters (number of chapters between the citations or citations within the same chapter);

[0029] with the help of the pages (number of pages between the citations or citations within the same page); and/or

[0030] a combination thereof.

[0031] The distance value can also be given with the help of the distance of the citations, such as in cm or inch. The methods for detecting the distance proposed here are exemplary and not concluding. Further methods for detecting the distance between the citations can be provided and/or combined with methods mentioned before.

[0032] In a further preferred embodiment of the invention, several preliminary similarity values can be calculated in case of multiple citations of the documents within the citation document (i.e. when a citation with regard to a document occurs several times). The similarity value for the documents can be calculated from the preliminary similarity values. The individual preliminary similarity values can be determined from distances, which, in turn, have been determined by means of different methods. This method can also be used when the citation of the documents occurs within different citation documents, that is when two documents are cited by one first citation document and at least one more citation document.

[0033] The similarity value can be calculated by averaging the preliminary similarity values. A weighting of the preliminary similarity values can be performed when averaging said values.

[0034] In an embodiment of the invention, the respective highest preliminary similarity value can be used in order to determine the similarity value CPI.

[0035] In a further preferred embodiment of the invention, a significance factor can be determined, wherein the similarity value together with the significance factor indicate the similarity of the documents to one another. The significance factor can depend on the number of the most frequently found preliminary similarity values or on the number of the highest preliminary similarity values.

[0036] Preferably, the method comprises a step for saving the similarity value for the documents on a memory device for finding and identifying similar documents, wherein the saving can comprise the following steps:

[0037] saving of the citation document and/or an identifier of the citation document;

[0038] saving of the (cited) documents and/or an identifier of the (cited) documents;

[0039] saving of the similarity value for the (cited) documents as well as of the significance factor, if required; and

[0040] saving of the preliminary similarity values for the (cited) documents, wherein an additional relation to the respective citation document is saved for the preliminary similarity values.

[0041] The method can also comprise a step, in which the distance values are saved between two citations, respectively. This has the advantage that the method for calculating the similarity values can change without having to calculate the distance values again. Thus, a reanalysis (parsing) of the documents is avoided.

[0042] The saving of the preliminary similarity values has the advantage that an update operation, which may be required after having added a new document to the stock of documents, can be performed efficiently, since preliminary similarity values having been already calculated can be used.

[0043] A further aspect of the invention is to provide a method for finding and/or identifying at least one document being similar to a document, wherein a similarity value is determined for the documents, wherein the similarity value indicates the similarity of the documents to one another, wherein the similarity value for the documents is calculated depending on a distance value between the positions of citations with regard to the documents within at least one citation document, and wherein the method comprises at least the following steps:

[0044] accepting the document or a document identifier, for which similar documents are to be found and identified;

[0045] detecting documents for which a similarity value is determined or determinable with regard to the accepted document; and

[0046] outputting the detected documents.

[0047] The document identifier can be, for example, a unique document identifier or a combination of several attributes enabling the identification of a document, e.g. a combination of information such as the document's author(s), publication year, and title.

[0048] The detected documents can be output as a list of documents including, for example, document titles and authors. This list may also comprise a link for downloading the respective documents. However, the detected documents can also be output directly, i.e. they can be, for example, directly displayed on a display device. This is particularly advantageous if, for example, only very few similar documents are detected. There may also be a combined output, i.e. a list of similar documents, wherein the first document from the list (i.e. the most similar document) is directly displayed on a display device.

[0049] A further aspect of the invention is to provide a system for performing the method according to the present invention.

BRIEF DESCRIPTION OF THE DRAWINGS

[0050] The invention is explained in detail with the help of the drawings. The drawings show:

[0051] FIG. 1 a method known from the state of the art for detecting similar documents;

[0052] FIG. 2 an example for detecting similar documents by means of the method according to the present invention; and

[0053] FIG. 3 a flow chart of the method according to the present invention.

DESCRIPTION OF A PREFERRED
EMBODIMENT

[0054] FIG. 2 shows an example which is used to explain a preferred embodiment of the invention.

US 2011/0264672 A1
Oct. 27, 2011

3

[0055] The basic assumption of the present invention is that the closer two citations with regard to documents are found within one document, the more similar the cited documents are. Similarity can mean that the documents cover similar or the same subjects or they comprise similar or the same arguments. FIG. 2 illustrates this.

[0056] In the example shown in FIG. 2, similar documents are detected for the document Input Document (ID). For this, the document Citing Document (CD) is analyzed and evaluated. The document CD includes a citation with regard to the document ID and a citation with regard to the documents D1 and D2, respectively.

[0057] The document ID is cited by the document CD in the same sentence (or paragraph) as document D2. It is therefore assumed that the two documents ID and D2 are very similar (in content).

[0058] The document D1 is cited in the same document CD as the document ID, but only in a later paragraph. It is assumed that there is a certain similarity with regard to document ID, but that this similarity is lower than the similarity between the document ID and the document D2.

[0059] In order to detect the similarity of the documents ID, D1 and D2 cited in document CD, the distance of the citations within the document CD is determined pairwise. The example shown detects the distances between the citation pairs (ID, D1), (ID, D2) and (D1, D2).

[0060] Similarity values are calculated with the help of the determined distances, indicating the similarity between the respective cited documents.

[0061] There are different or consecutive possibilities to determine the distance between two citations. The following examples are designated to determine the distance between two citations. This list of examples is not concluding and other methods suitable for detecting the distances can also be used.

[0062] Examples for detecting the distance between two citations:

[0063] character distance (number of characters between two citations)

[0064] word distance (number of words between two citations)

[0065] sentence distance (number of sentences between two citations)

[0066] paragraph distance (number of paragraphs between two citations)

[0067] chapter or sub-chapter (number of chapters or sub-chapters between two citations)

[0068] page (number of pages between two citations)

[0069] table or table elements (number of the table elements (columns and/or rows) between two citations)

[0070] absolute distance, for example in cm, mm, inch etc., between two citations

[0071] In case of the examples paragraph, chapter/sub-chapter, page and table, the value 0 can be assumed as distance when the citations are in the same paragraph, chapter/sub-chapter, page or table. In these cases, it is possible to use the alternatives character distance, word distance or sentence distance in order to improve the determination of the distance. The combination of these variants makes it, for example, possible to at first determine the distances between the citations only with the help of the paragraphs between two citations and to only use the method word distance for such citation with the citations being in the same paragraph.

[0072] After having determined the distances, a distance value is available for each citation pair (ID, D1), (ID, D2) and (D1, D2). The similarity values are then calculated from the distance values.

[0073] Depending on the distance or the distance value between two citations, a similarity value is calculated for the citation pairs. The similarity value is called citation proximity index (CPI). If two citations are directly next to one another (e.g. word distance=0), the similarity value can be, for example, determined to be 1, which would mean that there is a very high similarity with regard to the two cited documents. However, if there are several paragraphs between two citations or if the citations are in consecutive paragraphs, as the citations with regard to the documents D1 and ID in FIG. 2, a lower value can be determined as similarity value, which would mean there is an existing but low similarity of the cited documents. The determination of the similarity values is simple in this example. The similarity values can also be determined according to more complex algorithms.

[0074] Examples of similarity values CPI on the basis of different distances:

Distance	CPI
Two citations directly next to one another (character/word distance = 0)	1.00
Two citations in the same sentence	0.90
Two citations in two consecutive sentences	0.85
Two citations in the same paragraph	0.75
Two citations in two consecutive paragraphs	0.60
Two citations in the same chapter	0.50
Two citations in the same article	0.25
Two citations in the same book/conference/journal	0.05

[0075] In the example shown in FIG. 2, a CPI of 1.0 is determined for the document pair (ID, D2), since the citations are directly next to one another (word distance=0). A CPI of 0.25 is determined for the document pair, since the citations are in different chapters or paragraphs.

[0076] The similarity value can be determined hierarchically, as already mentioned above. If two citations are, for example, in different paragraphs, the exact word distance between the citations may be disregarded. This will be illustrated with the help of the following excerpt:

[0077] "[. . .] Some studies show that boys are better in mathematics than girls [1], [2]. Other scientists counter that the results may be in accordance with the facts, but this would be due to the prejudiced education of the children and not due to possible genetic differences [3], [4].

[0078] [. . .]

[0079] In his paper [5] John Doe brings up another interesting subject. [. . .]"

[0080] It becomes clear that the cited documents [1] and [2] must be virtually identical in content with regard to the subject as well as to the statement regarding this subject. The same applies to documents [3] and [4]. It is also clear that the documents [1] and [2] and the documents [3] and [4] bear a high similarity to one another; they deal with the same subject, but with different arguments. Although the document [5] is closer to the documents [3] and [4] than to the documents [1] and [2] with regard to the words counted (word distance), it does not bear more resemblance with the documents [3] and [4] than with the documents [1] and [2], since the citation [5] is in a new paragraph.

US 2011/0264672 A1   Oct. 27, 2011

4

[0081] In this example, the resulting similarity values would be:

CPI (1, 2) = 1	CPI (1, 3) = 0.75	CPI (1, 5) = 0.50
CPI (3, 4) = 1	CPI (1, 4) = 0.75	CPI (2, 5) = 0.50
	CPI (2, 3) = 0.75	CPI (3, 5) = 0.50
	CPI (2, 4) = 0.75	CPI (4, 5) = 0.50

[0082] As an alternative, the similarity values can also be determined in different ways, which will be shown with the help of the following example:

[0083] "Author A shows in [1] that boys are better in mathematics than girls. His experiments have been performed with the help of persons aged 18 to 25. [. . .]

[0084] He ascribes his results to the fact that [. . .]

[0085] However, author A also acknowledges that [. . .]

[0086] Author B shares author A's view [2]. In addition to that, author B, however, found out that [. . .]"

[0087] There are no citations in paragraphs two and three. Therefore, the paragraphs may be disregarded assuming that the text after a citation always refers to the citation until a new citation is mentioned. The citations [1] and [2] would have a similarity value CPI for "citations in two consecutive paragraphs" of 0.60 according to the list above.

[0088] The preceding examples only determined the similarity values of individual citation pairs. However, citations may also appear repeatedly in a text. In this case, the determination of the similarity value is explained with the help of an extension of the example mentioned above:

[0089] "[. . .] Some studies show that boys are better in mathematics than girls [1], [2]. Other scientists counter that the results may be in accordance with the facts, but this would be due to the prejudiced education of the children and not due to possible genetic differences [3], [4].

[0090] [. . .]

[0091] In his paper [5] John Doe brings up another interesting subject. On the basis of an idea according to [3], he examined whether [. . .]"

[0092] In this example, citation [3] is mentioned again, which enables further possibilities of combination or citation pairs. Disregarding the first occurrence of citation [3] at first would result in the following modified similarity values CPI:

CPI (3,1) 0.50

CPI (3,2)=0.50

CPI (3,4)=0.50

CPI (3,5)=0.90

[0093] Taking into account also the first occurrence of the citation [3], this results in additional similarity values, which have already been listed before with regard to this example. One way of determining the similarity value is to always use the respective largest similarity value of a citation pair. However, it may also make sense to perform a weighting.

[0094] The following becomes apparent from the last example: if the citations [3] and [5] are very similar (CPI=0.9) and the citations [3] and [4] are also very similar (CPI=1), there is a high probability that also the citations [5] and [4] are more similar than originally assumed (CPI=0.50). This problem is solved by determining the similarity value as mean value of both similarity values or by weighting the individual similarity values. This means that preliminary similarity val-

ues for the citation pairs are determined first, which are then used to determine the actual similarity value relevant for the detection of the similarity. This transitivity can be continued across unlimited numbers of levels.

[0095] The above examples always considered citations with regard to documents within one single document and then determined the similarity value for the cited documents.

[0096] The concept of calculation according to the present invention also applies to several documents citing documents, when two or more documents are cited from two or more documents. For example, the documents D1 and ID from FIG. 2 may be cited in another document CD2 (not shown here) apart from document CD.

[0097] In case of the analysis of several documents, different similarity values CPI can be determined for a citation pair, e.g. for the citation pair (D1, ID), since the citations in a first citation document CD are within the same paragraph, whereas the citations in a second citation document are in different paragraphs.

[0098] For this, the highest similarity value determined can be used to determine the actual similarity value for the two documents.

[0099] As an alternative, the highest similarity value will not simply be used for the citation pair in order to detect the similarity of the documents, but the similarity values are weighted in order to form a similarity value that way.

[0100] For example, the analysis of three citation documents for a citation pair may once lead to a similarity value of 1 and twice to a similarity value of 0.25. The final similarity value could be assumed to be 0.95, i.e. the similarity value of 1 is weighted more strongly than the smaller similarity values. Again, numerous other calculation methods can be used to determine the final similarity value.

[0101] In addition to the similarity values, a so-called significance factor can be introduced. This way it is possible to further enhance the information value with regard to the similarity of documents for different citation pairs with the same similarity value. When a first citation pair obtains a similarity value of 1 on the basis of one document and a second citation pair obtains a similarity value of 1 on the basis of five documents, respectively, the high similarity of the documents with regard to the second citation pair is more probable than with regard to the first citation pair. The number of the highest similarity values can be used as significance factor for a citation pair. In case the five similarity values 1.0, 1.0, 0.50, 0.25 and 0.25 are determined for a citation pair, the final similarity value could, for example, be 0.93 with a significance factor of 2, since the highest individual similarity value of 1.0 for the citation pair occurs twice.

[0102] FIG. 3 shows the main steps of the method according to the present invention in a simplified flow chart. In a first step S1, the citations with regard to other documents are determined within one citation document. The citation document as well as the cited documents may be electronic documents or so-called web documents. The method described before also applies to web pages.

[0103] After having determined the citations within a citation document, citation pairs are formed in a second step S2. In a third step S3, the distance values between the citations of the citation pairs are determined with the help of the positions of the citations of a citation pair. The determination of the distance values is performed as already explained before with reference to FIG. 2.

US 2011/0264672 A1

Oct. 27, 2011

5

[0104] In a final step S4, the similarity values are determined for each citation pair on the basis of the respective distance values. Step S4 may also comprise the variations for determining the similarity values described before with reference to FIG. 2, e.g. in case a citation pair occurs several times within a citation document or a citation pair occurs in several citation documents.

[0105] In an embodiment according to the invention, the citation documents and the cited documents are saved in a memory device. The cited documents may, in turn, serve as citation documents. The memory device, such as a data base, may also be provided to save the similarity values for the individual citation pairs.

[0106] In case a similarity value is determined from several preliminary similarity values (for example, in case a citation pair occurs several times within a citation document or in different citation documents), the preliminary similarity values can also be saved in the memory device for the respective citation pair. This has the advantage that not all the preliminary similarity values for a citation pair have to be determined again in case a citation document is newly added to the collection of documents.

[0107] As an alternative, the similarity values can be directly determined as reaction to a query. This is particularly suitable when only a small number of documents are involved.

[0108] According to the method, a searching person can predefine a document DI, for which the similar documents are to be detected. A processing device accepts the document DI (or an identifier of the document DI) and determines all the corresponding citation pairs. In case of the example shown in FIG. 2, the processing device would detect the documents D1 and D2 (wherein the citation pairs (DI, D1) and (D1, D2) have been detected). The similarity values 0.25 or 1.0 have been detected for the two citation pairs (DI, D1) and (D1, D2) and have been saved in the memory device. With the help of these similarity values, the processing device can sort the detected documents D1 and D2 according to the similarity and make them available as a sorted list to the searching person. In this example, the sort sequence would be D2, D1.

[0109] The underlying system, such as a computer or a computer network with connected memory device, may comprise an interface in order to also accept and process queries from the Internet for similar documents with regard to a citation document.

[0110] The block diagrams in the different depicted embodiments illustrate the architecture, functionality, and operation of some possible implementations of apparatus, methods and computer program products. In this regard, each block in the flowchart or block diagrams may represent a module, segment, or portion of code, which comprises one or more executable instructions for implementing the specified function or functions. In some alternative implementations, the function or functions noted in the block may occur out of the order noted in the figures. For example, in some cases, two blocks shown in succession may be executed substantially concurrently, or the blocks may sometimes be executed in the reverse order, depending upon the functionality involved.

[0111] The invention can take the form of an entirely hardware embodiment, an entirely software embodiment or an embodiment containing both hardware and software elements. In a preferred embodiment, the invention is implemented in software, which includes but is not limited to firmware, resident software, microcode, etc.

[0112] The invention can take the form of a computer program product accessible from a computer-usable or computer-readable medium providing program code for use by or in connection with a computer or any instruction execution system. For the purposes of this description, a computer-usable or computer readable medium can be any tangible apparatus that can contain or store the program for use by or in connection with the instruction execution system, apparatus, or device.

[0113] The medium is tangible, and it can be an electronic, magnetic, optical, electromagnetic, infrared, or semiconductor system (or apparatus or device). Examples of a computer-readable medium include a semiconductor or solid state memory, magnetic tape, a removable computer diskette, a random access memory (RAM), a read-only memory (ROM), a rigid magnetic disk and an optical disk. Current examples of optical disks include compact disk-read only memory (CD-ROM), compact disk-read/write (CD-R/W) and DVD.

[0114] A data processing system suitable for storing and/or executing program code will include at least one processor coupled directly or indirectly to memory elements through a system bus. The memory elements can include local memory employed during actual execution of the program code, bulk storage, and cache memories which provide temporary storage of at least some program code to reduce the number of times code must be retrieved from bulk storage during execution. Input/output or I/O devices (including but not limited to keyboards, displays, pointing devices, etc.) can be coupled to the system either directly or through intervening I/O controllers. Network adapters may also be coupled to the system to enable the data processing system to become coupled to other data processing systems or remote printers or storage devices through intervening private or public networks. Modems, cable modem and Ethernet cards are just a few of the currently available types of network adapters.

[0115] The description of the present invention has been presented for purposes of illustration and description, and is not intended to be exhaustive or limited to the invention in the form disclosed. Many modifications and variations will be apparent to those of ordinary skill in the art. The embodiment was chosen and described to best explain the principles of the invention, the practical application, and to enable others of ordinary skill in the art to understand the invention for various embodiments with various modifications as are suited to the particular use contemplated.

We claim:

1. A computer-implemented method for determining a similarity of documents (ID, D1), wherein the documents (ID, D1) are at least once cited by at least one citation document (CD), and wherein the method comprises at least the following steps:

determining the positions of the citations with regard to the documents (ID, D1) within the at least one citation document (CD);

determining a distance value between the positions of the citations within the at least one citation document (CD);

calculating a similarity value (CPI) for the documents (ID, D1), wherein the similarity value (CPI) depends on the distance value between the two citations citing the documents (ID, D1), and wherein the similarity value (CPI) indicates the similarity of the two documents (ID, D1) to one another.

2. A method according to claim 1, wherein different similarity values (CPI) are calculated for different distance values.

US 2011/0264672 A1   Oct. 27, 2011

6

3. A method according to claim 1, wherein a value between a first limit value and a second limit value is calculated as similarity value (CPI), and wherein the first limit value indicates a low similarity and the second limit value indicates a high similarity of the two documents (ID, D1) and vice versa.

4. A method according to claim 1, wherein the determining of the distance value comprises at least one of determining the character distance, determining the word distance, determining the sentence distance, determining the paragraphs, determining the chapters, determining the pages and a combination thereof between the positions of the citations.

5. A method according to claim 1, wherein in case of multiple citations of the documents (ID, D1) within the citation document (CD) several preliminary similarity values (vCPI) are calculated, and wherein the similarity value (CPI) for the documents (ID, D1) is calculated from the preliminary similarity values (vCPI).

6. A method according to claim 5, wherein the similarity value (CPI) is calculated by averaging the preliminary similarity values (vCPI).

7. A method according to claim 1, wherein in case of a citation of the documents (ID, D1) within different citation documents (CD) several preliminary similarity values (vCPI) are calculated, and wherein the similarity value (CPI) for the documents (ID, D1) is calculated from the preliminary similarity values (vCPI).

8. A method according to claim 7, wherein the similarity value (CPI) is calculated by averaging the preliminary similarity values (vCPI).

9. A method according to claim 6, wherein a weighting of the preliminary similarity values (vCPI) is performed when averaging.

10. A method according to claim 1, wherein in case of several preliminary similarity values (vCPI) the method comprises a step for calculating a significance factor, and wherein the similarity value (CPI) together with the significance factor indicate the similarity of the two documents (ID, D1) to one another.

11. A method according to claim 10, wherein the significance factor depends on the number of the most frequently found preliminary similarity values (vCPI) or on the number of the highest preliminary similarity values (vCPI).

12. A method according to claim 1, wherein the method comprises a step for saving the similarity value (CPI) for the documents (ID, D1) on a memory device for finding and/or identifying similar documents.

13. A method according to claim 12, wherein the saving comprises at least:

saving of the citation document (CD) and/or an identifier of the citation document (CD);

saving of the documents (ID, D1) and/or an identifier of the documents (ID, D1);

saving of the similarity value (CPI) for the documents (ID, D1); and

saving of the preliminary similarity values (vCPI) for the documents (ID, D1), wherein an additional relation to the respective citation document (CD) is saved for the preliminary similarity values (vCPI).

14. A method according to claim 13, wherein the saving further comprises:

saving of the distance values between the positions of the citations within the citation document (CD).

15. A computer-implemented method for finding and identifying at least one first document (D1) being similar to a

second document (ID), wherein a similarity value (CPI) is determined for the second document (ID) and the first document (D1), wherein the similarity value (CPI) indicates the similarity of the first document (D1) to the second document (ID), wherein the similarity value (CPI) for the documents (ID, D1) is calculated depending on a distance value between the positions of the citations with regard to the documents (ID, D1) within at least one citation document (CD), and wherein the method comprises at least the following steps:

receiving the second document (ID) or a document identifier, for which similar documents are to be found and/or identified;

determining first documents (D1) for which a similarity value (CPI) to the second document (ID) or to the document identifier is determined or determinable; and

outputting the detected first documents (D1).

16. A method according to claim 15, wherein the output order of the documents depends on the similarity values (CPI).

17. A method according to claim 15, wherein the similarity values (CPI) are determined after having received the second document (ID) or the document identifier.

18. A method according to claim 15, wherein the similarity values (CPI) have been saved in a memory device before having received the second document (ID) or the document identifier, and the similarity values (CPI) for finding and identifying are determined by query to the memory device.

19. A system for detecting a similarity (CPI) of documents (ID, D1), wherein the documents (ID, D1) are at least once cited by at least one citation document (CD), comprising:

at least one memory device for saving the documents (ID, D1) and/or an identifier of the documents (ID, D1);

a processing device being coupled with the memory device and being configured for

determining the positions of the citations with regard to the documents (ID, D1) within the at least one citation document (CD);

determining a distance value between the positions of the citations within the at least one citation document (CD);

calculating a similarity value (CPI) for the documents (ID, D1), wherein the similarity value (CPI) depends on the distance value between the two citations citing the documents (ID, D1), and wherein the similarity value (CPI) indicates the similarity of the two documents (ID, D1) to one another.

20. A system according to claim 19, comprising at least one interface in order to accept queries for similar documents with regard to a predetermined document via a LAN and/or a WAN, particularly the Internet or the World Wide Web, and to provide similar documents with regard to the predetermined document, wherein the interface is coupled with the processing device.

21. A system according to claim 19, wherein the processing device is further configured to determine documents, for which a similarity value (CPI) is saved with regard to a predetermined document (ID).

22. A data carrier product comprising a saved program code, being able to be loaded into a computer and/or into a computer network and being configured to perform the method of claim 1.

* * * * *

F   User Study Feedback

As part of the user study, participants had the opportunity to submit comments and suggestions on their perceived usefulness of the citation-based approach. Table 31 shows excerpts of responses collected in the user study.

Table 31: User Comments on CbPD

"[CbPD shows]... a similarity which I find valuable to see."
"[The citation pattern visualization] helped me come to a quicker conclusion. Sometimes [CbPD] helped either strengthen or weaken my opinion on similarity. For example, if shake & paste plagiarism also clearly shared citation patterns, I arrived at a conclusion more quickly[72]."
"...when many key words overlapped, but the citation patterns around shared words were unique, CbPD helps to show legitimate similarity."
"...[CbPD adds a]... new level of document similarity that I was unaware of before."
"Judging plagiarism is quick when two documents have text overlaps, but when the text is adjusted or rearranged, it is much more difficult to assess documents and to find any overlap in their content. It requires a deep background knowledge on the topic and also the cited works. The citation visualization really helps to better assess the content similarity when the text does not overlap. This makes it faster and easier, especially for an examiner who is not familiar with a particular topic!"

Some users expressed uncertainty regarding the value of citations. They felt citation-based similarity allowed them no quick way of knowing what similarity should still be considered "normal". However, the threshold problem for "acceptable" similarity also exists for character-based measures. The reality is

---

[72] Translated from German. Comment submitted by a General Medical Practitioner.

that no *quick* or *easy* fix exists to categorize a given similarity among documents as clearly suspicious.

One of the experts commented that for documents with high semantic similarity with no notable text similarity, the addition of very fine-grained text similarity visualization, i.e. ten or less matching characters was helpful for discerning if the patterns of medical key words, especially surrounding shared citations were suspiciously similar.

G   Reactions of Contacted Authors

Of the top-40 document pairs rated as most suspicious by user study participant, two publications had already been retracted. One publication [281] was retracted as a result of a previous email exchange we had with the earlier authors, while the other case [165] had already been retracted at the time of detection by the CbPD algorithms. We emailed[73] the authors of the remaining 38 earlier published articles asking them if they:

- were aware of the later published article?

- knew of any reasons which may explain the similarity of the later article?

- saw any indications for plagiarism?

The authors of 20 articles replied[74].

The authors of six articles confirmed the presence of plagiarism, one additional author confirmed plagiarism, but wished to take no action[75], and the authors of nine papers acknowledged similarities, but did not consider them as crucial enough to initiate a retraction process. The authors of two papers simply replied a "thank you" refusing to comment on plagiarism, and the authors of the final two publications replied they were not technically versed enough to utilize or make sense of the prototype visualization.

Many authors expressed gratitude for being made aware of the plagiarism of their work. Table 32 lists some of the email responses from the authors we contacted.

---

[73] All authors were contacted 2013-05-06, unless specified otherwise.

[74] As of 2013-05-31.

[75] Refer to the comment beginning *"I don't know if..."* on page 334 for an explanation.

Table 32: Original Author Comments on CbPD

"To be honest I am quite shocked. The resemblance is indeed more than striking. [...] your tool seems to be very efficacious indeed."
...the degree of overlap seems to me to be most consistent with over-reliance on our paper for language and structure by the authors of the later paper."
"I was not aware of this later paper and I do not know of any reasons which may explain the similarity of the later article to ours. *"The results which you have shown are mind boggling.. I simply don't know how to respond...I find no reasons for both the manuscripts to be so similar. Introductions can be similar to some extent, but almost the entire discussion seems to be copied as it is. Their images do not show any evidence of skin graft being used, where discussion mentions of skin grafts!!!* *...I see every indication for plagiarism in this particular article. It is definitely more than just coincidence. Unfortunately, our article has not even been cited by the manuscript."*
"...your approach is reasonable, and I applaud the success of your program"
"Your program is very nice and surprising! *We have not been aware of the existence of the later article."*
"Your work raises the question of reviewing. Why wasn't this detected by the reviewers?"
"I looked at your analysis and I am amazed. *We were definitely plagiarized and I was not aware of this article. [...] The best evidence is the results of your algorithm."*
"I'm quite surprised... I did not know that paper and I do not know its authors. *It seems that they just copied and pasted most of the discussion section and the bibliography of my paper without changing even a single word.* *I think this is a clear example of plagiarism"*
"I was not aware of this later published article. *I find no reason for the similarity (identity) of the articles. I am completely sure it is a case of plagiarism[76]."*

---

[76] Excerpt from an email exchange on 2012-09-03.

To guarantee anonymity to the individual authors quoted here, we do not disclose their names. Disclosure of full names is available only upon request[77].

The gamut of responses we received were in line with the types of responses collected in similar investigations of potential plagiarism. For a study examining precisely the responses of all involved parties that result from investigating plagiarism, refer to [202].

The responses we received from the original authors, who rejected the presence of plagiarism, showed that the opinions on what constitutes plagiarism continue to differ. A first case in which authors felt that high similarity was acceptable was in introductory or overview sections. According to one set of authors, introductory phrases *'set the stage'* of a paper and may be copied in publications, given that they serve to point out the scientific niche the paper will occupy. As one set of authors[78] argues, generic *'stage-setting'* statements were not part of the author's unique contribution and thus should not be viewed as plagiarism:

> *"the [...] sentences [...] are indeed similar. [They] 'set the stage'*
> *by pointing out how health care can be unsafe. They are not a part*
> *of the authors' unique contributions." T.A., B.G., L.S.*

A second case in which citation pattern similarity was viewed as justified by authors was for case reports and review studies. Such reports tend to follow standardized forms, often using boilerplate text, as pointed out by the following author:

> *"Both papers are study design papers of Dutch studies. The recent*
> *study was modeled using elements of the first study. Record review*
> *studies are highly standardized. This clarifies the similarities."*
> *M.B.*

---

[77] We also decided against using author initials, since the identity of the publications' original authors can easily be revealed once the retracted cases are made public. This would jeopardize the anonymity of authors who communicated confidentially with us by email.

[78] Excerpt from an email exchange on 2012-10-10.

A third example of author-approved citation pattern similarity affected review articles:

> *"the similarity [...] is normal because we wrote about the same*
> *topic and it is normal to use the same references because both*
> *papers are reviews and the field is so small (I mean the people*
> *working in the field are not so many so obviously we are all going*
> *to use the same references and same words)."*

A final – albeit a most controversial example of similarity considered "legitimate" – was pointed out by an author, who argued that the different definition on "acceptable borrowing" of text in developing countries should not be ignored:

> *"I don't know if there are technical criteria for declaring a*
> *document to have been plagiarized....My lenient reaction is no*
> *doubt colored by having trained many scientists from developing*
> *countries whose first language is not English. Not only must they*
> *rely on published English-language work to help them formulate*
> *wording for their own work, but the cultural norms for what is*
> *considered acceptable "borrowing" of language tend to be more*
> *permissive in developing countries than in the U.S."*

We were also reminded of the fear of consequences authors face for accusing others of plagiarism. The authors of one paper were not willing to approach the journal and expose the plagiarists themselves:

> *"We are not willing to do this job ourselves because this will lead*
> *to great conflict with the author of the second paper who is living*
> *in the same country, even though we do not know him personally."*

It was common for authors to express their disbelief and surprise of the plagiarism having gone undetected for so long. Many expressed their concern regarding the quality of peer review and the ability of current detection approaches to identify strongly disguised plagiarism forms beyond copy & paste. One author was of the opinion that automated plagiarism detection presented an important area of research, in which CbPD was:

> *"a useful step in development of more sophisticated methods."*

H Empirical Studies on Plagiarism Frequencies

Table 33: Studies Pertaining to North American Colleges

Source	Sample size, place and time of collection	Method	Results
[277]	447 undergraduates at one U.S. campus Spring term 1997	self-report survey	50 % copied from fellow students with their consent, 24.3 % without 35.6 % committed partial plagiarism
[45]	71 students at one U.S. campus Spring term 1998	self-report survey	67.2 % committed partial plagiarism 26.8 submitted a paper from an external source
[283]	698 students at nine U.S. campuses Academic year 1999/2000	self-report survey	19.0 % committed partial plagiarism "sometimes" 5.4 % submitted a paper from an external source "sometimes"
[176]	Unknown number of undergraduates at one U.S. campus publication date: Aug. 2003	self-report survey	47.1 % committed plagiarism
[220]	60,691 students at 67 U.S. institutions 21,649 students at 16 Canadian institutions Academic years 2002/2003, 2004/2005	self-report survey	38 % undergrad., 25 % grad. committed partial plagiarism 8 % undergrad., 4 % grad. copied from another source (within 12 months prior to the survey)
[46]	91 students at one U.S. campus Fall term 2004	self-report survey	53.2 % committed partial plagiarism 31.2 % submitted a paper from an external source
[223]	5,331 graduate students at 32 campuses in the USA	self-report survey	53 % of business majors, 43 % of other students cheated on written work

	and Canada Academic years 2003/2004, 2004/2005		33 % of business majors, 22 % other students literally copied from the internet (within 12 months prior to the survey)
[273]	1,225 students at one U.S. campus Observation period unspecified, publication date: Jun. 2007	self-report survey	62.6 % copied homework from fellow students 44.5 % plagiarized from internet 17.9 % copied term papers or projects from fellow students

Table 34: Studies Pertaining to Colleges Outside of North America

Source	Sample size, place, time of collection	Method	Results
[194]	518 students from three institutions in Singapore; Observation period unspecified; Publication date: July 2001	self-report survey	89.8 % plagiarized by paraphrasing 85.1 % copied literally from books, articles etc. 56.5 % copied papers from fellow students with or without their consent
[212]	954 students from four Australian universities; Observation period unspecified; Publication date: May 2005	self-report survey	81 % committed plagiarism
[83]	2002/2003: 145 undergraduates 2003/2004: 207 undergraduates from	Assign-ments checked with	~40 % of students had NOS>=20 % in both academic years analyzed[79]

---

[79] Non-Originality Score (NOS); documents scoring NOS>10 % are typically regarded as suspicious and likely to contain plagiarism.

	one institution in the UK	*OrCheck*	
[23]	182 graduate students from one institution in the UK Observation period unspecified; Publication date: 2006	Assign-ments checked with *Turnitin;* Suspicious documents inspected manually	*Turnitin* flagged 40.6 % of all documents as suspicious Manual inspection revealed 26 % of all documents contained actual plagiarism
[303]	159 students from one institution in the UK; Observation period unspecified; Publication date: June 2008	self-report survey	68.6 % plagiarized by paraphrasing (23.9 % frequently) 59.7 % copied material literally from books, articles etc. (24.5 % frequently) 21.4 % copied from fellow students (5.7 % frequently) 17.5 % submitted a paper from an external source, (3.7 % frequently)
[332]	322 undergraduates From three Swedish universities	self-report survey	61 % copied material literally from books, articles etc. 55 % copied from fellow students with their consent, 9 % without 31 % submitted a paper from an external source
[329]	~1,300 MA and PhD thesis at one Turkish university Submissions between 2001 and 2010	Assign-ments checked with *Turnitin*	22.3 % of thesis had 21 %<=x<=30 % NOS (NOS>15 % was considered suspicious by this study [85])

I Studies on Citation-based Similarity Measures

The following three tables summarize studies, which assessed the applicability of citation-based similarity measures for different retrieval tasks. Studies commonly analyzed the suitability of different measures for creating topic-centered clusters of research articles [4, 38, 39, 166, 167, 200, 244] or web pages [53, 54, 79, 86, 352].

Table 35 lists studies exclusively analyzing citation-based measures, while Table 36 outlines studies that compared character-based and citation-based similarity measures side-by-side.

Table 37 highlights studies that also evaluated hybrid measures, which combined both approaches.

Table 35: Studies Evaluating Citation-based Similarity Measures

Objective of Study	Similarity Measures	Gold Standard	Test collection
[86]: Find relevant web pages for given input URLs	Co-citation (CoCit), Companion	18 expert judgments	59 input URLs selected by experts, top-10 recommendations of each approach
[4]: Subject classification for research articles	BibCoup, Abstract keywords	1 expert judgments	43 IR articles
[295]: Perf. of similarity measures to identify research front	BibCoup, CoCit, Direct Citation	Topological clustering (defined criteria)	Articles retrieved by keyword search from SCI
[369]: Identify topically similar papers	BibCoup, CoCit, Amsler, Inter Conn.	Prediction of reference papers given in textbook chapters	DBLP and reference information crawled from MS Academic Search

Table 36: Studies Primarily Evaluating Citation-based Similarity Measures

Study, Objective	Similarity Measure	Gold Standard	Test collection
Comparison of similarity measures for topical similarity (our own study [134])	BibCoup, CoCit, Amsler, Co-citation Proximity Analysis, CoCit, Lucene	Information content analysis derived from MeSH thesaurus	~260,000 documents from the PubMed Central Open Access Subset
[39]: Subject clustering, creation of topic maps for research articles	CoCit, Vector Space Model (VSM)	1 expert interview per analyzed domain	~3,400 and ~1,300 articles from two research fields
[352]: Web page clustering	BibCoup, CoCit, anchor texts	Relevance judgment by the authors	200 web pages for each of 8 topics
[168]: Evaluate suitability of similarity measures to identify research front	BibCoup and CoCit combined with title keyword clustering	None; clustering derived from assumptions made	~73,000 environmental research articles from SCI

Table 37: Studies Evaluating Hybrid Measures

Study, Objective	Similarity Measures	Gold Standard	Test collection
[166]: Subject clustering, creation of topic maps for research articles	BibCoup, VSM of titles and abstracts, chi-square combination of both	MeSH	5,188 papers retrieved by journal selection, keyword search etc.
[53, 54, 79, 80]: Subject classification for web pages	BibCoup,CoCit, Amsler, Compan., kNN with tf/idf VSM, SVM, Naïve Bayes classifier	Expert classifications	2 sets of manually pre-classified web pages; in [79] further ~6,600 articles from ACM DL
[3]: Subject classification for research articles	BibCoup, term-based approach, combination of both	One expert clustering	43 IR articles
[167]: Subject clustering, creation of topic maps for articles	Various citation-based, tf/idf VSM, linear combinations	*External:* Thomson Reuters Essential Science Indicators	~6 million papers, ~8,000 journals from Web of Science
[200, 201]: Clustering of research articles	character-based, various citation-based LSI of binary article cross-citation, combination of text- and citation-based measures	*Internal:* Mean Silhouette Value, Modularity	

J Overview of Selected PDS

Given the fast-paced changes in the software landscape for plagiarism detection, this section presents some established systems that are well-maintained and find widespread use for the comparison of academic documents.

Table 38 presents PDS that focus on collusion detection by employing a user-defined corpus. PDS that compare documents to external collections are typically web-based. Major vendors, including *Ephorus*, *SafeAssign*, *Turnitin*, and *Urkund*, maintain large indices of the web and exclusive non-publicly available content, including journal articles, books, and prior works submitted for inspection. Turnitin calls itself the global leader in PD and claims to continuously index ~24 billion web pages, ~250 million student papers, and ~100 million books and periodicals [164]. The comparison algorithms of all commercial PDS are trade secrets. However, given the size of the reference collection, we conclude that the systems must apply approaches requiring low computational effort, which suggests commercial PDS most likely use fingerprinting.

Table 39 summarizes systems that check documents against an external collection. The last columns in both tables list publications that offer details on detection procedures and system performance. Information on the exact algorithms used in commercial tools is not publicly available.

Table 38: PDS for Document Comparisons within a User-Defined Corpus

System/ Manufacturer	Detection Approach	License/Costs	Source
AntiPlagiarist [2]	**client software:** local installation **procedure:** word-based string matching	Commercial $34.95	[355]
CopyCatch [60]	**client software:** local installation **procedure:** string matching	Commercial individual price	[50, 89, 353]
Encoplot [143]	**client software:** local installation **procedure:** fingerprinting using 16-character-grams	Freeware; Open source	[142, 143]
Ferret [186]	**client software:** local installation **procedure:** word-3-gram fingerprinting	Freeware	[22, 203, 204]
Sherlock [184]	**client software:** local installation **procedure:** word-n-gram fingerprinting	Freeware; Open source	[184]
WCopyFind [35]	**client software:** local installation **procedure:** word-based string matching	Freeware; Open source	[94, 282, 355]

PDS that compare documents to external collections are typically web-based. Major vendors, including *Ephorus, SafeAssign, Turnitin*, and *Urkund*, maintain large indices of the web and exclusive non-publicly available content, including journal articles, books, and prior works submitted for inspection. *Turnitin* calls itself the global leader in PD and claims to continuously index ~24 billion web pages, ~250 million student papers, and ~100 million books and periodicals [164]. The comparison algorithms of all commercial PDS are trade secrets. However, given the size of the reference collection, we conclude that the systems must apply detection approaches with low computational effort, which suggests commercial PDS most likely use fingerprinting.

Table 39: PDS for Document Comparisons with an External Collection

System/ Manufacturer	Detection Approach	License/Costs	Source
Copyscape [60]	**client software:** web-based system **input:** URL or plain text (max. 2,000 words) **procedure:** chunking and selection strategy unknown, chunks searched with Google	Commercial $0.05 per scan	[282, 353, 356]

Docoloc [93]	**client software:** web-based system **input:** single or multiple documents **procedure:** selection of (5-9)-word-grams, which the system searches with Google	Commercial €264 p.a. max 5,000 pages	[145, 251, 282, 355, 356]
Ephorus [100]	**client software:** web-based system **input:** single or multiple documents **procedure:** chunking and selection strategy unknown, comparison to indexed www and repository of prior submissions	Commercial individual price	[282, 355, 356]
PlagAware [207]	**client software:** web-based system **input:** single document **procedure:** chunking and selection strategy unknown, web search for chunks, string matching on retrieved results	Commercial €0.01–0.03 per 250 words	[355, 356]
Plagiarism Detector [300]	**client software:** local installation **input:** single or multiple documents **procedure:** chunking and selection strategy unknown, chunks searched with Google, Alta Vista and Yahoo	Commercial $49.99–79.99	[260, 355, 356]
SafeAssign [34]	**client software:** web-based system **input:** single or multiple documents **procedure:** chunking and selection strategy unknown, comparison to www, exclusive content, and repositories of prior submissions	Commercial individual price	[282, 353, 354, 356]
Turnitin [164]			[50, 84, 89, 157, 282, 353, 354, 356]
Urkund [271]			[282, 355, 356]

Index